Living with Class

Living with Class

Philosophical Reflections on Identity and Material Culture

Edited by Ron Scapp and Brian Seitz

palgrave
macmillan

First published in 2013 by
PALGRAVE MACMILLAN®
in the United States—a division of St. Martin's Press LLC,
175 Fifth Avenue, New York, NY 10010.

Where this book is distributed in the UK, Europe and the rest of the World,
this is by Palgrave Macmillan, a division of Macmillan Publishers Limited,
registered in England, company number 785998, of Houndmills,
Basingstoke, Hampshire RG21 6XS.

Palgrave Macmillan is the global academic imprint of the above
companies and has companies and representatives throughout the world.

Palgrave® and Macmillan® are registered trademarks in the United States,
the United Kingdom, Europe and other countries.

ISBN: 978–1–137–32678–2 (HC)
ISBN: 978–1–137–32681–2 (PBK)

Library of Congress Cataloging-in-Publication Data is available from the
Library of Congress.

A catalogue record of the book is available from the British Library.

Design by Integra Software Services

First edition: December 2013

I really would have liked to contribute to this volume, but I had to work.

Jens Veneman

Contents

List of Illustrations

Figures

Tables

Introduction: Working Class

Ron Scapp and Brian Seitz

Do the Math

99%? The numbers just don't add up, since the complementary figure is far less than 1%, which leaves a lot more slop than any legitimate accountant might expect or be willing to sign off on. But since we've experienced a crisis that illuminates the material discrepancy of these percentages, let's revisit some historical constellation points to help provide context.

One might start approaching these numbers, this constellation, with reference to the collapse of the Soviet system. The fruit of a classless society appears to be little more than managerial elites transmogrified into billionaires whose children attend fancy schools in Switzerland, England, and the United States. This reality is a peculiar part of the variegated phenomenon of "state capitalism." At the innovative, cutting edge of this historically recent socioeconomic mutation are Russia and China, each a unique formation, and each, too, a radical reconfiguration of class and the material culture that those countries had revolted against, only to find themselves now among the most recent representations of the ever-widening gap between those who count and those who get counted upon to labor and sustain the new math. This new calculation, "the slop" we noted above, signals the difference between those who have and those who have immeasurably less to little to nothing, a difference that is not just a distinction. And what if this difference or fissure were not about "a system of oppositions"?[1] Or: what about Marx minus dialectics, social class headed into not the Hegelian inevitable but the truly unknown, gated communities a bulwark against global warming and other material realities?

Elsewhere, on the tangent of the European arc of subtraction—as in the deletion of the social welfare state as we know it—reduction in the name of austerity and fiscal accountability continues to diminish the living conditions of those many whose numbers steadily grow but seem to matter less and less. Dubai World aside, "home ownership" sounds wholesome, but only if one ignores the fact that mortgages mean that it's the banks doing the actual owning. Take Ireland, for example. There, people did not really lose their houses, since the properties were essentially foreclosed upon the signing of the mortgage, and the owners thus never occupied them in any meaningful future sense beyond embodying an act of the imagination, the wholesome veneer of which—*home*—barely masked a consumerist fetishism of ownership, centered in this case on the false security of "real" estate. A similar scenario holds true in the United States, where the territory contains the tensions between working class Americans going into foreclosure, the wealthy Koch brothers' deep background funding of the Tea Party and, perhaps surprisingly to some, the Public Broadcasting Service, and the right's and neo-liberals' successful push for the extension of Bush-era tax breaks for the top 2% of the US population. Well, let's round that up (up, up) to the top .05%.

England remains a socioeconomy driven by class distinctions. *Traditional* class distinctions have been rendered semi-shambolic: From the tabloid standpoint, and while Kate and the Queen are doing their best, the Royals are an object of scandal pretty much on the same level as the tragic Amy Winehouse, while Mick Jagger is, bafflingly, a Knight (and Keef—aka, Keith Richards—mocks him for it). At the same time, though, posh neighborhoods of London house foreign billionaires, who, at the top end, own premier sports franchises. In fact, a conspicuous proportion of wealthy British residents are citizens of other countries, including former colonies (Britain does not care how the money was obtained, just so long as it flows into and through London's financial district). At the same time a significant percentage of poor Britons descend from the former colonies: unemployment among the youth of those descendants is at record levels, levels that fuel the nihilism that has been an element of literal riots.

The level of anger arising from the financial meltdown in the United States would seem to provide the basis for "accountability" on Wall Street. But the anger quickly turned on itself. Spearheaded by working class people inclined against their own interests, Main Street quickly returns to the fantasy of the market to resolve the disparities to be found across the nation regarding health care, education, and social security. Stocks go back up and the market is back in business, while Main Street continues its downward slide.

All of these reference points highlight the combustible dynamics of a global economy driven to an extreme that the most orthodox of Marxists could not have anticipated, and only very attentive economists predicted (in such detail anyway). Although this book is not an effort at resuscitation, the class-conscious philosophy of Karl Marx remains oddly relevant. This may seem to be an impossible calculus, and yet its manifestations are not completely incoherent and in fact intimate an uncanny logic, perhaps even a logic of revolution, if not one determined by the fantasy of dialectical resolution.

Sciences of Wealth

Through a range of vistas, and as observers of culture, one thing we are attempting to revisit here is the very presumption that there is a "science of wealth." A recent statistical study concludes that, as indicated by the inaccuracy of their inevitably narcissistically smug predictions, CEOs actually tend to know jack about economy. Even if Adam Smith and his invisible hand continue to empleasure (some of) and pain (many more of) us, suggesting that something "real" is unfolding and can be observed and studied, we also continue to be harried by the least imaginative students of capital (e.g., Alan Greenspan, et al.), who manifest the baffling impression that Ayn Rand was a philosopher rather than a pedestrian ideologue—a scientist of wealth, who chose fiction to explicate her "theories," clumsy fictions that get rewritten by contemporary authors of wealth on CNBC, Fox Business, and just about anywhere multinational corporations have the inclination to publish reports, which means just about everywhere.

Although deeply cynical, the agenda of the neo-cons was successful, if measured by flow into their growing bank accounts while the nation's reserves are depleted. And the same is true for the neo-liberals.

Conclude that socialism matters but may not count?

The neo-*coms*—neo-communists, our locution—appear, according to news sources, not to have an agenda as such, but . . . they do have a lifestyle. Witness the look of Occupy Wall Street—from grunge to business suits as camouflage—and their alleged lack of a clearly articulated agenda according to the liberal media, which, however, was coupled with lucid anger, that the media (of both right and left) duly noted. As a result, the global economy, including the labor force that sustains it (we're talking about people who actually work rather than go to offices), has been stretched to its limit, has spread to all corners, as has the growing militarization of the response that has spread to contain the disruption of business, which has never been as usual.

So, those of us who do not claim, who cannot claim, any "scientific" approach but nevertheless continue to shop, buy, and consume, and do so with a mixture of measured pleasure and genuine caution, concern, anxiety, of, that is, worry and obligation, are forced to step back and reflect on the interaction and play of facts and data that get reported everyday. *Living with Class* is our attempt to gather additional information from a varied group of ethno-philosophers of different forms of wealth who together share, here, their descriptions, assessments, strategies, and conclusions about the state of affairs regarding money, poverty, bank accounts, property, investments, loans, profit and wages, and labor, to name a few areas of concern.

Without Class

What is a person worth? More precisely, how much does one cost? The question is answerable within the context of a well-established class structure. A laborer is worth so much, an undocumented laborer so much less, etc. A CEO, even a bad one (well, they are a bad species?), is worth many more times the cost of even the best employee. There are exceptions, for sure—rare as they really are—but within the class system, we live with the identity and material reality that we are placed in or move up and down to—and live we do, however well or not.

How these differences come to be determined is all about a strange alchemical synthesis of the cost of living and surplus value, that is, the origin of profit. Marx was the first to understand this, but his understanding was crippled by his desire to maintain his system, which was synonymous with his insistence on "science." Consequently, his explanations for surplus value and thus, by extension, for social class never, finally, made sense, especially to those counting pennies at either end of the economic continuum. This is because there is nothing scientific or precise about the conditions that make it possible for one person to be scrambling to be malnourished while another person is commanding outrageously large bonuses simply because he—and it is typically a he—has figured out how to get away with pillage, most dramatically in the least productive domain, the world of investment banking, which produces nothing material, but only wealth based on exotic schemes and machinations.

But the question regarding one's worth gets easily complicated if we move beyond class, if, that is, we were to imagine living without class. The question then becomes much more philosophical and far less a matter of economics, per se.

Without class the math stops. Quantifying a person's identity and value then shifts to another plane, a metaphysical one that requires a new matrix of accounting for oneself or another. Now the question is a matter of quality, of character and disposition: Is Luis worthy of my friendship? Is Xinghua a good woman? Living without class has been the goal, the dream that still lingers. But it is less and less the ambition of still many more who have placed their bets—their fantasies—of living with class via credit debt or lotto (typically both). Without class, the absence of class becomes the backdrop, the palimpsest for living with class and all of its inequalities and harsh realities. The reasonable becomes the fruitless, while the pointless and the absurdity of buying your way up and/or out becomes the pragmatic strategy for continued survival and living. One's identity becomes perversely meshed with the very material cultural that so many of us have managed to render ethereal due to the various practices of reimagining our lives through the possibility of repositioning ourselves, of placing ourselves, somewhere better than we find ourselves at any given moment—regardless of how good or bad the moment may be—of living with class as we have come to understand it.

The numbers don't add up, as far as we can tell, and nor should they. The chapters in this volume, however, make a case for another kind of counting and/or calculus, another attempt at considering and reconsidering the very numbers and ways in which people survive, thrive, and struggle, by accident and by design. The fact that around the world we are witnessing the continued growth of and disparity between the wealth gained by the super-rich and the decline in the standard of living of the poor and working poor should cause all of us to take a pause and rethink the very dynamic and nature of class as presented and maintained by all involved (super-rich, rich, wealthy, wealthy enough, almost wealthy enough, not wealthy enough but working, the working poor, the poor and the impoverished). We hope that the eclectic chapters in this volume will contribute to such reconsideration of the lives of all who are otherwise shaped by class.

Note

1. Stiegler, Bernard, *For a New Critique of Political Economy*, trans. Daniel Ross (Cambridge: Polity Press, 2010), p. 15.

CHAPTER 1

Class Dismissed: The Issue Is Accountability

bell hooks

As a society we continue to be silent when it comes to issues of class. This silence helps perpetuate the myth of abundance—the assumption that one of the most outstanding features of a democratic society is that class does not matter since everyone can move up the class ladder.

More than ten years ago, in the preface to *Where We Stand*, I wrote:

> Many citizens of this nation, myself included, have been and are afraid to think about class. Affluent liberals concerned with the plight of the poor and dispossessed are daily mocked and ridiculed. They are blamed for all the problems of the welfare state. Caring and sharing have come to be seen as traits of the idealistic weak. Our nation is fast becoming a class-segregated society where the plight of the poor is forgotten and the greed of the rich is morally tolerated and condoned.

Unfortunately, these words remain an accurate description of class dynamics today. While there was once a United States that allowed poor and working folks to gain class mobility, to change and shift class positionality, this is no longer possible. In these hard times of economic crisis shifting one's class location is no simple matter. Currently, many more of our nation's citizens find themselves descending rather than ascending the ladder of upward class mobility.

Indeed, one positive impact of the recent economic crisis is that it has compelled masses of citizens to acknowledge class and class differences, and more importantly to face that exploitive and oppressive class hierarchies uphold dominator culture. Becoming aware of class difference that perpetuates domination—a predatory oligarchy where those with the greatest class power control and exploit everyone—has changed the way all of us experience class.

Ironically, this awareness has not made it easier to have open discussions of class. In this imperialist, white supremacist, capitalist patriarchy, it is easier for everyone to talk about race, gender, and even sexuality than to talk about class. Despite censorship and silencing, awareness is growing—a developing class consciousness is emerging. The movement for social justice "Occupy Wall Street" is a fine example of this new trend.

Despite the power of the Occupy movement, it is unfortunate that many radical young folks find it more compelling to critique and condemn the rich and the super-rich than to challenge each other and everyone else to examine our class values, our class allegiances. It is so much easier to condemn the rich and the super-rich than to engage in vigilant critical evaluation of all our relationship to capitalism. In his insightful book *How Much Is Enough*, Arthur Simon explains:

> Capitalism stimulates and thrives on our human desires to possess more, a desire that instinctively gravitates towards greed, which tends to create disparities that make some rich while leaving many impoverished. It is good at generating wealth, not so good at spreading it around . . . it is simply driven by the profit motive.

The free enterprise capitalist system with its insistence on unlimited growth nourishes greed. As stated in *Where We Stand*, "greed has become the common bond shared by many of the poor and the privileged."

All of us who live within the capitalist system, who benefit from its largesse, are vulnerable; we all have within us the capacity to nurture a relentless and brutal greed that simply does not invite emphatic concern and compassion for those who are less fortunate, especially the poor. Journalist Hervé Kempf, in *How the Rich Are Destroying the Earth*, challenges all of us to acknowledge the connection between the greed of the rich and our own greed. With keen insight he highlights the reality that "material growth intensifies environmental degradation," which wreaks its most devastating havoc on the poor and indigent. Explaining further, Kempf contends:

> The oligarchy also exercises a powerful indirect influence as a result of the culture attraction it consumption habits exercise on society as a whole . . . People aspire to lift themselves up the social ladder, which happens through imitation of the superior classes' consumption habits. Thus, the oligarchy defuses its ideology of waste throughout the whole society.

Hence masses of people from all class locations are driven by shared greed. Again, while radical folk from all class may have sharp critiques of the rich and super-rich, there is little discussion of the way in which greed articulates itself in all our daily lives.

Continued silence around the issue of class on the part of aware privileged class folks (including many progressives) stems from the individual and collective fear that the spotlight of interrogation will shine on us. And, the fear is that this light will show that in the final analysis our collective greed, our commitment to materialism, overconsumption, and waste, is a bond shared with the predatory oligarchy. A perfect representation of how this fear of interrogation silences is the conservative media's response to Tavis Smiley and Cornel West's efforts to highlight the issue of poverty in this nation. They began with a poverty tour that culminated with the publication of their book *The Rich and the Rest of Us*. Readers of the book, progressives and conservatives alike, interrogated where the authors stand, where earning millions places them. Again and again they were harshly critiqued about their stance. Much of this critique was aimed at defusing and obscuring the central focus on the issue of poverty and the plight of the poor. This mean-spirited critique functions as a means of oppressive censorship, letting folks know (especially radicals and/or leftists) that any call for an emphasis on poverty will be regarded as hypocritical and therefore not genuine.

The Rich and the Rest of Us offers astute insights about the way in which the rich and superrich constitute a predatory oligarchy that restricts public freedom and aims to destroy the spirit of democracy. However, Smiley and West do not hold the poor and the rest of us accountable for our continued support of the culture of greed. In conversation with Cornel West, I have shared my concern that the representation of the poor as always and only victims is a portrait that differs from conservative images primarily in intent and perspective. Smiley and West speak and write with genuine compassion about the poor, expressing their concerns in fairly clear plain language, and yet what they offer as a means to end poverty is not ways to dismantle predatory economic systems, which would include an understanding of the way all of us embrace hedonist materialism, overconsumption, and waste. Hence the vision of an end to poverty they offer promotes changes that would enable the poor to join the rest of us in choosing a lifestyle that is not sustainable given the current global crisis, economic and environmental.

Affirming that the rich and the rest of us continue to dream of moving on up (rising up the class ladder), *Time Magazine*'s feature story "Can You Still Move Up in America?" begins with the following declaration:

America's story, our national mythology, is built on the idea of being an opportunity society. Americans care much more about being able to move up the socio-economic ladder than where we stand on it. We may be poor today, but as long as there is a chance that we can be rich tomorrow things are OK.

Until all our nation's citizens can accept that beginning with the super-rich and rich, we must all learn to live more simply to create sustainable life for all living creatures.

Let us remember, as stated in *Where We Stand: Class Matters*:

The poor may be with us always. Yet this does not mean that the poor cannot live well, cannot find contentment and fulfillment.... Solidarity with the poor is not the same as empathy. Many people feel sorry for the poor or identify with their suffering yet do nothing to alleviate it. All too often people of privilege engage in forms of spiritual materialism where they seek recognition of their goodness by helping the poor. And they proceed in the efforts without changing their contempt and hatred of poverty. Genuine solidarity with the poor is rooted in the recognition that interdependency sustains the life of the planet. That includes the recognition that the fate of the poor both locally and globally will to a grave extent determine the quality of life for those who are lucky enough to have class privilege. Repudiating exploitation by word and deed is a gesture of solidarity with the poor.

More importantly, when we all understand the fundamental link between hedonistic materialism and the environmental destruction of the planet, we can all work together "to live simply, so that others may simply live." Without shifting class location we can refuse to participate in class domination. We can dismiss and devalue class by refusing attachment to privilege class value and status. Without this dismissal, solidarity with others is impossible.

The movement to change our thinking about poverty must begin with reframing how all of us see and relate to the experience of living poor. This means that while those with privilege can acknowledge the pain and injustice of poverty caused by greed and exploitation, we can refuse to dehumanize poor folk by recognizing them as participants and choice-makers when the issue is of overconsumption and waste. Each of us, no matter our class, has to decide what to do with what we have. To live in brutal poverty that is imposed by imperialist, white supremacist, capitalist patriarchy does not preclude anyone from choosing to reject mindless consumerism, and overconsumption. Yes, even the poor can choose to live simply. When poor and working class folks choose to live with integrity, respecting stewardship of the planet and its resources, no one pays attention.

While pundits tell us the rich set the standards that masses of poor and working class embrace and mimic, they do not talk about critically conscious poor people who make progressive choices about how to live in the world. Significantly, they do not call attention to the fact that the progressive radical poor have much to teach the affluent about ways to live that honor sustainable life practices.

Devoted religious circles are perhaps the only place in our nation where living in poverty is seen as an experience that can deepen spiritual practice and faith. In such circles, efforts to change negative perceptions of poverty are linked to radical calls for global justice. Our passion for justice must be the force undergirding efforts to envision new economic systems that are sustainable, that make sharing resources commonplace.

When we choose to live with less, embracing simple ways of being and living in the world, we are doing the work of justice-making. There can be no love without justice.

CHAPTER 2

Letter from a Lovelorn Pre-Radical: Looking Forward and Backward at Martin Luther King Jr.

Kevin Bruyneel

In July 1952, 23-year-old Martin Luther King Jr. made the following statement: "So today capitalism has outlived its usefulness. It has brought about a system that takes necessities from the masses to give luxuries to the classes."[1] He did not say these words from the pulpit nor during one of the many political speeches he gave during his lifetime. He did not write them for a newspaper editorial nor any document produced for public consumption, such as his 1963 "Letter from Birmingham Jail." But he did write them in a letter. It was a private letter to Coretta Scott, whom he had started dating earlier that year. The King, who wrote this letter, had just finished his first year of graduate school at Boston University and he was serving as the associate pastor of the Ebenezer Baptist Church in Atlanta, Georgia. He was not yet *Dr.* King. He was not yet the public, political figure whose status and popularity in the dominant American collective memory is equal to, if not greater than, the nation's most exalted presidents. Tracing King's popularity from its lows to its present highs reveals that the transformation of King's status in US history and in the nation's collective memory is startling.

In August 1966, Dr. King was viewed favorably by 33% and unfavorably by 63% of the Americans polled.[2] While his leadership role in the Civil Rights Movement never made him very popular nation-wide, his approval ratings suffered further during the mid- to late 1960s when his politics and public claims turned increasingly towards efforts to achieve economic justice. He worked on the Poor People's Campaign that planned to demand from the US federal government "a $30 billion annual investment in antipoverty measures, a government commitment to full employment, enactment of a guaranteed income and funding for the construction of 500,000 affordable housing units per year."[3] King's vocal opposition to the US war in Vietnam also diminished his popularity with the US population. In our time, however, Dr. King has an almost unanimous approval rating. In August 2011, Gallup's survey found that 94% of respondents viewed King favorably and only 4% unfavorably.[4] Given his actual views, we can see that King's almost sainted status today is built upon a mythical construction of the man's politics and political identity. A central component of this myth is the productive absence of King's views and actions concerning class politics and economic inequality in the United States. This productive absence helps reinforce the prevalent notion that the American nation lives without class as a vibrant political concern—that it is a "classless" society. This chapter is an effort to refuse this absence as part of a politics of reclaiming a more radical King whose memory can be mobilized to support, among other things, a class-based, anti-capitalist politics in the United States.

While one can trace and reveal King's views on class in a number of ways and more easily, such as with his work on the Poor People's Campaign, I center my effort by attending to the content, tone, form, and context of the young King's brief letter to his future wife. It is a letter written in and for the private realm, and while it sets out King's more radical views on politics and economics as carried out in the public realm, it also offers insight into his gendered view of domestic relations. As such, this personal letter provides us a way to paint a wider picture of what we mean by living with class in the United States, as it points us to the mutually constitutive relationship of race and class and also to the notion of *living with* as a reference to domestic relations, and as such the gendered construction of the private realm that is fundamental to the structure of liberal capitalist societies. As well, in the private realm we reveal ourselves more than we do in the public realm, often in both positive and negative ways. In this regard, King's letter to Coretta Scott is an example of political scientist James Scott's notion of the private or "hidden transcripts," which is the "discourse that takes place 'offstage', beyond direct observation by powerholders," in contrast to the "public transcript" discourse that occurs onstage, in full view of powerholders and the public.[5] I will draw a connection between the private and public transcripts of Dr. King's political views later in this chapter. I now turn to consider the young King's less guarded hidden transcript, written before he took up his role under the glaring lights of the American political stage.

"Love is such a dynamic force, isn't it?" King's question to Coretta Scott reflects the tone and substance of the letter's first few paragraphs, indicative of a youthful, romantic note rather than a political tract. King begins by admitting to being in a "better mood" upon receiving Scott's most recent letter. Prior to her latest missive, Scott had angered King by not agreeing to meet with his parents and stay with his family on her next trip to Atlanta. He confesses that his "heart . . . had well-nigh grown cold toward you," but that the "stormy winds of anger" toward her could not upset the "solid foundation" of love that King feels toward Scott. Unsettled by her refusal to abide his wishes, King's words take on a saccharine flourish, such as "my life without you is like a year without a spring time." And it forces him to reveal his vulnerability to her: "Darling, I miss you so much. In fact, much to [sic] much for my own good. I never realized that you were such an intimate part of my life." Her refusal of his request to stay with his family has exposed his dependence upon her and his lack of authority in the relationship. It also led him to deploy evocative imagery to describe his vision for their relationship: "Can you imagine the frustration that a King without a throne would face? Such would be my frustration if I in my little kinghood could not reign at the throne of Coretta."[6] The metaphor is tortured and apt, both reflecting a familiar gendered imagery of domestic relations and foreshadowing the status that King as a person and a myth would eventually assume in American political culture.

My purpose in analyzing the intimate aspects of this letter closely is not to critique King personally, for there is nothing wrong on their face with what he says here—they are standard words of love, desire, and courtship. Instead, there are two more generalizable and connected reasons why I pay close attention to King's more intimate words to Coretta Scott. The first is that his rendering of the power dynamic in his relationship with Scott—he the King, she the throne—resonates as a common construction of a patriarchal domestic household. While he professes to place her *as* the throne as a way of honoring her—note she is not *at* her own throne, such as at his side—King is also clear that he is the one that reigns; it is his "kinghood." Here, King's words reflect a familiar gendering of the private and public spheres in liberal societies, where he is the *king of his castle*, as the saying goes, and her domestic power is symbolized in the naming of the throne after her: the throne that does not leave the kingdom. This metaphor points to the gendered dynamics of living with class; for many women, that means living with and within a patriarchal private realm in liberal capitalist societies.

The second reason for paying due attention to King's vision of his domestic "kinghood" and Coretta Scott's place in it comes with the awkward transition his letter makes from entreaties of love to a discussion of his views on economics, politics, and religion in public life. As if symbolizing the manner in which the gendered domestic sphere provides the foundation for the engagement of ideas and actions in a predominantly masculine public sphere, King's letter first sets a foundation of his priorities for the intimate, private sphere of his love life and upon that basis awkwardly and suddenly vaults into the concerns of public life. This transition starts by his granting that the topic of love is too "ineffable to be grasped by the cold calculating heads of intellect," and then the next paragraph sharply shifts the discussion to "something more intellectual," as he puts it.[7] It is ironic and fitting, then, that it was Scott's gift of Edward Bellamy's book *Looking Backward* that was the vehicle through which King shifts the letter's focus from their personal relationship to matters generally deemed more of public debate and concern. Published in 1888 and one of the most popular books of its time, Bellamy's utopian novel has its protagonist, Julian West, fall asleep in the late nineteenth century and wake up in the year 2000. Upon waking, he discovers that the United States has become a socialist utopia, where, among other things, private property and industry have been nationalized and the nation is a class-less society in a material sense, as opposed to the contemporary liberal sense of ideologically disavowing class dynamics.

Bellamy's book is a direct critique of capitalism and also an effort to reimagine how the nation could reorganize itself, politically, economically, and socially. Scott's inscription on the book prompts him to engage these topics: "Dear Martin: I shall be interested to know your reaction to Bellamy's prediction about our society. In some ways it is rather encouraging to see how our social order has changed since Bellamy's time. There is still hope for the future . . . Lest we become too impatient. Coretta"[8] With the rest of the letter, up until the last two paragraphs, King analyzes Bellamy's book as a way to articulate his own views. As to the tone of the letter, the rhetorical flourish and insecurities of an intimate love letter are suddenly gone, left behind, for a tone of intellectual engagement and political assessment. Like the shift from the intimate private sphere to the open and impersonal public sphere, the letter itself seems to be split into two realms, representing and reflecting the private/public split of liberal political societies. I refer to this development as fitting and ironic because it takes Scott's gift and her prompting inscription to serve as the basis for King to shift the letter's focus and provide the basis of the subsequent elaboration of his views. This dynamic between Scott and King is thus emblematic of the foundational, often hidden, role that the patriarchal private realm provides as the support structure for the existence of a predominantly masculine public realm. The love letter part of the letter is over, for now, but it has set the table, in the metaphorical sense and in a literal sense too if one accounts for the material conditions and demands of the gendered sociopolitical order, for the rest of the discussion.

In now focusing his attention on discussing Scott's gift, King refers to Bellamy as having the "insight of a social prophet" and the "mind of a social scientist," and defines his own views through his reading of *Looking Backward*. He tells Scott that he "welcomed the book because much of its content is in line with my basic ideas. I imagine you already know that I am much more socialistic in my economic theory than capitalistic."[9] King goes on to suggest that capitalism began with the "high motive" of blocking "the trade monopolies of nobles," but became "victim to the very thing it was revolting against." And here we is where get his line about capitalism outliving its usefulness, about it now serving the interests of the new noble classes, the bourgeoisie and the owners of capital. Thus, he concurs with Bellamy's vision of the "gradual decline of capitalism." In this regard, King reads Bellamy's work as an assessment of the potential for the evolutionary transformation of the organizing economic structure of the nation. In particular, King concurs with Bellamy's "evolutionary rather than the revolutionary" approach to such a transformation, seeing it as the most "sane and ethical way for social change to take place." King's only quarrel with Bellamy on this matter is that "I don't think he gave capitalism long enough time to die. It is probably true that capitalism is on its death bed, but social systems have a way of developing a long and powerful death bed breathing capacity . . . . Capitalism will be in America quite a few more years my dear."[10] King has diagnosed the problem with capitalism as fostering the exploitation of and extraction from the masses. But what we do not get from the young King is a cure to the disease he has diagnosed. Rather, he looks for and desires capitalism's demise via evolutionary development, over time, but not through active revolutionary resistance. As such, we do not get an articulation of a politics of class and anti-capitalism, or a politics of any real sort. On this matter, he is still hesitant.

King argues, through Bellamy, that even those more socialistic in their thinking, such as himself, are just going to have to live with capitalism, and thus class inequality and tensions, for quite some time. King tells Scott he would "welcome the day to come when there will be a nationalization of industry," and that we need to "hope, work, and pray in the future we will live to see a warless world, a better distribution of wealth, and a brotherhood that transcends race or color. This is the gospel that I will preach to the world."[11] King's aims and hopes accord with where his public life and political activism will move over the next decade and a half, as he will eventually and openly draw the connections between US empire, class inequality, and racial injustice. But for now, still three years from serving as a leader of the Montgomery Bus Boycott in 1955, King is struggling with the relationship between the theological and the political in seeking to grasp how to bring about change in the American social order. We see this in how he distinguishes himself as a socialist but not a communist, because for King the latter implies signing on to a revolutionary approach that believes "killing a thousand people will bring about a good end." And as he maintained throughout his political career, "destructive means cannot bring about constructive ends." As well, as it concerns Marxism and communism, King sets himself apart by "being an idealist" rather than a "materialist," and would "reject Marx at this point."[12] And this is where the tensions among King's theological, economic, and political views come to the fore. These are tensions that as a young man he is still trying to resolve and make sense of as he looks forward to what he foresees to be some form of career in public life.

King does concur with Marx in one regard, which is that religion can "become a tool of the middle class to keep the proletariant [sic] oppressed. To [sic] often has the church talked about a future good 'over yonder' totally forgetting the present evil over here." He does not say what this evil is—it could be capitalism or racial segregation or war, or all three. He does promise to "avoid making religion what Marx calls the 'opiate of the masses'." At the same time, King's idealist/non-materialist approach means that he does not see the achievement of "better economic and social conditions" to be the fundamental cure to what ails the US social order. Rather, to him, "ultimately, our problem is [a] theological one. Man has revolted against God, and through his humanistic endeavors he has sought to solve his problem by himself only to find that he has ended up in disillusionment."[13] While at this point in his life the preaching of the Gospel and the role of theology remains the singular way in which King imagines a form of public subjectivity for himself, we also see here that he is comfortable with Marxist class analysis and discourse. The seeds of a pre-radical are evident here, if not yet blossoming. He speaks of the tensions and inequities between the bourgeoisie and the proletariat, and views capitalism to have turned from a positive to a negative influence on the US social order. At this time, though, he is still not comfortable with reliance upon the "humanistic endeavors" of public life to bring about change—seeing them as too walled off from theological imperative and guidance. He is only able to caution himself to not allow his preaching of the Gospel to become a means to perpetuating the disempowered, oppressed condition of the working class. As such, he is not able to address the other side of the question: not only what serves in the oppression of the proletariat, but even more importantly what would serve to foster their liberation? King's only answer seems to be time: more time for capitalism "to die" and to be replaced by the evolutionary emergence of a new economic system. Thus, writing in 1952, as King works out his views on the role of the economic system and theology in public life, he persistently elides the one element that could serve to animate people's public engagement with regard to both realms: that element being the political.

Regarding systemic economic change, King openly resists the revolutionary in favor of the evolutionary. As to the role of humanistic endeavor, King deems it the path toward disillusionment or violence rather than fulfillment and peace. In all, King expresses anxiety about advocating direct human action in public life as a way to address and solve problems in our world. He is fearful of the human potential for violence and disenchantment. At a more fundamental level, I argue that what we are witnessing here within the safety of the hidden transcript of private realm communication is King seeking to both imagine and work out his role in public life as he looks forward to his status as a future leader of a congregation, obviously unaware of the profound national role he is about to take on. He believes the Church has a responsibility to publicly name present evils in our time and space, and yet he is decidedly uncomfortable with human action, let alone revolutionary action. Politics is about many things—power, identity, and interests to name but three central components—but as much as anything it involves human action in the world, in public life, on the public stage. And truly radical, democratic action in the world cannot predefine its own ends, cannot dictate its consequences, but rather must be willing to act for the very purpose of bringing something new and unforeseen into the world. As political theorist Hannah Arendt notes in this regard, "the fact that man is capable of action means that the unexpected can be expected from him, that is he able to perform what is infinitely improbable."[14] The King of 1952 is right that violence and disillusionment are ever-present potentialities in the human endeavor of public action that seeks to change the social and political order, such as efforts to bring an end to capitalism, formal segregation, and imperial wars. And this is the very experience of action that King lacks at this point in his life. It is for this reason that I deem this letter to be, in one sense, a letter from a pre-radical, one who has not as yet learned about politics through performing on the public stage. Eventually, he will become the Arendtian actor who performs the "infinitely improbable," but he is not quite there yet.

Looking forward to another of King's letters, his most famous one, the aforementioned "Letter from Birmingham Jail," we see the transformative effects of now Dr. King's active political engagement since 1955. The letter, composed on scraps of paper as he sat in a Birmingham jail in April 1963, is posed to the white liberal clergymen who claimed to support the goal of King and Civil Rights Movement. But these clergymen had issues with the direct actions of the movement, and they suggested that King not move so fast and cause so many problems, because they argued racial equality would be achieved with time, inevitably. In the 1963 letter we can imagine the older Dr. King writing also to the younger King on this theme of time. Where the King of 1952 wrote of the need for evolutionary rather than revolutionary change, implying that we would have to wait for capitalism to die over time, the Dr. King of 1963 has come to realize that

> it is a strangely irrational notion [that] there is something in the very flow of time that will inevitably cure all ills. Actually, time itself is neutral; it can be used either destructively or constructively . . . . time itself becomes the ally of forces of social stagnation. We must use time creatively, in the knowledge that the time is always ripe to do right.[15]

While the King of 1952 was referring to capitalism and of 1963 to racial segregation, the political principle remains the same: if there is an injustice that needs to be addressed—and to the King of 1952 capitalism had become an unjust economic system and for the King of 1963 it was the injustice of formal segregation—then one must act, engage in human endeavor, to expose tensions and generate crises in the public realm so as to compel social change.

As I look forward and backward in grasping King's thoughts, words, and actions, I draw out three generalizable insights. The first is a lesson regarding the importance of witnessing King's own struggles and development in coming to terms with politics as both a contingent and a necessary human endeavor. The second is that we have an even greater basis for refusing the productive absence of class from the dominant collective memory of King's politics and political identity. And the third concerns the difficult, sometimes blurred, and often under-acknowledged relationship between the private and public realms in liberal capitalist societies, and the gendered implications of that relationship. Next, I address all three in turn, and then draw the chapter to a close by returning to King's letter to Coretta Scott.

While I argue that as it concerns capitalism and class inequality, King held a relatively consistent critique throughout his adult life, with regard to taking action in the public realm to turn these critiques into transformative praxis we witness King struggling with how to reconcile his theological commitments to justice with his anxieties about the potential consequences of revolutionary action in the public realm of humanistic endeavors. While his concern with "humanistic endeavors" points to his concern that without the guidance of God there is significant potential for violence and disillusionment, as we see with the "Letter from Birmingham Jail" posed to liberal clergymen, these men of God who were not engaging in public action, King had come to realize that political action was a fundamental and necessary human enterprise for generating change. Those who pleaded with him to slow down on the premise that the wheels of God or time would bring about justice were now speaking to a Dr. King who now knew that revolution and not evolution was the path to social, economic, and political transformation. In this regard, then, it is worth appreciating the honesty with which the young King struggles with—and thus does not easily romanticize— the complexities and contingencies that go with bringing one's theoretical and philosophical views into practice through praxis, the expression of words and deeds in the public realm. With the 1952 letter so situated, we then get a more complex picture of the development and manifestation of the political identity of Dr. King, one which is far too flattened and simplified in the nation's collective memory today.

The way in which the American nation remembers Martin Luther King Jr. matters a great deal, especially for American politics and political discourse. In our era, his more radical politics have been productively excised from his legacy, leading to what Dr. Cornel West has popularly termed the "Santa Claus-ification" of King—turning a radical, historical, and divisive human actor being into a warm, inoffensive, mythical figure that is adored by all. In many ways, King has become an empty signifier that almost anyone across the US political spectrum can ventriloquize so as to advocate their own social and political views, to become whatever we need him to be. The effort to refuse and fight against this contemporary mnemonic production is not about staying true to King's legacy for its own sake, but rather it is a matter of being attentive to and engaged with the way in which his legacy is deployed powerfully in contemporary political discourse. I suggest that there are two ways in which unearthing his critique of capitalism within his 1952 letter to Coretta Scott serves this effort to deconstruct the myth of King. First, it shows that within the offstage comfort and cover of the private transcript of his personal letter—where he is not carefully crafting a message for a public audience—we get a direct sense of King's concerns with capitalism as articulated early in his adult life. And secondly, we have the basis to deploy Dr. King's memory as a substantive basis for contemporary claims regarding the politics of class, and can do so with the knowledge that we are speaking about commitments he held throughout his adult life, not just at the end. As noted, over time, Dr. King's class politics became more public and precise, but the letter to Coretta Scott demonstrates that this was not a view he arrived upon after the Civil Rights Movement was able to achieve legislative successes with the 1964 Civil Rights Act and the 1965 Voting Rights Act. Rather, the critique and concern with capitalism produced and shaped Dr. King's politics throughout his adult life. His view of the intimately tied relationship between race, class, and militarism was a consistent view, not one that simply emerged in the late 1960s.

Thus, by taking a perspective that looks forward and backward in King's life, we unearth the deeper, historical foundations of the claims he articulated later in his life, such as in important and celebrated speeches as the one that he gave to the 10th annual convention of the Southern Christian Leadership Conference (SCLC), in Atlanta, Georgia, on August 16, 1967. Here we can make the connection between the hidden transcript of his personal 1952 letter and the public transcript articulated on the stage of the 1967 SCLC convention. In this speech, Dr. King's critique of capitalism is crystal clear, as he asks: " 'Why are there forty million poor people in America?' And when you begin to ask yourself that question, you are raising questions about the economic system, about a broader distribution of wealth. When you ask that question, you begin to question the capitalistic economy." And then he asserts that "one day we must come to see that an edifice which produces beggars needs restructuring." He makes clear that he is not a communist, which he deems to "forget that life is individual," but he is also not a capitalist, which "forgets that life is social." What he wants, as seen with the Poor People's Campaign, are programs for full employment, adequate housing, and a guaranteed annual income. He also wants an end to the Vietnam War. And in this regard, his critique of capitalism is intertwined with his critique of racial oppression and US militarism: "when I say question the whole society, it means ultimately coming to see that the problem of racism, the problem of economic exploitation, and the problem of war are all tied together. These are the triple evils that are interrelated."[16] In his 1952 letter he said he hoped for a day when there would be a better distribution of wealth, a warless world, and a brother-hood that transcends race. And on the public stage 15 years later, he articulates and calls for action to reorganize the social and political order by addressing the interrelationship between race, class, and militarism, as the mutually constitutive nodes of exploitation, oppression, and domination in and of the United States. This is the Dr. King that lived with class as a pressing political concern through-out his adult life, and the one that needs to be fought for in our contemporary political discourse that invokes King's legacy, as so much of American political discourse indeed does. But to draw out and argue for the radical King as against the mythical King requires that we pay due attention to the forms of oppres-sion and inequality that were too often constitutively absent from Dr. King's own claims and political priorities. I refer here to an evil that King did not mention in his 1967 SCLC speech, that of patriarchy and gender-based oppression, which points us back to the relationship between the private and public spheres in liberal capitalist societies.

I turn again to what Dr. King did say during the SCLC speech, as a way to shed light on what he did not say. In setting out what sort of public action was required to overcome racial inequality and oppression so as to achieve justice and dignity for black Americans, King asserted the following, all in the same paragraph: "the Negro must rise up with an affirmation of his own Olympian manhood"; "reach down to the inner depths of his own being and sign with the pen and ink of assertive manhood his own Emancipation Proclamation"; declare "I am somebody. I am a person. I am a man with dignity and honor"; and also "stand up and say, 'I'm black and I'm beautiful,' and this self-affirmation is the black man's need, made compelling by the white man's crimes against him."[17] The masculinist language here is no mere placeholder for a generalized and non-gendered black American subjectivity. Even if Dr. King meant it that way, and the distinctiveness of the phrase "Olympian manhood" would indicate he did not, what matters here is that he constructs a "subject of liberty" that is male, which is a familiar, even hegemonic, construction in the free subject in political theory and discourse, as noted by feminist political theorist Nancy Hirschmann.[18] In Dr. King's vision, black American males who are actively engaged in public life constitute themselves as truly emancipated subjects, free not just on paper as written in laws and proclamations, but as constructed through their actions on the public stage of politics. When we pair this masculinist discourse with the fact that Dr. King leaves patriarchy out of his list of the intertwined evils of racism, economic exploitation, and war, we then get a clearer sense of how women and the private sphere serve as mutually constitutive, productive absences in King's vision for a re-imagined US social and political order. In the entire 1967 SCLC speech, women are referred to only twice, once as a "wife," whose personal family tensions with husband and children will be alleviated through greater economic equality, and once in the pairing of "men and women, however black them may be," who should be judged on the "content of their character and not on the basis of the color of their skin."[19] Being judged on gender identity is nowhere mentioned. The point of drawing out this constitutive absence is to not engage in my own myth construction, to be as clear-eyed as possible as to his politics. As well, while I do see Dr. King's politics as much more radical than is accounted for in the nation's dominant collective memory, the inability to address gender oppression and the private sphere undermines, in particular, his critique of capitalism.

As Hirschmann argues in her work on gender and liberty in political theory, "freedom could be defined as abstract choice for men only because women were bound to aspects of life that are not necessarily chosen."[20] In other words, men can imagine and construct themselves as independent subjects because they are dependent on the work done by women in the private sphere. This work, to which women are bound if not by law in liberal spheres then even more pro-foundly by the construction of women as naturally domestic subjects defined by their ties to children and the family, is the hidden, under-acknowledged struc-tural undergirding of the seemingly autonomous realm of public life in liberal polities. To critique economic exploitation and capitalism without drawing out the forms of exploitation that shape women's role in the private sphere is to then leave productively absent from one's critique a fundamental pillar of the liberal capitalist social order. While, without doubt, Dr. King engaged in a profound critique of the American social and political order in his SCLC speech, I believe we actually build upon rather than detract or dismiss his efforts by engaging in an honest and rigorous assessment of the work that the absence of gender and the private sphere does to what are otherwise quite radical political views. To reveal the deeper historical roots of this absence in the 1967 SCLC speech, then, I take us back to King's 1952 letter to Coretta Scott, back to the hidden transcript.

Scott's gift of Bellamy's *Looking Backward* prompted King to expound and reveal his views on many topics: capitalism, revolution, Marxism, communism, religion, idealism, materialism, humanism, the relationship between means and ends in politics, wealth distribution, war, and race. But he did not say a word about gender, or more specifically the status of women. In the letter, King claimed that he had "just completed" Bellamy's book and found it "fascinating and stimulating."[21] As such, it is worth noting that King had not a word to say about the status and liberation of women that is so evidently part of Bellamy's utopian vision. The passages on gender roles and the status of women are not obscure parts of Bellamy's text. To the contrary, they are filtered throughout and sometimes posed at length. For example, at one point, Julian West learns from his twenty-first century era friend, Dr. Leete, the difference for women between living in the year 2000 as compared to those in 1887:

> It seems to us that women were more than any other class the victims of your civilization. There is something which, even at this distance of time, penetrates one with pathos in the spectacle of their ennuied, undeveloped lives, stunted at marriage, their narrow horizon, bounded so often, physically, by the four walls of the home, and morally by a petty circle of personal interests. I speak now, not of the poorer classes, who were generally worked to death, but also of the well-to-do and rich. From the greatest sorrows, as well as the petty frets of life, they had no refuge in the breezy outdoor world of human affairs, nor any interests save those of the family. Such an existence would have softened men's brains or driven them mad. All that is changed to-day. No woman is heard nowadays wishing she were a man, nor parents desiring boy rather than girl children. Our girls are as full of ambition for their careers as our boys. Marriage, when it comes, does not mean incarceration for them, nor does it separate them in anyway from the larger interests of society, the bustling life of the world. Only when maternity fills a woman's mind with new interests does she withdraw from the world at a time. Afterward, at any time, she may return to her place among her comrades, nor need ever lose touch with them.[22]

Take note of the importance that is placed upon removing the constraints of the private sphere and also challenging the presumed domestic status of women. Women's liberation requires not being "stunted by marriage" and "bounded... physically, by the four walls of home." The socialist Bellamy recognizes the physical, emotional, and developmental constraints that the private realm places upon women, including the presumption that their lives are defined by marriage to a man and as mother to his children, and that alone. Rather, in Bellamy's utopia, marriage and maternity are not forms of "incarceration" but options of real choice, and these are choices that do not prevent women from engaging in the "breezy outdoor world of human affairs," from pursuing the "full ambition of their careers," and taking her place in the public world "among her comrades." Bellamy is drawing a direct connection between freedom from the private realm and the capacity of women to be subjects of liberty in public life. If anything, the private/public split seems rather blurred in Bellamy's utopia, as even if a woman "withdraws from the world at time," she need "never lose touch with" her comrades.

One cannot say for certain why King did not offer any commentary or thoughts on gender in his 1952 letter, given that he would have read such elaborate and lengthy passages in *Looking Backward*. It is entirely possible that while King was in accord with Bellamy on much of his radical reimagining of the social order, the fundamental reordering of gendering relations and the relationship of the private to the public spheres fundamentally upset his patriarchal and theological worldview. We might also speculate about whether, in asking him what he thought about "Bellamy's predictions about our society," Coretta Scott may have wanted King to think and comment on this utopian reimagining of the role of women in society. In the end, we do not know for sure. But what we do know is that just as with the 1967 SCLC speech, the role of women in his 1952 letter stands as a productive absence. There are many lessons to take from Martin Luther King Jr.'s legacy: his actual historical and political legacy, not the mythical one. To critique him on the matter of gender is not to undermine the claim that he was a radical in many ways and that his memory as a radical does and should remain a substantiated resource for political claims in our time. But it also serves to once again show us that politics is a fundamentally and inescapably human endeavor, and it is thus fraught with the contingencies, imperfections, and limitations of human capacities. We witness these very human elements in King's concluding words to Scott in the 1952 letter.

After thanking Scott "a million times for introducing" him to such a "stimulating book," King shifts the discussion from matters public, political, and intellectual back to the personal and private. He returns to the issue of her earlier refusal to stay with his family, remarking: "I see you are much more influenced by other people than you are by me, as maybe you would rather spend your vacation with them since they have all the answers." And then, after reminding her "how nice 'I've been to you in the past,'" he surmises about her: "Oh well I guess all of us have a little of the unappreciative attitude in us." He still holds out hope she will change her mind and that they will not have to "break up about this trip."[23] His tone and words at the end of the letter are clearly that of a man who is feeling hurt and vulnerable, and it leads him to lash out, at times quite passive-aggressively. But what, then, to make of this? To be honest, I pondered not including these more intimate words in this chapter. For one, I do not see them to be necessarily pertinent to his political identity and politics. I am strongly opposed to the moralization of politics, and the accompanying tendency toward a focus on personal character rather than substance, policy, and publicly avowed and practiced commitments. King and Scott were married in 1953, so whatever issues they may have had at this time—and in their marriage as well—is not what I deem fodder for valuable political analysis. I do not think we learn much in that regard. That said, I end with these words in the spirit of refusing to reproduce the saintly myth of Dr. King that has taken hold in the American collective memory. His politics was more radical, much more radical, than his myth allows, or could ever allow in the US context. At the same time, even his radical politics involved its own productive absences, and thus serve as a chastening lesson for any of us concerned with imagining and enacting a more just world. In the end, in his public and personal life, Dr. Martin Luther King Jr. was, of course, human, all too human, and it is on that basis that we should assess him, draw lessons from his politics, and turn to his complex and substantiated political words and deeds as a resource for generating a social and political order that moves closer to, and hopefully even beyond, his radical vision.

Notes

1. Martin Luther King Jr. to Coretta Scott, personal correspondence. July 18, 1952. Atlanta, GA. As reprinted in *The Papers of Dr. Martin Luther King Jr.: Volume VI: Advocate of the Social Gospel, September 1948–March 1963*. Clayborne Carson, senior editor (Berkeley: University of California Press, 2007): 125. Hereafter cited as King to Scott. The letter can also be accessed at The Martin Luther King Research and Education Institute website, sponsored by Stanford University. http://mlk kpp01.stanford.edu/index.php/encyclopedia/documentsentry/to_coretta_scott.

2. Jeffrey M. Jones. "Americans Divided on Whether King's Dream Has Been Realized," *Gallup Politics*. August 26, 2011. See answers to "Views about Martin Luther King Jr." http://www.gallup.com/poll/149201/Americans-Divided-Whether-King-Dream-Realized.aspx (accessed: September 4, 2011).

3. Mark Engler. "Dr Martin Luther King's Economics: Through Jobs, Freedom," *The Nation*. February 1, 2010. http://www.thenation.com/article/dr-martin-luther-kings-economics-through-jobs-freedom# (accessed: August 15, 2011).

4. Jones (2011). See answers to "Views about Martin Luther King Jr."

5. James Scott. *Domination and the Arts of Resistance: Hidden Transcripts* (New Haven, CT: Yale University Press, 1992): 4, 2.

6. King to Scott: 123.

7. King to Scott: 123.

8. King to Scott: 124. Scott's inscription is dated April 7, 1952.

9. King to Scott: 123, 125.

10. King to Scott: 125.

11. King to Scott: 126.

12. King to Scott: 125.

13. King to Scott: 125.

14. Hannah Arendt. *The Human Condition* (Chicago and London: University of Chicago Press, 1958): 178.

15. Martin Luther King Jr. "Letter from Birmingham Jail," April 23, 1963. Birmingham, AL. This letter can be accessed at The Martin Luther King Research and Education Institute website, sponsored by Stanford University. http://mlk kpp01.stanford.edu/index.php/resources/article/annotated_letter_from_birmingham/ (accessed: May 3, 2013).

16. King. "Where Do We Go from Here," *Southern Christian Leadership Conference*, 10th Annual Convention, August 16, 1967. This letter can be accessed at The Martin Luther King Research and Education Institute website, sponsored by Stanford University. http://mlk kpp01.stanford.edu/index.php/kingpapers/article/where_do_we_go_from_here/ (accessed: May 5, 2013).

17. King. "Where Do We Go from Here," August 16, 1967.

18. Nancy Hirschmann. *The Subject of Liberty: Toward a Feminist Theory of Freedom* (Princeton, NJ: Princeton University Press, 2003): 41.

19. King. "Where Do We Go from Here," August 16, 1967.

20. Hirschmann (2003): 32.
21. King to Scott: 123.
22. Edward Bellamy. *Looking Backward, 2000 to 1887* (public domain book, Kindle version): 119 (e-book page). First published in 1888 (Boston: Ticknor & Co.).
23. King to Scott: 126.

CHAPTER 3

In Search of a New Left, Then and Now

Dick Howard

Why This, Why Now?

When Ron Scapp and Brian Seitz asked me to participate in this collective adventure, the journal *Platypus* had just published a rather long biographical interview with me. This format permitted me to bring together personal experience with theoretical reflection. Doug LaRocca, whom I'd never met, had "discovered" my *Specter of Democracy*; we then talked, on tape, and he did a first edit of my rambling reflections. I then reworked the material, trying to stay within the informal but comprehensive structure of our conversation (which can be found at http://platypus1917.org/2012/10/01/petrified-relations-must-be-forced-to-dance-interview-with-dick-howard/). Unfortunately, questions of copyright prevented its republication in this volume. In its place, I agreed to return briefly to put some of the themes invoked in that interview. I've introduced subtitles in the text in order to recall the liveliness of the question-and-answer format of the dialogue.

The emergence and the unexpected resonance of the appeal of the "99%" that coincided with the disappointment of the hopes kindled by the election of Barack Obama have led many to search for a "New Left." The label recalls those tumultuous years in the late 1960s when the civil rights movement joined the anti–Vietnam War protests to create a youthful social movement that was indeed new. The first problem with drawing an analogy to our day is that there is no "old left" dogma that needs to be rethought; Marxism is dead, Russia is Putin, China is roaring capitalism, Castro is dying, and Chavez is dead. What ideology could the 99% challenge? Some talk generally about fighting "hegemony," but in the last resort, their claim is moral: the good reject the bad, the many the few, the commoners the elite. This is pristine, pure, and self-satisfying, but it avoids the need to think about the kind of *politics* necessary to realize their goals. I don't mean to say that the 99% need to become policy wonks. They, we, need to understand the changed vision of the political that could accompany their appearance on the public stage. Only when their political impact has been realized can the policy wonks step in.

Having been a participant in the earlier New Left, I have tried to understand the splinters left by its implosion and to capture its spirit in work I've done over the years. I will try to summarize briefly here some of the stages in that search and the questions it raises in a way that will prove suggestive to those who seek to understand the *political* potential of the "99%."

Trying to Become Revolutionary

In the 1960s, the old left was communist. As the heir to the 1917 Russian Revolution, it maintained a mythical legitimacy, despite its gray failures and its compromises with the ruling classes of the West. A new left had to show that really existing communism was unfaithful to its own revolutionary premises. It could appeal to largely unknown but creative thinkers building from the communist tradition. That was why Karl Klare and I edited *The Unknown Dimension: European Marxism since Lenin* (1972). It is hard to remember that four decades ago, the works of thinkers like Lukács, Bloch, Korsch, and Gramsci were largely untranslated; that the Frankfurt School was known largely through the work of Marcuse, and some early texts of Habermas; and that creative philosophers like Sartre, Della Volpe, or Althusser were rethinking Marx's presuppositions. Today most of them are known, but the excitement and incitement brought by their work has fizzled as they have been claimed by the academy. Looking back, it is significant that the last chapter of *The Unknown Dimension* presented the theories of a "new working class" that were being developed by Serge Mallet and André Gorz. Theory was not the only domain that was changing and challenging.

The goal of my early work was to challenge the identification of Leninism with revolutionary thought and action. That was why I had edited the *Selected Political Writings of Rosa Luxemburg* (1971). However, my early enthusiasm for Luxemburg was shaken while preparing a paper for an international conference on her work in Italy in 1973. Why, I asked, was Luxemburg at once the most creative Marxist of her generation, and yet the most dogmatic adherent to the literal words of Marx? How could she be satisfied that she had refuted her revisionist opponents simply by showing that their arguments were refuted by Marx's texts? The search for answers led me to investigate more closely what I called *The Marxian Legacy* (1977). The first chapter of that book underlined the paradoxical combination of creativity and dogmatism in Luxemburg. The paradox continued to occupy me over the years as it reappeared in one or another thinker or movement; I came back to it directly a decade later in a revised second edition of the *Legacy* (1988). Was their something in Marx's own work that affected the way in which his heirs appropriated his thought during the century after his death? I was led to rethink the implications of my earlier book *The Development of the*

Marxian Dialectic (1972). I had asked how and why the young Marx, a serious critic of Hegel and theorist of alienation, had turned his attention to political economy. I thought at the time that this new stage represented the overcoming of mere philosophy. Now I had to ask what was "political" about the economy? This was the first of my repeated rereadings of Marx and attempts to understand his legacy.

Rethinking Revolution

When I reconsidered Marx, in a book titled *From Marx to Kant* (1985), I tried to understand his work in the broader context of the philosophical movement of German idealism, which began with Kant's creation of critical philosophy and which reached its theoretical height with Hegel's encyclopedic system. I suggested that there are three ways of doing modern philosophy: the critical, the originary, and the constitutive. Kant's critical philosophy looks to the empirical world and tries to understand its conditions of possibility; his approach is critical insofar as it shows the limits of rationality. Hegel's originary philosophy tries to understand how the really existing world acquires a rational form through its own self-development; the real and the rational are shown to be ultimately identical. Marx's constitutive philosophy transcends the subjective limits of the Kantian critique and inverts the Hegelian idealism; for him, the rational must be made to be real by the intervention of practical agency. In this way, it appears that Marx's method is the culmination and therefore the transcendence of German idealism. But why, then, did I suggest the move from Marx to Kant? The first reason was political: the constitutive theory that eliminates the need for philosophy turns out to be one explanation of the *totalitarian* politics, which cannot be blamed on a Leninist, or Stalinist, deformation of the Russian Revolution. When put into practice, Marx's theory had unintended consequences that needed to be explored, both from the standpoint of theory and from that of politics.[1]

Marx's model of revolution was built on the French example, where the overthrow of the monarch was followed rapidly by the proclamation of the republic in 1791. The republic in turn became increasingly radical, demanding not only formal political rights but social equality under the leadership of Robespierre and the Jacobins. But the progression was halted by a reactionary coup d'état. Marx and his heirs assumed that the reaction triumphed because economic conditions were not yet ripe; the nascent proletariat was too weak to impose its demands. "Well grubbed, Old Mole," Marx liked to say, assuming that the revolution continued to work underground, waiting for its time. Marx's confidence was based on his assumption that history follows a progressive logic which is rooted in material, and primarily economic, conditions. The problem, however, is that this vision does not leave much room for political creativity, even from someone like Rosa Luxemburg.

At this point, I began to wonder what could be learned from the other great revolution, the American? Was it simply a "bourgeois" triumph preparing the path for capitalism? Or did it have something to teach would-be revolutionaries?

Had I been wasting my time studying French history while disdaining my own? One thing I had learned from studying France was how to write in French. That led me to accept a proposal to write *La pensée politique de la Révolution américane* (1987). Coinciding with the bicentenary of the US constitution, this volume was a small part of the wave of antitotalitarian political thought known as the "second left."[2] What was revolutionary about the American experience, I argued, was the political creativity illustrated by the changed perspectives during the three phases of action: the anticolonial movement, the Confederation, and the creation of the constitution. Although this part of the story is well known, its significance only became clear with what its contemporaries called the "revolution of 1800." Elected after a bitter campaign in which each side denounced the other with rhetorical thunder adapted from the calamitous events in France, Jefferson's presidency was the first time in history that power passed peacefully from one party to another. The parties did not at first appreciate the significance of the event. When outgoing president Adams signed the "midnight appointments" of party loyalists, Jefferson's allies refused to issue their papers, asserting that they now incarnated the popular will. This conflict was resolved in 1803, when the Supreme Court affirmed, in *Marbury v. Madison*, that the origin and legitimation of power lies in the constitution.

Read in the context of the critique of totalitarianism, what was revolutionary in the American revolution was the gradual recognition that while the origin of power lies in the popular will, that will can never be incarnated by any party or any particular institution. When I returned to this American political history, I titled the book *Aux origines de la pensée politique américaine* (2004), stressing that the long (and at times troubled) history of American democracy can be understood as a series of contests among parties and institutions whose claim to speak for "the people" or to represent the popular will is challenged by other parties and institutions, maintaining a dynamic of renewal. There is a contest among the three branches of the federal government, but there are also conflicts between the claims of the federal, state, and municipal governments, as well as diverse demands from social and economic actors, including even the 1% against the 99%. It is these clashes—and not the elimination of conflict—that are essential to democratic life.

This interpretation of the American revolution as democratic also explains the theoretical reason for my return *From Marx to Kant*, which I reaffirmed in the revised edition (1993).[3] Kant distinguishes two modes of judgment in his *Critique of Judgment*. The first is subsumptive; it begins from a universal law in terms of which particular facts can be interpreted. The second is reflective; it begins with the particular and searches for a more general explanation of its claim to significance. Subsumptive judgments occur in the domain of science; reflective judgments belong especially to the aesthetic sphere. Although Kant does not draw this implication (but Hannah Arendt does), judgments of taste are similar to political claims. When I say that something is beautiful, I cannot appeal for justification to universal and objective laws; I must convince others to adopt my point of view, to understand why I have made this claim and why they should agree with me. The same reasoning applies to political judgments, whose validity depends neither on their subsumption under objective laws, nor does it depend on external constitutive action that imposes the revolutionary's vision on a passive world. Some of the implications of this changed perspective on political judgment were developed in two collections of essays published in the subsequent years, *The Politics of Critique* (1988) and *Defining the Political* (1989). The Fall of the Wall in 1989, after the emergence of an opposition building on institutions of civil society, was an unexpected confirmation of the anti-totalitarian spirit of a new left.

The Lure of Antipolitics

The Specter of Democracy (2003) begins with a series of citations from "The Communist Manifesto," which are a brilliant description of the emergence of modern democratic *society*. The rise of the bourgeoisie destroys "all fixed, fast-frozen relations" while "all new formed ones become antiquated before they can ossify. All that is solid melts into air, all that is holy is profaned." Marx's rhetoric is familiar; the vision of a history based on class struggles that are at last going to culminate in the negation of the negation is captivating. But Marx's title is telling: he will make "manifest" the inevitable course of historical necessity. There is place for judgment in this tableau, and no space for political initiative. Great forces are invoked, collisions are predicted, the end is inevitable. Yet Marx's pamphlet speaks also in the name of a political party. Why would one join? The appeal, clearly, is to the desire to be on the right side of History. The promise of communism is to eliminate those uncertainties that are essential to a democratic politics in which individuals have to express and defend their own judgment *not* in the face of History but along with their fellows. Marx describes brilliantly the emergence of the "specter of democracy," but his communist vision dissolves its dynamic by eliminating the space of political judgment by integrating the individual into a greater whole.

In the Introduction to *The Specter of Democracy*, I described two experiences that have continued to influence my thinking. The first took place when I was a student in France in 1966, still trying to learn the language. At my first Parisian demonstration against the war in Vietnam, I was caught up in the world historical spectrum evoked by the rhetoric of the speaker. Joining the applause, I noticed that the speaker was also applauding. Ah, I thought, this is no bourgeois egoist; his words are the wisdom of history, a revelation of its truth, the manifest certainty of revolutionary triumph, and I am participating in it! Of course, my participation was passive; it was an example of what I have come to call *antipolitics*, the illusion of politics that in the last resort brings the destruction of the space of politics. The dilemma became clear with the second experience, this one in Prague in 1967. I had become friends with a group of oppositional students, who explained to me that they had gotten in trouble with their government because they had organized a demonstration against the American war in Vietnam. I didn't understand; after all, their government opposed the war.

The difficulty, they explained, was due to the fact that *they* had organized the demonstration. Their refusal to accompany passively the necessities of history as deciphered by the Communist Party was a threat because it was based on their desire to participate actively in the political debate.

The lure of antipolitics does not entice only Marxists, nor does it attract only those on the left side of the political spectrum. In my repeated attempts to understand the paradoxes of democratic politics, I became increasingly aware that what I call "the political"—that symbolic framework which defines the space in which collective action becomes possible and meaningful—is inseparable from its paradoxical opposite, the lure of antipolitics. That is the claim that animates the reconstruction of the history of political thought proposed in *The Primacy of the Political* (2010). To make a long story short, Plato's appeal to the philosopher-king can be seen as the origin of antipolitics, for which Aristotle criticizes him explicitly. In the context of a different understanding of "the political," Saint Augustine pursues the Platonic claim, while Saint Thomas provides his political counterpart. In the same way, in a new political framework, Luther and Calvin offer the poles of antipolitics and politics; later, as the framework of political changes, Hobbes and Locke develop new variants of the same polarity. The paradox is not limited to the realm of theory; it appears as well in the polarity of the French and American revolutions. Of course these polarities are not pure; *The Primacy of the Political* describes as well sometimes stuttering and sometimes hefty attempts at openness.

But that is another story.

The 99% and the Search for a New Left

The intuition that unifies the work I've sketched here is that a New Left goes together with the emergence of a new definition of the political. That was what Marx offered when he turned from philosophy to political economy to search for the solution to what he called "the riddle of history" in a revolution to overthrow capitalism. That was, however, an anti-political definition of politics; it was the expression of Marx's constitutive philosophy that left no room for political judgment. But, bearing in mind the paradox of the political, Marx describes brilliantly the reality of an emerging democratic *society*. This is the political side of his legacy that should be preserved. To make it fruitful, it will be necessary to see whether and where there is a new sense of the political emerging today while also remaining alert to the inevitable temptations of the emergence of new forms of antipolitics. This is the challenge posed by the emergence of the 99%. The "old" New Left of my time imploded because it was unable to sustain this challenge. If the temptation of antipolitics is to be avoided today, we'll have to do better.

Notes

1. I cannot develop here the importance of the critique of totalitarianism, a touchy subject, particularly before the collapse of communism in 1989 when many feared

that criticism somehow was disloyal to the leftist cause. I will return to the concept when I discuss the "lure of antipolitics," of which totalitarianism is the modern form.

2. To my way of thinking, "*la deuxième gauche*" was a French variant of the New Left, with which I had been involved since my student days at Nanterre in May 1968. But that is another story.

3. Rereading these remarks, I'm struck by the fact that I have published revised or new editions of several books, as well as collections of essays that might have been reworked into more unified volumes. The reason for this, I think, is that I write for the present, not for the academy, let alone for eternity, expressing judgments and trying to justify them.

CHAPTER 4

The Status of Class

Stanley Aronowitz

C. Wright Mills famously amended the standard historical materialist theory of class. While not denying there is a ruling elite, and that the largest corporations were crucial among its constituents, he added two institutional orders: the top brass of the military and what he termed "the political directorate"—those perched at the pinnacle of national politics. At the same time, he offered a controversial judgment. If the criterion of class was power, Congress was relegated, in his schema, to the middle levels of power. Underlying his idea of class rule was the concept of historicity. And ownership and control of the decisive means of material production represented a central but not exclusive constituent of class power.

Mills's magisterial *The Power Elite* was published in 1956. He stated plainly that his theory was valid for the present (1956) and implied that it might be altered by altered circumstances. So, capitalist society did not produce classes ahistorically as many Marxists believe. Specifically, the accumulation of capital and its imperatives are not exclusive determinants of class power. Classes are emergent and are likely to change constituents. Based on his previous studies of the US labor leaders and the middle "classes"—old and new—Mills concluded that, in contrast to his earlier view that the rise of militant industrial unions had produced "new men of power," the constellations of workers and intermediate occupational and political formations did not constitute classes or elites in the historical sense. They had, by the mid-1950s, remained "dependent variables" in the economic and political system of power. Thus, Mills introduced two new criteria for evaluating the conditions of social conflict: does a social formation pose a challenge to existing power relations that force the elites and the rest of society to address its demands, and whether the subaltern social formations that constitute a class in the historical sense are indeterminate, and not a fixture in social relations.

Even the composition of the ruling elite may be in flux. For example, in the era of the national security state, the military plays a much more powerful role in the constitution of the political directorate than at any time in US history. This has been the case since the Cold War and its permanent war economy and continuous foreign wars. The professional politician who challenges the military-industrial complex is not likely to win a place, let alone the key place in national political power. Similarly, the key powers with the corporate capitalist sector are no longer large industrial production, corporations such as autos, and steel. We now live in the thrall of finance capital: principally investment banks and large insurance corporations. They call the tune for both domestic and offshore investment, both at the level of capital goods such as machinery and durable consumer goods like autos and housing. The open question today regarding the role of large corporations is the position of the giants of the new media. Are they creatures of finance capital? Or are they a separate sector that, given their wealth and cultural reach, constitutes an independent power center?

In this perspective, workers and their organizations become classes when they bid for power and propose to upend existing relationships and their force is great enough to cleave society. Such was the Egyptian protest. Had it refused to disperse after the fall of Mubarak and successfully neutralized the military—which had temporarily supported the uprising—it could have secured power. However, its internal divisions were too severe, so it permitted the military to win political hegemony. At this writing, the Turkish popular struggle to capture urban space is not concluded. Its ostensible goal, to protect a park from government plans to privatize much of it, has begun to escalate into a demand that the religious party's prime minister step down. The popular forces are mostly secular. Will they forge a coalition that bids for political and social power?

Antonio Gramsci has suggested that class power is the expression of a "historic bloc" rather than of a single formation. The bloc usually consists of diverse social formations. The Russian, Chinese, and Cuban revolutions were actually coalitions whose members disagreed about the direction of the revolution, but united around the objective of overturning the prevailing oligarchies. Similarly the French and American uprisings were comprised of disparate and even antagonistic formations. The Parisian proletariat joined the bourgeoisie that promised equality. When that promise was betrayed, a section of the subalterns formed the "Conspiracy of Equals," whose leader, Gracchus Babeuf, was executed in 1797 by the counterrevolutionary Thermidor. Again, after the British were vanquished by 1781, the struggle about the constitution among the American rebels devolved around issues of whether to have a lower and upper legislature, an independent Supreme Court, and, above all, a series of rights that protected the citizenry against the arbitrary powers of the central government. The outcome of these struggles was never truly resolved; power, however, resides, to this day, in the hands of a ruling bloc that has successfully relegated workers, the middle class of small entrepreneurs to, at most, middle levels of power in states and local communities, and, then, only for limited periods.

An objection to these formulations might be: aren't the workers and the poor social classes? Yes, but only for brief periods have they constituted class power in the historical sense. The industrial workers of the 1930s came close to class power, but were finally integrated into the prevailing system by the New Deal, even though the reforms of 1935–38 were the outcome of factory occupations, mass demonstrations, and strikes. The black freedom movement achieved class power in the 1960s when it chose to circumvent legislation in favor of direct action in some of the most visible sites of racial apartheid. That the movement was itself cleaved into a radical, direct action wing and a liberal, democratic wing did not thwart its achievement. But, it should be remembered that when Rev. Martin Luther King Jr. began to extend the movement's purview to issues of economic equality and justice, he was assassinated. It is one thing to integrate a lunch counter; it is another to demand recognition of black labor's power.

We would need to recognize Shulamith Firestone's claim that women are a class. I would amend her theory by insisting that women became a class in the historic meaning I have outlined when the whole society was forced to respond to the demands for abortion rights, workplace equality, and a new relationship between men and women in the bedroom. In this connection, *Roe v. Wade* (1973) was the outcome of women's struggle to become a class. The movement's direct confrontations with male power combined with the organization, ideologically as well as politically, of women of different social formations produced the Supreme Court decision. But women and black power proved historically limited. Their achievements could be and, in many respects, have been reversed, which reflects the indeterminate nature of class. As Adam Przeworski has argued, most struggles are about class formations rather than class struggles. And this formula is no less true of divisions among elements of the ruling elites. The ruling class does not directly rule; that is the function of the political directorate. But if the elite of power is itself a historical formation, how it works requires constant analysis and revision. This may disturb the dogmatists. But if that analysis does not take place, arid conceptions pollute the intellectual environment.

Now we must undertake a fresh analysis of rule: what are the global rulers? Are there more than a single power bloc, that is, can China, India, Russia, and Brazil (the BRIC countries) be considered, potentially, a rival bloc to the US-led Western alliance? Are foreign relations merely an efflux of existing power elite interests or are there genuine national interests at play in diplomacy and wars? Answering these and other questions are vital for grasping the nature of class power.

CHAPTER 5

"Fix the Tired": Cultural Politics and the Struggle for Shorter Hours

Kristin Lawler

In the spring of 2012, McDonald's began airing a series of commercials exhorting Americans not to "be a chicken" and to "take back your lunch!" The television spots feature a multicultural crew of cubicle slaves aghast at, but clearly a little seduced by, the audacity of their colleague, a black woman inciting a mini-revolt by heading out to McDonald's for a lunch break. The ad encourages the audience to join the woman, as an Asian male coworker does, in striding out of the office and into the local Mickey D's—here portrayed as an urban outdoor café. The ads were part of the "It's Your Lunch—Take It!" campaign, dominated on social media by red posters with messages like "A sesame seed of REVOLT has been planted" and "OVERTHROW the noon meeting!" And while much of the progressive blogosphere was horrified by the corporate appropriation of the revolutionary and disruptive discourse newly in the air since the Occupy-dominated fall of 2011, the fact that one of the world's most sophisticated market research and advertising design behemoths chose to sell burgers and chicken sandwiches by attempting to tap into Americans' discontent with the contemporary crisis of overwork through which they have been suffering speaks to something more than just McDonald's craven pursuit of profit.

It is material evidence for a growing exhaustion on the part of the American working class, and points, I'd like to propose, to the cultural conditions for the possibility of its overcoming. The vast majority of workers in this country have seen their hours of work increase—about 180 additional hours per year in comparison to 1979—and their average pay stagnate over the last 30–40 years, and this trend has only been exacerbated as the Great Recession that began in 2008 effectively doubled the unemployment rate, so that those "lucky" enough to have a job have been, by all indications, working scared—longer, harder, and without much of a peep.

In 2010, US worker productivity surged as a result of massive layoffs in the wake of the financial crisis (doubling from the 2009 rate, which was double that of 2008). This is only the most recent iteration of a trend that's been in evidence since the early 1970s, when the Keynesian wages-for-productivity deal between capital and labor was definitively called off. Now, with every new crisis and subsequent "jobless recovery," those fortunate enough to earn a paycheck in the aftermath tend to keep their heads down and accept doing the job of two or more people, "multitasking" (which all the research shows is not actually possible), or, more and more, forgoing essentials of a decent life, of which lunch may be just a minor example.

The Work Ethic and Its Discontents

Not surprisingly, people are stressed. And although pharmaceutical companies incessantly offer up a plethora of chemical solutions to the resulting epidemic of American anxiety and social disconnection, it seems the pills are not quite doing the job. According to the American Psychological Association's 2011 "Stress in the Workplace" study, 36% of workers report experiencing work stress regularly (other studies put the percentage at 40) and 49% attribute a significant part of this to low wages. But it's not just the money—43% of workers surveyed are unhappy due to heavy workload, 40% due to the unrealistic expectations of their employers, and 39% of workers report long hours as a major source of stress.[1]

One-third of workers report having serious trouble balancing work and life—and like all surveys that measure unauthorized attitudes, this is most likely underestimated. Arlie Hochschild's ethnographic work on families and children has for decades now made the case that overworked (and especially inegalitarian) two-income families suffer. In her most recent work, *The Outsourced Self*, Hochschild discusses the penalties imposed on the personal sphere by "the unforgiving demands of the American workplace," and finds that children—70 percent of whom live in households in which all the adults work—are the most harshly punished of all. Hochschild quotes economist Sylvia Hewlett's *When the Bough Breaks: The Cost of Neglecting Our Children*: "compared with the previous generation, young people today are more likely to commit suicide; need psychiatric help; suffer a severe eating disorder; abuse drugs; be the victim of a violent crime."[2]

The increasing penetration of what Herbert Marcuse calls the "performance principle"—the imperative that every moment and every iota of the natural world be made to produce at optimum efficiency, an imperative that he, following Marx and Max Weber, sees as the defining feature of contemporary capitalism—into educational institutions means that kids suffer at school, too. Subject to an increasingly stressful regime of testing and homework that leaves many plagued by depression and anxiety, children and teens are increasingly likely to use performance-enhancing and mood-altering drugs in an attempt to keep up with it all. New numbers indicate that 11% of American schoolchildren, and one in five teenage boys, have been labeled with "attention deficit hyperactivity disorder" (ADHD)—an overblown medicalization of what amounts to kids' old-fashioned resistance to the intensified workload. Today, the newest drug trend in middle-class high schools is the abuse of Adderall, an ADHD drug that helps the kids focus. (You know when teens do drugs for work rather than play, something has really changed.) And the talk among the new billionaire educational "reformers" and the officials directing their project is that what we really need to do is eliminate summer vacation for kids!

This ethos, having saturated elementary and secondary education with its relentless regime of testing, assessment, and endless work, now has higher education clearly in its sights, demanding an end to the "useless" thinking that characterizes a broad liberal arts education and an intensified articulation of the undergraduate degree to the requirements of corporations—the very corporations that make profit from the desperate overwork of their employees. Colleges and universities, at one time at least in part a space to develop thinking outside of the standard "good = profitable," are being squeezed under a new regime disguised with the terms "accountability" and "outcomes assessment," but which is actually a strategy to bring one last somewhat intellectually unruly place under rational, and increasingly corporate, control.

Public support for these policies is bought with the withdrawal of government funds from higher education, funding without which the expansion of college from elites to a significant mass of Americans never existed, and probably can't be viable. (This is a central piece of a broader political strategy known as "starving the beast"—underfunding public services so that they don't function properly, and on that basis making a case for their transformation and privatization. It applies to both public colleges and universities and privates, which rely on public support to operate.) And this is happening at precisely a moment when we desperately need *more* real thinking, not less.

For instance, the ecological costs of what economist Juliet Schor calls the "business-as-usual economy" are, it goes without saying at this point, severe. The environmental crisis that we face demands attention, presence, critical thinking, creativity—precisely the qualities that overwork and its concomitant stresses so severely impede. Capital's logic—what Jock Young, following Marcuse, calls the "ethos of productivity"—holds that anything worth doing can be quantitatively measured in terms of what it produces, rather than what it is *in itself*. This logic, applied to the natural world, has ushered in the contemporary era of chronic catastrophe. Planet Earth has a brilliant ability to purify itself, innovate solutions, and heal from toxins when it's given a break. But the productivist ethic spares nothing—and no bit of mountaintop or shale rock or ocean is left just to *be*. From the perspective of capital, the natural world is little more than a resource to be extracted productively or a dump for the effects of profit-making production. Thinking beyond the ethos of productivity that, as Heidegger illustrates, frames our "world picture" is basically a matter of survival at this point.

The plague of overwork and the culture that supports it has even more immediate consequences: people's very physical safety is at risk. Americans fell in love with the heroic Captain Sully Sullenberger after he successfully landed a jumbo jet on the surface of the Hudson River in 2009. Sadly, they didn't pay much attention when he testified before Congress shortly afterward that if people want brilliant, highly trained, experienced pilots like him to fly their planes safely, they'll have to support the pilots' union in fighting for it—since the airlines themselves wage a relentless battle in every contract negotiation to allow planes to be flown by far less experienced pilots working 80-hour weeks for close to minimum wage.

A few weeks after Sully's "miracle on the Hudson," a smaller, regional jet crashed in upstate New York, killing everyone on board and one person on the ground. It had been flown by two inexperienced, underpaid pilots who were later found to have been suffering from fatigue. In another of many examples, New York City in 2012 shut down a number of Chinatown-run bus companies for safety violations to which attention was brought by a horrific, deadly highway crash caused by one of many exhausted and underpaid drivers. And "distracted driving"—otherwise known as the attempt to multitask behind the wheel—is now, with fatigue, the leading cause of auto accidents.

What unites all this is very simple. According to the UN's International Labour Organization, Americans work 137 more hours per year than Japanese workers, 260 more hours than British workers, and 499 more hours per year than French workers.[3] America is the only rich country without any mandated time off, and its workers continue to be the most productive, per hour, on earth. Why do we work longer and harder than folks in other highly wealthy countries? The answer points to the importance both of culture and of movements: the decline of organized labor in the United States during the past 40 years, and the cultural ideology of the work ethic into which American workers, more than others around the world, are socialized.

This work ethic, first outlined by Max Weber in his well-worn classic *The Protestant Ethic and the Spirit of Capitalism*, grounds a culture in which hard work in itself is a moral imperative and laziness, in itself, is a sign of moral turpitude. America, more than any other nation, has been culturally shaped by the "spirit of capitalism"—the idea, as Weber says, "so familiar to us and yet really so little a matter of course," that the combination of hard work and a compulsion to save and accumulate money characterizes the ethics of the morally upright man. What unites the two, hard work and penny-pinching, is an ascetic avoidance of any behavior that's spontaneous or hedonistic. In this ethic, the good is identified with a detached, calculating attitude toward the moments of one's life and our natural surroundings; the bad or unethical is identified with the "spontaneous enjoyment of life," in whatever forms it takes. This ethic—the privileging of work, thrift, and calculating detachment over play, hedonism, and spontaneity— was the characteristic feature of the Puritan culture that founded a significant portion of America, and that is central to the operation of capitalism still.

For although this essentially Puritan culture encourages us to equate being "productive" with being a moral, ethical person, the "work ethic" at this point is little more than a cultural strategy to dupe workers out of understanding the simple fact that what we're really seeing here is as old-fashioned as those McDonald's ads are trying to look: the class struggle. In Weber's analysis, capitalism, once it becomes dominant, no longer needs the ascetic culture that built the bourgeoisie. However, this originally Puritan class became so successful that their Calvinist values are now a tenet of our culture. So Americans are not working longer and harder for less because they necessarily believe it's the right thing to do—although the ideological dominance of the work ethic demands at least lip service, and the ideological apparatuses of the state, as Louis Althusser showed us long ago, *do* punish perceived resistance. And they are not working so hard because there's not *enough* to provide for people outside of the regime of endless work, as the current scarcity-dominated corporate-funded media discourse would have us believe. Both in the long and the short term, it's not real material scarcity but the unevenness of the struggle between capital and labor that accounts for where American (and, increasingly, European) workers are today.

In fact, the massive implementation of labor-saving technologies makes possible the ancient dream of human liberation from alienated labor, articulated early on by Aristotle in *Politics*: "if the shuttle would then weave, and the lyre play of itself; nor would the architect want of servants, or the master slaves." But freedom is not an automatic result of technological "progress." Without a fight, capital will take the gains in increased profits—after all, profit is the driving force behind innovation to begin with. Technological innovation is *both* capital's response to workers' waging of struggle—if workers were like robots (work much, desire little), there would be no need for capital to replace them with robots—*and* the freedom-or-destitution stakes of the struggle itself. Who wins will determine whether labor-saving technology will fulfill the dream of more leisure and freedom for all or whether it will continue to throw masses of workers into penury while the rest work desperately to keep a paycheck.

The Greatest Refusal

In this struggle between capital and labor, it seems that the bosses are winning the cultural as well as the material battle, in the United States at least. However, the American work ethic is just never completely internalized by the working class, I would argue, simply because ultimately it's an iteration of the logic of capital. Human beings just do not live according to the same logic that corporations do. Simply put, there is an opposing logic at work within the capitalist system—what Stanley Aronowitz, in *The Crisis of Historical Materialism*, calls "the counterlogic of the working class." If the logic of capital is the push for profit, and ever-greater profit through the exploitation of labor—more and more production for low and declining wages—the opposing working class counter-logic becomes the locus of any real resistance to the crisis of overwork we've been outlining.

Italian autonomist Marxist Antonio Negri calls this the "refusal of work"— the mass insubordination to capital's demand that all moments of life and pieces of the natural world be alienated and made productive rather than enjoyed in themselves. For both Aronowitz and Negri, the essence of working class struggle is everything that people do outside of and in opposition to the logic of capital.

Harry Cleaver, in his introduction to Negri's *Marx beyond Marx*, summarizes it thus:

> Capitalism is a social system with two subjectivities, in which one subject (capital) controls the other subject (working class) through the imposition of work and surplus work . . . therefore, the central struggle of the working class as an independent subject is to break capitalist control through the refusal of work . . . in the space gained . . . the revolutionary class builds its own independent projects—its own self-valorization.[4]

This self-valorization consists of all the independent, self-directed activities that people engage in as a result of their own desires and aspirations and that are by definition antagonistic to capital's push to increase profit quantitatively on the back of labor. Some of it is active and productive, some is passive and receptive, but it's all a product of the individual constituting time on his or her own terms. It's fundamentally different from the colonized time that constitutes life at work.

Even during a moment characterized by massive worker insecurity, the existence of this counter-logic remains easy to spot, if you know where to look. The mobilization of it is another question, to be discussed below. But there are certainly plenty of contemporary signs pointing to a substantial subterranean resistance to the demand that all life be subordinated to paid labor. The trend is apparent in the products both of the critical infrastructure of academics and intellectuals and of commercially produced popular culture. Sadly, where it can't be found right now is in its original home—in the organized American labor movement.

Still, a discourse around shortening the hours of labor *is* emerging to make sense both of the double crisis of overwork and unemployment, and of the budding resistance to this state of affairs. In June 2012, a front page article in the *New York Times* Sunday Review section, entitled "The Busy Trap," pilloried the middle-class professional's seeping fetish of equating being "crazy busy" with having a life that matters; the author finishes his ode to idleness and pleasure with the assertion that "life is too short to be busy."[5]

Robert and Edward Skidelsky, in their 2012 book *How Much Is Enough?*, discuss a 1930 John Maynard Keynes essay that predicts that as technological progress makes each hour of labor more productive, average hours of work would decline, so that by 2030, the workweek would be around 15 hours. According to the authors, "he looked forward to a moment when the spontaneous, joyful attitude to life now confined to artists and free spirits was diffused through society as a whole."[6] Although the authors attribute overwork in the face of high technology to a rising material standard of living, and make a case, neither innovative nor particularly strong, for an embrace of material austerity as the road to freedom in time, it is the 15-hour workweek idea that's gotten the book the most attention.

In a similar vein, the Center for Economic Policy and Research proposed a shorter workweek as part of the solution to global warming in early 2013. The logic was similar to that of the Skidelskys—that less work is synonymous with decreased consumption and thus with an improvement in the natural environment. The reality, though, is that only *some* forms of consumption are environmentally damaging. Eating out in restaurants, for example, is far more efficient and ecologically friendly than are private meals at home. And compostable, environmentally friendly packaging, like organically grown food, is actually *more* expensive, not less. Far more accurate in terms of economics (and way more fun) than this austere, patrician line on leisure and consumption is the sentiment of the old labor movement song: "Whether you work by the piece or by the day, decreasing the hours increases the pay."[7]

And in early 2012, the New Economics Foundation, a British think tank, came out for a 20-hour workweek as the solution to the technological displacement of jobs, as well as to the other overwork-fueled social problems. One of the authors of the report asserted that "there is a great disequilibrium between those who have got too much paid work, and those who have got too little or none."[8] The report garnered a great deal of play as an innovative idea that made sense. But there was no discussion of how a 20-hour week might actually be accomplished aside from the usual milquetoast "government should mandate it." That exhortation might be a nice way to end a paper, but it's no strategy for social transformation.

Even the anodyne, business-friendly TED Talks have gotten in on the action. One recent speech-maker extolled the importance of work–life balance and even of leisure, but again without saying a word about the history of the capital/labor struggle over work time, the outcome of which actually determines how long and how hard people are working.

And in June 2012, highly influential left-wing talk show host Bill Maher ended his HBO show with a lamentation that America is "the only country where no one really gets the day off." Pointing to the six-week paid vacations and mid-day siesta breaks enjoyed by Europeans, he answers his own question—why the difference?—by asserting rightly that Americans are working scared, terrified to lose their jobs because we're the only "big-boy" country in which unemployment means total destitution. And unlike many of those who criticize overwork in America, Maher acknowledges that it's the decline of the union movement that is to blame.

The Folks Who Brought You the Weekend

The problem, as Maher points out, is that the organized labor movement has been in massive decline for decades, under relentless attack by the union-busting and outsourcing that have characterized capital's post-1973 neo-liberal agenda. The bumper-sticker version of this insight puts it well: "The Labor Movement: the folks who brought you the weekend"; it's a reminder that the labor movement and the question of hours are linked not only in terms of the problem of overwork but also of its solution. According to David Roediger and Philip Foner's *Our Own Time*, the seminal study of the movement for shorter hours within American labor, "the length of the workday has historically been the central issue raised by the American labor movement during its most dynamic periods of organization."[9] The authors go on to demonstrate the way in which the shorter hours' demand, both as a means to share the work during times of high unemployment and as a means to the enjoyable life that capitalist "progress" can technically make possible with a minimum of toil, has been the most inspirational that the labor movement has ever put forth.

And according to Jonathan Cutler, author of *Labor's Time*, a study of the shorter hours movement within the 1950s' United Auto Workers-CIO, when after much internal struggle the union effectively abandoned the syndicalism of the hours' demand for union president Walter Reuther's corporatist push to make labor a partner in managing production (and society), it lost its ability to inspire and thus to mobilize workers in the face of increasing employer aggressiveness. According to Cutler's analysis, the demand for a 30-hour workweek at 40 hours' pay was consistently the most popular issue among the union's rank and file. He argues that the demand, in addition to potentially ameliorating the desperation accompanying unemployment, is inherently solidaristic across lines of race, ethnicity, and gender—lines that capital has always used to divide and conquer the working class. Roediger and Foner again:

> Reduction of hours became an explosive demand partly because of its unique capacity to unify workers across the lines of craft, race, sex, skill, age, and ethnicity. Attempts by the employing classes to divide labor could be implemented with relative ease where wage rates were concerned . . . With regard to hours, the situation was different . . . thus the shorter working day was an issue that could mitigate, though not completely overcome, the deep racial and ethnic divisions that complicated class organization in the United States.[10]

McDonald's unwittingly makes this case with the fascinating racial politics of its "take back lunch" campaign—gender and racial-ethnic difference is elided in the appeal to a seemingly universal desire for leisure. And this universality is central to the shorter hours strategy.

Because, fundamentally, the question of hours is a question of overall labor supply. A shorter-hours labor strategy pushes to restrict the supply of labor provided to capital while avoiding the unsustainable exclusiveness of the old AFL craft union version. If the push for a shorter workday or week is to be successful, everyone has to be *in*. When people work less, this becomes a means to the leverage provided by an undersupply of labor relative to demand, as well as being something valuable *in itself*. And the inherent solidarity of the strategy extends to the unemployed as well: as AFL President Samuel Gompers said in 1887, "so long as there is one who seeks employment and cannot find it, the hours of labor are too long."[11]

The globalization of capital's supply chains makes a solidaristic labor supply strategy even more crucial, as the fortunes of one nation's workers, waged and unwaged, are increasingly, and more and more visibly, tied to those of all other nations. Any "us" and "them" strategy pits workers against workers in an ugly race to the bottom in which we all supposedly have to work harder to compete with the (fill in the blank) workers who will work more for less. This is precisely the reason that if the organized union movement is to successfully mobilize the resources it still commands—16 million US members and over ten billion dollars in dues revenue, still not quite something to sneeze at—it must rethink many things, from its codependent relationship with the Democratic Party specifically and fetishizing of electoral politics more generally, to its focus on defending the benefits of its own members rather than on a broader working class strategy, to, most important, what Aronowitz has criticized as its focus on "jobs, jobs, jobs." The latter is simply not what moves people. Movements need many things, but an inspirational discourse may just be the most important. Defending and demanding jobs and more jobs has not succeeded. The history of the labor movement shows, however, that the push for freedom has.

There is plenty of evidence that the popularity of the shorter hours' demand could be more powerful today than ever. For one thing, the fact that overall US worker productivity was down 1.9% in the fourth quarter of 2012, after growing only anemically in 2011, even though the high unemployment rate barely budged, seems to be a sign that the strategy of working folks to death may just be hitting a wall. The market research firms that drive big advertising certainly seem to think so.

What Commercials Signify

For example, an ad for Carnival Cruise Lines features a middle-aged dad letting loose on the dance floor to the tune of "I Don't Want to Work," as his son's voice-over reflects on how "different" dad seems on vacation. "What's going on with Dad?" the boy intones over images of the father laughing and goofing off with his kids and romancing his wife. "He seems different. He's not tucking in his shirt. He's not talking about work. He's not checking messages every nine seconds . . . and now this?"

This is just one of many leisure industry ads that highlight the personal joy and family connections that leisure promotes and overwork warps. Corona beer commercials for years now have used the popular metaphor of the beach for leisure and relaxation and counterposed this image with those of the workaday world, from which it is assumed that viewers want a respite (and can supposedly get it by drinking a Corona—which is probably a start, given Roy Rosenzweig's claim in *Eight Hours for What We Will* that the eight-hour movement of the late 19th century originated in the working class culture of leisure and conviviality of the pubs).

Cheetos is currently selling tortilla chips with a spot in which its hipster cheetah mascot joins two construction workers in disco dancing around a construction site and joyfully ignoring the boss' frustrated exhortations to get back to work. A particularly striking ad in the same campaign depicts a bank teller shrugging in the face of armed robbers bursting in and screaming; the cheetah next to her says lazily, "we're on break," as they both chomp chips and refuse to take responsibility for defending the bank's financial interests. The ads end with the tagline "Take a Cheetos Break."

And a new "Take Back Your Summer" ad campaign for Las Vegas tourism dramatizes a grim-looking workplace ceremony in which a silver-haired boss awards a middle-aged man with a certificate honoring his not having taken a vacation day since 1997. The worker responds by screaming "Certificate? Certificate?" and running around the room, ripping up the said certificate and the sad-looking "celebrate" sign hung comically in the corner. The ad ends with an image: "Vegas. TAKE your vacation!"

Other ads in the campaign highlight workers "making their escape" from their dehumanizing offices, breaking out of the workplace paramilitary style, as though it's a prisoner-of-war camp. A few images are even more explicitly political: a worker stands on her desk, Norma Rae style, holding up a "Vacation Now" sign and saying, "I have 47 vacation days! That is insane! They're our days! Let's take back our summer!" Another depicts a well-attended rally about which one participant explains, "we're rallying everyone to use their vacation days this summer . . . how many do you have?" Assorted workers—white collar, construction, and service—tell how much vacation time they've accumulated but never used, because, as one of the workers says in another spot, "*nobody* takes their vacation days."

Highly significant here is the way this politics plays in terms of the Social Security/retirement age debate, one of today's most important contemporary questions of labor supply and work versus leisure. An older fellow bikes up to the rally and asks, "I'm retired. Can *I* take a vacation?" One can practically hear the shrill conservative response in the awkward pin-drop silence that follows the question. When a rally leader cries, "sure. You've earned it!" and the crowd explodes in celebration, the commercial implicitly demonstrates a key political reality. To the extent that the retired and the still working refuse to be pitted against one another, the rally, a political attempt to transform a work-obsessed culture, can continue. These ads are, I am arguing, highly significant as evidence of a widespread, subterranean refusal of work and its attendant resentments into which advertisers are trying to tap.

They also provide evidence to refute the idea, widely accepted in leftist circles, that advertising in particular and commercially produced culture more generally has no subversive political content. I've argued elsewhere[12] that it's high time for progressives to abandon the idea that consumer culture functions only to prop up the current, exploitative capitalist order, the very one that keeps the masses chained to their cubicles (or wherever they work). This idea has a couple of main incarnations. First, Birmingham center theorists like Dick Hebdige argued that cultural opposition, like that of the punk rockers that the Birmingham Centre for Contemporary Cultural Studies (BCCCS) famously studied, to capital is "real" but inevitably gets swallowed up by the system and packaged for sale, stripped of any but surface, meaningless opposition. More recently, Thomas Frank in his 1997 *The Conquest of Cool*, posits oppositional popular culture as a product of capital, specifically the hucksters on Madison Avenue, because if a person wants to be "cool" and distinguish him or herself from the masses, that person must continually buy something new in order to maintain this distinction. Either way, rebellion seems just another mode of incorporation into the system.

However, the truth is that the real political significance of commercial culture is in the contradictory ways its message overflows its formal, system-perpetuating functions. As Ellen Willis said of the 1960s' counterculture, arguing against "standard leftist notions about advanced capitalism—that the consumer economy makes us slaves to commodities, that the function of the mass media is to manipulate our fantasies so we will equate fulfillment with buying the system's products," she asserts that

> these ideas are at most half true. Mass consumption, advertising, and mass art are a corporate Frankenstein; while they reinforce the system, they also undermine it . . . the mass media helped to spread rebellion, and the system obligingly marketed products that encouraged it, for the simple reason that there was money to be made from the rebels who were also consumers. *On one level the sixties revolt was an impressive illustration of Lenin's remark that the capitalist will sell you the rope to hang him with.*[13]
>
> (emphasis added)

As much fun as it is to trace what Daniel Bell called the cultural contradictions of capitalism, though—and all the subversive effects that commercial broadcasts of countercultural content, like rock and roll, or surfing, for instance, have had—this is simply not enough. For one thing, the capitalist will as just as easily sell you the rope to hang *yourself* with. The Vegas commercials and ones like them may be getting more prominent, but they are by no means the only cultural messages on television today. Campbell's soup advertises a liquid food that you can drink at your desk or wherever it is you are hurrying off to. There is even a toy foot spa for little girls, called Orbeez, the ads for which portray preteen girls stressed after a hard day, trying to relax by bathing their feet. Assorted television, radio, and print spots support the still-dominant discourse that says there is an individual solution to the structural problem of what might be called the "energy crisis" of the overworked American employee (and student). In this case, the advertisers are not tapping into subversive desire but into the exhaustion and desperation felt by time-poor workers of all stripes.

Fix the Tired

One of the most ubiquitous of these aims is to sell "5-hour Energy," a liquid stimulant that comes in single-serving plastic bottles meant to be ingested in one quick quaff. The advertisements have many iterations, but generally hew to the same theme. A typical one opens with a classic blues track, wailing repeatedly "I'm so tired..." behind images of workers of all collars wilting from exhaustion at their desks and on construction sites. The gravelly voiced, oh-so-sympathetic narrator gives voice to what we all know: "Tired sucks.

Not end-of-the-long-day tired, but middle-of-the-day, places-to-go, things-to-do, deadlines-to-meet, but all-I-want-to-do-is-close-my-eyes tired. 5-hour Energy fixes tired fast. One shot. Back to work. Problem solved. 5-hour Energy. Fix the tired."

Probably the most discouraging of these ads, from the perspective I've outlined, are the spots that highlight workers who simply don't have the time or energy to brew even the morning cup of coffee with which sleep-deprived workers fuel their workday, and used to at least feel they had a few moments to enjoy. In another ad, a bed-headed young woman is trying to find the energy to work out on her home exercise equipment—an activity broadly encouraged these days as one key to being happier and more productive under the stressful circumstances. In the commercial narrative, 5-hour Energy makes the woman's routine on her glorified hamster wheel possible. It seems only a matter of time before the little stimulant is portrayed as the way to find the energy to do yoga, or meditate, or any of the other new-agey ways that will purportedly make us all more "sane" and "relaxed." Can the 5-hour Energy solution for finding the strength to pick up the Prozac bottle to make tolerable the misery of overwork be far behind?

Sadly, the 5-hour Energy "solution" is emblematic of much of what is discursively held out to workers as the way to navigate this deadly state of affairs. (In more ways than one—the substance has been cited in numerous reports of deaths to the Food and Drug Administration.)[14] Along with ingesting the little drink (and then throwing away the hard, tiny plastic bottle), we are exhorted to get yet another debt-funded degree, to work harder, to stay at work longer, to multitask better, and to forget everything else that makes life worth living while we spend all of our time working to afford student debt, food, gas, and health care.

A new Hormel ad campaign celebrates this explicitly: one of its "Hardest Working Women" ads begins by panning over a cubicle decorated with family photos and drawings by children. The woman at the desk looks tired but determined; the narrator intones: "Your desk. It's where you spend a lifetime. So your kids can go to college. So you can actually visit that beach displayed proudly on your monitor. For that, you work through lunch. Or, as we like to say, lunch through work." The microwave meal is touted as "desk drawer to hot and ready within 90 seconds." And the campaign includes a "Hardest Working Women" contest, in which family and friends are invited to nominate hard-working women to win a three-day trip to NYC (flying coach) worth approximately $4,900. This year's winner received a makeover and a spot on Oprah's new show, along with a certificate that reads:

> Today we celebrate Crystal ... Crystal puts in long hours at the medical clinic that she runs, is an active mom to three young children, serves as her daughter's Girl Scout troop leader, donates to charities and is a serious couponer. According to her husband, she puts all of these responsibilities before herself time and again.

The Return of Cultural Politics

Clearly, advertisers know that there are two tendencies out there with respect to work: docility born of desperation and resistance born of the desire for something more. They are agnostic with respect to which tendency is preferable—in this, the hedonistic commercial side of capital is a highly unreliable ally of its Puritan, production-directing brethren. What advertisers are *not* equivocal about is how collective action is produced: they know that when you appeal successfully to a deeply held sentiment, be it a desire or a fear, you have the ability to move masses of people to do the same thing, all at once. Advertisers and the corporations they serve seek commercial collective action—everybody buys the same thing at the same time. But this is certainly not the only kind of collective action that people can be inspired to engage in.

Commercial appeals to both desire and fear abound, because both drive working class strategies in the contemporary absence of a vibrant labor movement. Which pitch workers choose depends on more than admen, though. As American Studies scholar Michael Denning puts it, "subaltern experience does not necessarily generate social criticism and cultural resistance; the possibility of popular political readings of cultural commodities depends on the cultivation, organization, and mobilization of audiences by oppositional subcultures and social movements."[15]

I think it's clear that there is a massive resistance to work and overwork, and a desire for freedom and pleasure, that characterizes both the working class in general and the contemporary moment in particular. Imagine if the labor movement—as it has before, with great success—worked to mobilize the radical cultural politics of freedom that are so clearly available in order to agitate for a shorter workweek.

Consider May Day. The late-nineteenth-century labor movement mobilized the already-existing pagan spring celebration in order to demand the eight-hour day. After the Haymarket massacre in May 1886 at a shorter-hours rally, May 1 became the International Workers' Holiday, which it's been ever since. Both American politicians and the more conservative elements of the union movement itself worked to suppress the essentially Dionysian cultural politics of the May Day holiday, largely by replacing it with September's more austere and work-affirming "Labor Day" and officially renaming May Day "Loyalty Day." Still, the May Day tradition remains important, both as an ongoing locus of labor activity and as a reminder of the incredible power that's unleashed when the widespread cultural desire for freedom is mobilized—not just to sell products but actually to gain freedom.

Capital really does make technically possible freedom in time as well as material abundance, even as it disavows this potential in favor of a discourse of artificially perpetuated scarcity deployed to maintain control over an always potentially restive working class. While ideologists insist that *"there just isn't enough"* for people to escape the austerity of work without end, global economic output continues to rise. It's only invisible because it is more and more concentrated in the hands of the world's very wealthiest entities—and this massive inequality leads to economically devastating speculative bubbles as well as to penury and overwork among the mass of workers, waged and unwaged. Right now, advertisers are hedging their bets on which is the more powerful popular mover—desperation or desire. For the moment, they are playing both sides. If the American union movement embraced its own most powerful traditions—radical cultural organizing and the push for shorter hours—I'd say the smart money would bet on freedom.

Notes

1. American Psychological Association and Harris Interactive. "Stress in the Workplace: Survey Summary," March 2011. http://www.apa.org/news/press/releases/phwa-survey-summary.pdf.
2. Hewlett, Sylvia, quoted in Arlie Hochschild. *The Outsourced Self: Intimate Life in Market Times* (New York: Metropolitan Books, 2012).
3. International Labour Organization, Conditions of Work and Employment Programme. "Working Time in the Twenty-First Century," October 2011. http://www.ilo.org/wcmsp5/groups/public/—ed_protect/—protrav/—travail/documents/publication/wcms_161734.pdf.
4. Cleaver, Harry, in Antonio Negri. *Marx beyond Marx: Lessons on the Grundrisse* (Brooklyn: Autonomedia, 1991): xxiv.
5. Kreider, Tim. "The Busy Trap," *New York Times*, July 1, 2012.
6. Skidelsky, Robert, and Edward Skidelsky. *How Much Is Enough? Money and the Good Life* (New York: Other Press, 2012): 16.
7. The anti-consumerist line on leisure has a long aristocratic history, as does its counterpart in mass fantasy. Sebastian de Grazia, in his 1962 *Of Time, Work, and Leisure*, compares the dream of Utopia—a world of "meaningful" leisure without alienated work—to the folk dream of Cockaigne, or "The Big Rock Candy Mountain." The latter is a dream not of cultured leisure but of, as de Grazia dismissively puts it, "ease and abundance." Then and now, both classes of the anti-work dream are with us. I am making the case that American advertisers are looking to tap into what inspires large numbers of people. Luckily for those who don't want their leisure policed by the guardians of high culture, The Big Rock Candy Mountain wins out in popular culture every time.
8. New Economics Foundation, *Twenty-One Hours: Why a Shorter Working Week Can Help Us All to Flourish in the 21st Century*, January 2012. http://neweconomics.org/sites/neweconomics.org/files/21_Hours.pdf.
9. Roediger, David, and Philip Foner. *Our Own Time: A History of American Labor and the Working Day* (New York: Verso, 1989): vii.
10. Ibid., p. viii.
11. The term "unwaged work" is probably a more useful one than "unemployment," though: simply put, not everyone who works earns a wage. There is a seminal, unwaged sector of the working class—those, like women, children, students, casual workers, even modern-day slaves, whose labor of reproduction makes the whole system of production possible. As Silvia Federici and the Wages for Housework

movement have made clear in their groundbreaking analyses, any true working class solidarity must include an overcoming of the artificial waged/unwaged divide. This is why a culture of resistance to work in all its forms, rather than the defense of the jobs of waged workers, is so much key to the transformation of working class fortunes.

12. Lawler, Kristin. *The American Surfer: Radical Culture and Capitalism* (New York: Routledge, 2011).

13. Willis, Ellen. *Beginning to See the Light: Sex, Hope, and Rock and Roll* (Hanover, NH: Wesleyan University Press, 1992): xvi.

14. Meier, Barry. "Caffeinated Drink Cited in Reports of 13 Deaths," *New York Times*, November 14, 2012.

15. Denning, Michael. *The Cultural Front: The Laboring of American Culture* (New York: Verso, 1998): 64.

CHAPTER 6

Literary and Real-Life Salesmen and the Performance of Class

Jon Dietrick

Early in the 1962, film adaptation of Meredith Willson's 1957 play *The Music Man*, "Professor" Harold Hill (Robert Preston), having just arrived in River City, Iowa, runs into a retired con man and former associate named Marcellus Washburn (Buddy Hackett). As the two catch up, Washburn asks Hill what his current line is, noting, "Last I heard you were in steam automobiles." "I was," replies Hill. "Well, what happened?" asks Washburn, to which Hill replies, "Somebody actually invented one."[1] Here, in case we missed the point of anvil salesman Charlie Cowell's (Harry Hickox's) thundering denunciation of Hill in the film's opening scene, we are introduced to Hill's *modus operandi*: he capitalizes on ordinary, middle-class Americans' hope and wonder—and greed— by selling them an advance interest in something that does not exist: yesterday it was steam automobiles, today boys' bands.

In the summer of 1990 I got to witness firsthand a group of modern-day Harold Hills undergoing what, if this were a case for Harvard Business School, might be termed their "Steam Automobile Dilemma." The setting wasn't a close-knit, sunny Midwestern town but the drab and dingy Wall Street offices of a small, disreputable, soon-to-be defunct brokerage firm where I had taken a summer job as a "cold caller" while enrolled as an English major at Hunter College. The cold caller's job was to screen prospects for a small team of young brokers. The firm that hired me specialized in "penny stocks," or very low priced stocks (usually under $5 a share), trading not on any national exchange but on what brokers called the "pink sheets" (yes they were actual printed sheets, and they were pink), a designation that meant that the stocks were not registered with the Securities and Exchange Commission and the companies issuing the stocks had no reporting requirements. The particular pink-sheet-listed stock my team was selling was called American Safety Closure, and the company's steam automobile was something called a "recyclable plastic tamper-evident safety closure."

The pitch, which I heard repeated endlessly that summer, was meant to appeal to two paradoxically opposed concerns dear to many of the middle-class investors at all likely to buy from men like my bosses: "consumer safety" and the "heavy hand" of government regulation. It began like this: "Do you remember the Tylenol scare of the early 1980s? Where several people died after taking poisoned capsules? Well Mr. _____ that single event launched what is today a $5 billion industry:[2] tamper-evident safety closures." That was the consumer safety angle. The government regulation piece of the narrative involved onerous community recycling laws and the costly process of chopping the tiny metal tamper-evident cap rings (remember those metal caps and rings?) from the necks of plastic soda bottles before they could be recycled. Enter American Safety Closure and their patent on a plastic cap with a plastic tamper-evident ring that could be melted down with the bottle in a recycling facility, thus apparently saving the soft drink industry from total collapse. At some point soon, of course, all the major soft drink makers would need this technology and right now ASC owns it. So how many shares can I put you down for?

I should add here that at this point I, the relatively naïve 20-year-old English major newly arrived in the city from small-town Pennsylvania, believed that a company called American Safety Closure had an existence independent of the brokers' sales pitch, a telephone number with answering machine in Hempstead, New York, and a stock price listed on a pink sheet of paper; that they had indeed developed a recyclable plastic tamper-evident safety closure; and that it was only a matter of time before the big bottlers signed a deal with the company or purchased it. Of course, none of this was true.

The steam automobile moment came one afternoon when a prospect informed—mid-pitch—the second most powerful of the three young brokers who employed me that he was at that moment looking at a 2-liter bottle of soda that had what was unmistakably a plastic tamper-evident cap. The cap had obviously been invented already and was being used by at least one soft drink company.

What happened next was a brilliant bit of improvised dishonesty on the part of the senior-most broker in the room. Seeing that his underling was blowing the sale and gathering from his responses what had happened, he grabbed the phone mid-conversation, pretending to be the same broker the prospect had been talking to for going on ten minutes now, and explained that the tamper-evident cap the man was looking at was made from poly*urethane* and could not be melted down with the bottle during recycling, but that American Safety Closure's patented cap was made from poly*ethylene* and *could* be recycled along with the bottle.

Now I don't know if my boss had this bit of (wholly fabricated) information at the ready to overcome this objection, but the intensity and urgency of his performance, coupled with the surprised reaction from everyone else in the room, told me this was most likely a completely improvised moment. This man was not a chemist. In fact what was remarkable about his education was how adroitly he had been able to avoid it. Having been raised in a very wealthy, incredibly well connected New York family that counted former US presidents, ambassadors, and some of the most powerful men on Wall Street in its line, this guy had managed to come through his formative years knowing very little about anything except how to get people to give him money. When our paths crossed he was 28 or 29 years old and attended a weekly meeting of Narcotics Anonymous at Trinity Church, and I was told by a friend of his (I have no way of knowing if it's true—a lot of stories circulated about the man) that the job on Wall Street was a sort of "last chance" favor from a relative who was a judge following his being arrested for selling cocaine. When I met him he was trying to complete a Bachelor's in Business at NYU, and a young Indian woman he paid as an assistant would regularly be doing his homework in a corner of the office. I'm fairly confident he was not schooled in the chemical composition of various forms of plastic.

In any case, the polyurethane–polyethylene improvisation would certainly not be the last time I would see this man come up with a brilliant lie very quickly. I also don't remember if that particular prospect was convinced, or convinced enough to buy shares in American Safety Closure. But the writing was on the wall, and before the summer ended the Wall Street penny stock version of Harold Hill's being "run out of town on a rail" had occurred: the stock price sank, heavily margined customers made furious phone calls to the office, the number in Hempstead was disconnected, lawsuits were filed. One day I showed up for work and the phones, most of the furniture, and nearly all of the employees had disappeared. But my boss was there and he said he wanted to talk to me.

The firm was closing. He'd let go most of his other cold callers and assistants (the young Indian woman who had been doing his homework was unceremoniously fired), but there was a silver lining. He'd just been offered a job as a broker at a major firm and he wanted me to come with him, continue working as a cold caller for a few more months, and eventually take the exam to become a licensed stockbroker. What about this firm? What about American Safety Closure? What about the soft drink industry?! How was it possible that a "major firm" offered him a job after he'd basically destroyed most of his clients *and* this firm? Then he told me everything. American Safety Closure only existed as an idea to make brokers money. There was no patented technology for a recyclable plastic tamper-evident safety closure, or if there was, that patent was not owned by American Safety Closure. American Safety Closure probably didn't own pens. And the brokerage firm was always more or less a temporary arrangement, its eventual dissolution a foregone conclusion. It also existed only to make a small group of brokers money. The major firm that now wanted him knew how the game was played and didn't worry itself about his angry clients or anything else. They knew he'd made a lot of money for himself and for his firm while it lasted, and they knew he'd likely do it again, and they wanted a piece of it.

After listening to all this I told my boss that I didn't feel good about lying to people to make money. Then he told me two things: that he wanted me to come with him because I reminded him of himself when he was a few years younger, and that I had to shed my "middle-class morality."

Leaving aside for the moment the advice about my middle-class morality—a term, by the way, that sounded as odd coming from this man as the polyurethane/polyethylene line—the idea that I could have reminded my boss of himself at any point in his life seemed on the surface risible. I came from poor people in the economically depressed, ecologically exhausted coal country of northeastern Pennsylvania. He grew up on the North Shore or "Gold Coast" of Long Island (famous as the setting for Fitzgerald's *The Great Gatsby*), the scion of an old blue-blood New York family with the most powerful of ties both on Wall Street and in Washington. Yet in the years since this encounter I have come to understand something.

If there was one thing my boss and I had in common it was that we both had much practice performing class, though of course we came at the performance from opposite places. Very few of the people this man did business with came from the same class background he did. His success, therefore, depended on his constructing a middle-class persona by which he could relate to his prospects and clients. In fact this persona even had its own name. If his name were Joseph Preston Tisch (this was not his name, but the pseudonym I've created retains, I think, the class associations of his actual name), his clients all knew him only as "Joe Tisch," his friends and family only as "Preston Tisch." He maintained pretty much a firewall between the two personas, and as were his other employees, I was instructed never to refer to him by his upper-class middle name if I wasn't absolutely certain that another party to the conversation was not a client or a prospect.[3]

For my part, I had been constructing a class persona at least since I was 16 years old and saw *Breakfast at Tiffany's* beamed into my parents' run-down working class living room. The move to New York when I was 18 was certainly part of this construction, as was to a certain degree my choice of major: English Literature. Having moved away I pretty quickly shed most aspects of the working class Pennsylvania coal region dialect my childhood friends still use today. And then there was Wall Street.

Most people who knew me then were more or less shocked that I took even a summer job on Wall Street, so at odds did it seem with my ethical and political convictions (I had belonged briefly to a college socialist organization), and even with my personality, which always tended toward the shy and reserved. From the perspective of the performance of social class, however, the job made a kind of sense. Selling is of course a highly performative endeavor. As Timothy Spears writes in his cultural history of the early-twentieth-century salesman, the salesperson effaces his own personality and attempts to become "all things to all men."[4] This was as true of the men with whom I worked on Wall Street in the early nineties as it was of the turn-of-the-century "drummers" Spears discusses. To my interview for the job as a cold caller I brought my brother's blazer, three sizes too big for me, draped over my arm (I was fortunate that the oppressive heat that day made this move seem almost plausible), and I bought my first tie in Chinatown on the way down to Wall Street from my West Village hovel. It was a cheap like-ness of the blue tie with white polka dots Steve Martin was then sporting on the cover of *GQ*, and I had to ask the old Chinese man who sold it to me to tie it for me. I would not have said this then, but I was preparing for a role. It was this sense of playing the part of a social class from which you did not come, I have come to think, that my boss saw that we shared, though of course the stakes were not the same in our respective cases.

The "middle-class morality" I was urged to slough off is interesting in this sense. The first use of the term I can locate is in a play, and one very much con-cerned with the performance of social class: Shaw's 1912 *Pygmalion*. The term is introduced not by the controlling professor of phonetics and professional lan-guage coach Henry Higgins, nor by his Cockney-turned-"duchess" student Eliza Doolittle, but by Eliza's ne'er-do-well father, Alfie. When he hits up Higgins for money in exchange for letting the good doctor experiment on his daugh-ter, Higgins and his companion Pickering object to paying him for his daughter on moral grounds. Through Alfie, Shaw deconstructs this "morality" and reveals it to be nothing more than a means to keep people like Alfie, "the undeserving poor," as he calls himself, from changing their economic or social situation for the better. "What is middle class morality?" asks Alfie rhetorically: "Just an excuse for never giving me anything."[5] The upper-class Higgins and the Cockney Alfie Doolittle come from very different worlds. What they share is an understanding of the performative aspect of social class. When asked if there is a living to be made in phonetics, Higgins replies "Quite a fat one," since "This is an age of upstarts. Men begin in Kentish Town with 80 pounds a year, and end in Park Lane with a hundred thousand. They want to drop Kentish Town; but they give themselves away every time they open their mouths. Now I can teach them."[6] Of course Higgins's passing off Eliza as a duchess is evidence of this, and near the end of the play Alfie has come into some money and shows up aping the dress and manners of the upper class.

The conservative Midwestern American setting of *The Music Man* does not at first glance share much with Shaw's London. But Wilson's 1912 America is also surely "an age of upstarts," and one in which the middle-class individualism of the Victorian period has led to (among other things) a burgeoning consumerism combined with an extreme sentimentalism. The boys' band is just the kind of quaint, old-fashioned, communal organization the town believes can stave off the dangers of all that un-chaperoned freedom of the "pool hall." Of course that band is sold to them by the slick, amoral Hill, a rootless, modern traveling sales-man (assisted by Washburn and also by Tommy Djilas, the town hoodlum). The children will be "taught" to play their instruments via the seemingly very mod-ern "think system," a preposterous method of imbibing musical facility obviously modeled on similar self-help (and perhaps especially language-learning) "systems" that proliferated throughout the nineteenth century (and that still do today).[7] And the instruments and uniforms will be gotten through the then-modern method of mail order. We see how much excitement mail order purchasing causes when everyone in the town—even the mayor—drops everything at the announcement that the Wells Fargo Wagon has arrived. It's even an occasion for a song celebrating consumerism: "O-ho the Wells Fargo Wagon is a-comin' now/Is it a prepaid surprise or C.O.D.?"[8] All the civic pride and concern for the community is forgotten in an instant at the thought of a truck full of consumer goods, because, as the song goes, "It could be something for someone who is no relation, but it could be something special just for me!" And as with Higgins and Alfie Doolittle, and as with me and my boss on Wall Street, Wilson's play also has two characters who share an understanding of the performative aspect of social class. If River City's mayor refuses to be fooled by the slick Harold Hill, that is because the mayor is, like Hill, consistently engaged in the performance of class. He sets himself up as the moral guardian of the community, but his comically botched speeches made up of nonsensically thrown together bits of famous American orations (including the Gettysburg Address) attest to the fact that he is involved in a performance. And it is the mayor, after all, who owns—quietly—that threatening pool hall.

It was ultimately this understanding of class performance that my boss and I shared. I accepted his offer and worked with him for a time at the bigger firm, and even acquired my license to be a stock broker—but whether it was because I continued to be needled by that "middle-class morality" or because I simply was not cut out to be a salesman, I left Wall Street within a couple of years and set my sights on graduate school and an eventual career as a drama professor. I had and still have a great love of reading, and I find teaching mostly very rewarding. But I am sure that on some level I also find attractive the class performance that being a professor involves, at least for this working class Pennsylvania boy.

Notes

1. *The Music Man*, digital stream, Directed by Morton DaCosta (Los Angeles: Warner Bros, 1962).
2. The $5 billion figure was completely made up, and brokers would sometimes show off by exaggerating the number wildly ("what is today a $600 billion industry!") in a bid to demonstrate one of their favorite sales maxims: "it isn't what you say; it's how you say it."
3. Still on Wall Street, today this man works with a much, much more "exclusive" clientele and he now uses his middle name professionally.
4. Spears, Timothy, *100 Years on the Road: The Traveling Salesman in American Culture* (New Haven, CT: Yale University Press, 1995), 1.
5. Shaw, George Bernard, *Pygmalion*, public domain (Kindle version), loc. 644.
6. Shaw, loc. 220.
7. Anyone using Facebook today certainly has not been able to avoid the "Language Professors Hate Him" ads promoting a system of instant language acquisition.
8. *The Music Man*.

CHAPTER 7

Money Changes Everything? African American Class-Based Attitudes toward LGBT Issues[1]

Ravi K. Perry, Yasmiyn Irizarry, and Timothy J. Fair

Americans' attitudes toward LGBT issues are projected to continue shifting through the twenty-first century.[2] According to scholars, polling data, and pundits, Americans are showing increasing support for issues such as the right to marry and the elimination of barriers in federal immigration for LGBT persons, among other issues.[3] In addition, a number of national polls have found that, generally speaking, Americans' attitudes toward nonheterosexuals are increasingly positive.[4]

Although for many years, minority communities have been labeled as largely conservative on questions of LGBT rights, since President Obama announced his support of the right for same-gender-loving individuals to marry in May 2012, scholars, LGBT advocates, and others have speculated on the ways his announcement may impact the African American community's views of LGBT issues.[5] In fact, some journalists have noted the significance of the White House picking African American ABC News correspondent Robin Roberts to announce the president's position.[6] Interestingly, during the same period, the NAACP's Board of Directors voted to support same-sex marriage, citing it was a civil rights issue.[7]

Polls released after these announcements suggest a slight, but statistically significant jump in African American support for the right of same-sex couples to marry.[8] Pundits and advocates have since speculated that despite prior portrayals of a black antigay agenda, there exists a diversity of opinions in the black community and that many African Americans have since as far back as the modern American Civil Rights Movement in the 1960s been vocally supportive of issues relating to LGBT rights.[9] However, as polls from the later part of 2012 indicate, the presumed Obama effect on African American attitudes toward LGBT issues dissipated. Once again, the speculation turned to black conservative opinions on a host of social issues, re-invoking the storyline that the black vote helped defeat the right for same-sex couples to marry in California.[10]

The African American community's attitudes toward LGBT-related issues seemed to be one of paradox. While many projected that they would develop increasingly positive attitudes post Obama's announcement, there seemed to be no sustained effect in later polls. Furthermore, when states and localities began to introduce same-sex marriage related bills, many African Americans were clearly on the opposite side of this fight. The battle lines around North Carolina's antigay Amendment One in 2012, in part, describe the shift. While the state's NAACP stood in solidarity with the position set by its national office, many African American pastors were against it.[11] A national group of black pastors spoke at the National Press Club, openly advocating for black Christians to withdraw support from the President in his bid for reelection in November 2012.[12] Meanwhile, other Church leaders in the North Carolina Amendment One debate took a middle ground approach. Although they could not encourage their congregations to support marriage equality because their religious beliefs stood in conflict with the issue, they did personally choose to view marriage inherently as a civil rights question.[13]

At the same time that North Carolina debated Amendment One (which ultimately passed and did amend the state's constitution to define marriage as between one man and one woman), heavily black middle-class states such as Maryland were preparing their stand on this issue as well.[14] Maryland is in many ways unique, both because it has a heavy black Democratic influence in Baltimore and in Prince George's County—a Washington DC suburb with one of the largest numbers of black middle- and upper-income communities in the nation—and because it ultimately became the first state (along with Maine) to put the question of same-sex marriage to voters and have voters approve.[15] Although both states are below the Mason–Dixon line, Maryland did what North Carolina could not.

The role of the black community in working either to secure passage or to deny passage of the 2012 marriage rights question is representative of the diversity of opinions within the black community. One of the things we discovered during our investigation into black Americans' opinions on two questions respective to LGBT rights was that shifts in attitudes toward LGBT issues began much earlier than many suggest. As others have noted, General Social Survey trends suggest that blacks' negative attitudes toward homosexual sex and the right to marry have been decreasing since as early as 2004.[16] In the aggregate, this trend indicates that blacks' attitudes mirror the shift in attitudes for the larger (mainly white American heterosexual) community throughout the country.

This, however, is not where the story ends. As the 2012 marriage rights anecdotes respective to the efforts at the ballot box to enact pro- and anti-same-sex marriage laws in Maryland and North Carolina portray, the black community's views are diverse. This diversity, as it turns out, is in part due to class-based differences; however, for blacks, they manifest in ways that contradict broader trends, as well as class differences in whites' attitudes toward LGBT rights. Examining race and class trends in attitudes between 2004 and 2010 (before the aforementioned marriage debates in states such as Maryland and North Carolina in 2012), we show how blacks of various SES classes, on the one hand, are less likely to disagree with the right of homosexuals to marry, even though an overwhelming majority of middle-class blacks continue to believe the act of homosexual sexual relations remains "wrong."

Historic LGBT Attitudinal Trends

Homophobia, discrimination, and violence against homosexuals persist within the United States, as research shows that pervasive attitudes of homophobia are highly correlated with antigay behavior.[17] The sexual orientations of individuals under the LGBT umbrella have been the driving force behind biased perceptions of nonheterosexuals on both a collective and individual level.[18] As a result, a significant number of LGBT individuals have experienced physically violent treatment because of their sexual orientation.[19] These negative attitudes have also influenced local, state, and federal policies, thus restricting LGBT individuals' and couples' access to services, such as workplace health insurance benefits available to married couples.[20]

Prior research shows that most Americans held unfavorable attitudes concerning the morality of homosexuality into the 1990s.[21] However, more contemporaneous studies suggest that Americans are expanding their view of civil rights, and that these more inclusive and liberal perceptions are improving attitudes toward gays and lesbians.[22] For example, some companies have established classes geared toward reducing negative attitudes toward homosexuals in the workplace.[23] Additionally, many high schools and colleges have established support groups for students who identify as gay or lesbian.[24] More recently, American attitudes toward openly LGBT elected officials have also started to shift, with about 68% of respondents in a 2007 Gallup survey indicating that they would vote for a well-qualified gay or lesbian American for President.[25]

As attitudes toward homosexuality continued to shift, research on attitudes toward homosexuality has consistently examined three indicators: race, religiosity, and political philosophy. This research suggests that those who are more religious, attend church more frequently, and espouse conservative philosophies have more negative views of homosexuality.[26] Conversely, scholars find that liberals often have more favorable attitudes toward homosexuality than those of conservatives.[27] Scholars have also attempted to distinguish attitudinal differences toward homosexuality by race. For example, Gates found that many African Americans do not equate the struggle for civil rights for blacks with the struggle of gay and lesbian inclusion in American policy discourse.[28] In fact, there has been a long-held belief that African Americans are more likely to be homophobic than whites, despite the fact that previous research has diverged on whether African Americans are less favorable toward homosexuality.[29]

Although much of the literature on attitudes toward homosexuality and LGBT rights has focused on differences across demographic subgroups, little attention has been paid to class differences in LGBT attitudes. The purpose of this chapter is to examine differences in attitudes toward homosexuals by socioeconomic status and to explain how these differences vary for whites and blacks.

The Road toward Black Acceptance of LGBT Rights/Actions

In 2004, then-Senator Obama gave the keynote at the Democratic National Convention in Boston, MA. As the only black US senator, Obama's speech was heralded as the beginning of a new era, with many speculating that he would one day become President. In this same year, Massachusetts—the first state to legalize same-sex marriage—began issuing licenses. And just one year prior, the United States Supreme Court, in a 6–3 ruling in *Lawrence v. Texas*, struck down the sodomy law in Texas and, by extension, invalidated sodomy laws in 13 other states, making same-sex sexual activity legal in every US state and territory. Yet at the time, American public opinion on LGBT issues and marriage was largely congruent—a majority of Americans thought it was wrong and both major political parties were silent about the question.

Fast forward to 2008; in just five years since the *Lawrence* ruling, several public opinion surveys suggested that Americans' views on same-sex marriage were evolving. This was also evident throughout President Obama's first presidential campaign, where he was regularly asked his opinion on the issue, and fittingly indicated his response was evolving. Despite the fact that LGBT issues did not have majority support in 2008, slowly, views began to change. With a significant LGBT voting bloc in the 2008 presidential election, these communities made their voices heard, and for the first time in recent American political history, the Democratic Party appeared, at least to some extent, responsive to their interests. Cautiously, yet consistently, President Obama in his first term began using administrative policy to unravel federal law and programs that served to marginalize the LGBT community. Though not legislation—and as such, policies that can be reversed with a new president—these policies have been significant in their attempt to address policy inequality for the LGBT communities.[30]

Given the increased support for LGBT-related sociopolitical rights, our argument concerning class effects within the black community is framed around two broad contextual trends: how certain advancements and increasingly favorable attitudes toward homosexuals and LGBT issues resulted in shifts in policy and attitudes while simultaneously in other jurisdictions, policies and attitudes remained stagnant. At the time of this writing, a decision in *Hollingsworth v. Perry*, a case regarding California voters' ban on same-sex marriage via the passage of Proposition 8, was just rendered at the United States Supreme Court. Confirming oral argument testimony, and early projections, the justices ruled that bans on same-sex marriage are unconstitutional, thereby making it national policy to enforce what many believe to be a civil right.[31]

The Proposition 8 context is critical background for this chapter as the immediate and sustained aftermath of the vote largely centered on how conservative religious groups, Latinos, and African Americans pushed the proposition over the edge.[32] Many believed this to be an ironic occurrence—how black Californians can, in one breath, cheer the election of the first black president as a major civil rights victory for the nation and the world, and yet, at the same time, vote to deny civil rights to a group of marginalized American citizens.

Since the passage of Proposition 8, other states (through legislatures, Supreme Courts, and/or voter-initiated ballot-box referendums) have taken up the marriage question—with mixed results. Meanwhile, the African American LGBT community has become more vocal and more active in the LGBT rights movement. There has also been a rise in the strong presence of organizations that seek to address the health, welfare, and policy needs of minority LGBT community members, including, but not limited to, the National Black Justice Coalition, the Hispanic Black Gay Coalition, the Barbara Jordan/Bayard Rustin Coalition, the Here to Stay Coalition, Black Lesbians United, the Zuna Institute, and the Center for Black Equity, to name a few.

The expansion of advocacy groups that address the issues and interests of black LGBT communities is relevant to our discussion herein because they have played a large role in helping to shift attitudes in their black communities respective to LGBT issues. While these efforts seem to be fruitful in the aggregate, as we discuss in our analyses, many members of these communities, including those who have more elevated social standing, have yet to be ardent supporters of the very concept these organizations seek to represent—freedom of sexual expression. That many black middle-class heterosexuals have yet to support the act of sexual expression suggests the process of developing strong allies to push the agenda forward continues.

Considering LGBT Attitudes by Race *and* Class

Scholars find that, collectively, blacks have developed increasingly positive LGBT attitudes over the past several years. Lost in this debate, however, is the discussion of how these opinions vary by class, and, more specifically, how race and class intersect to shape LGBT attitudes. With data from the General Social Survey (GSS)—a nationally representative sample of noninstitutionalized, English-speaking adults—we explore how the intersection of race and class influences attitudes toward two dimensions of LGBT issues: sex and marriage.[33] The data stem from four waves of the GSS: 2004, 2006, 2008, and 2010. In all four waves, random subsamples of respondents were asked, "What about sexual relations between two adults of the same sex—do you think it is always wrong, almost always wrong, wrong only sometimes, or not wrong at all?," and "Do you agree or disagree that homosexual couples should have the right to marry one another?"[34]

Since our focus is on negative attitudes, valid responses for both questions were recoded into dichotomous measures. Respondents who said that same-sex relations were "always wrong" or "almost always wrong" were coded as 1, and those who responded "wrong only sometimes" or "not wrong at all" were coded as 0. Likewise, respondents who "disagreed" that homosexual couples should have the right to marry were coded as 1, while those who "agreed" or "neither agreed nor disagreed" were coded as 0. Table 7.1, which presents distributions for the analytical samples across all four waves, shows a decrease in negative attitudes toward same-sex sexual relations and same-sex marriage over the six-year period. Although promising, these trends are tempered by 2010 figures showing that over 50% of Americans view same-sex relations as almost always or always wrong and that about 40% of Americans still disagree with homosexual couples having the right to marry.

Although negative attitudes toward same-sex sexual relations and same-sex marriage have declined across all racial groups, stark racial differences persist, as blacks are much more likely than other racial groups to espouse negative perceptions (see Figure 7.1). In contrast, scholars find that markers of middle- and upper-class status, such as higher levels of education and income, are associated with more positive social attitudes. To approximate class, we draw on the GSS socioeconomic index, a measure of social standing derived from respondents' education, income, and occupation.[35] For our analyses, we divided the socioeconomic index measure from each wave into four quartile categories that are the basis of our class comparisons. Descriptive analyses suggest that a larger proportion of lower-class individuals do espouse negative LGBT attitudes compared to those from the upper class (see Figure 7.2).

While it is difficult for our socioeconomic status indicator to establish qualitative congruence with regard to class status, we assume the bottom quartile is reflective of lower-income and lower working class status Americans, as descriptive statistics for this category show a weighted average family income of just over $40,000 for whites and around $34,000 for blacks, and only 5% of Americans in this category have a bachelor's degree or higher, while over 30% have not completed a high school degree. The second quartile, which has a weighted average family income of around $53,000 for whites, but under $35,000 for blacks, is likely representative of working class Americans. In this quartile, only 9% of Americans have a bachelor's degree (3% for blacks), but an overwhelming majority (86%) have completed at least a high school degree. The third quartile, which has a weighted average income of about $70,000 for whites and $57,000 for blacks, is most likely representative of the lower middle class. In this category, over 30% of Americans have at least a bachelor's degree and another 12% have an associate's degree, but very few have advanced degrees (6%). Last, the top quartile is representative of upper-middle-class and upper-income Americans. In this quartile, nearly 40% of Americans have family incomes over $100,000, and about 14% have family incomes over $150,000. In addition, two-thirds of Americans in this group have at least a bachelor's degree and nearly 30% have graduate degrees.

Although increasing social class is associated with more positive attitudes, subsequent analyses suggest that the influence of class on LGBT attitudes is not independent of race. Using logistic regression techniques, we estimate the likelihood of espousing negative LGBT attitudes, while accounting for various

Table 7.1 Frequency distributions of negative attitudes toward same-sex sexual relations and marriage rights (General Social Survey: 2004–2010)

	Total		2004		2006		2008		2010	
	Freq.	%	Freq.	%	Freq.	%	Freq.	%	Freq.	%
Same-sex relations are wrong										
Almost or always	2,742	56.9	496	62.1	1,055	60.2	649	55.6	542	50.9
Sometimes/never	2,080	43.1	303	37.9	697	39.8	519	44.4	561	49.1
Total	4,822	100.0	799	100.0	1,752	100.0	1,168	100.0	1,103	100.0
Same-sex marriage right										
Disagree	2,618	49.4	617	55.5	955	52.4	589	47.9	457	40.2
Neutral/agree	2,682	50.6	495	44.5	866	47.6	641	52.1	680	59.8
Total	5,300	100.0	1,112	100.0	1,821	100.0	1,230	100.0	1,137	100.0

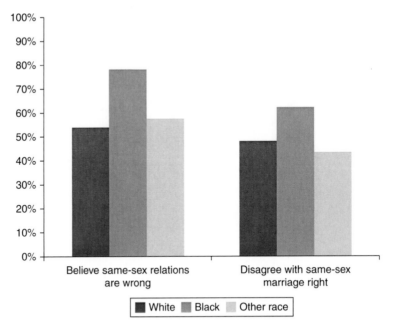

Figure 7.1 Weighted percentage of respondents with negative attitudes toward same-sex sexual relations and marriage rights by race

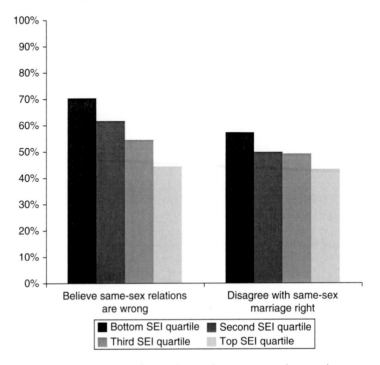

Figure 7.2 Weighted percentage of respondents with negative attitudes toward same-sex sexual relations and marriage rights by socioeconomic index quartiles

background characteristics including gender, age, religiosity, political affiliation, and region. Age includes four categories: 18–29, 30–44, 45–59, and 60 and up. Religiosity includes three categories—mainline Christian/Catholic, conservative Christian, and other/no religion—that are based on the RELTRAD procedure.[36] Political affiliation includes three categories: Democrat, independent (including those who lean Democrat or Republican), and Republican. Last, I include controls for region: Northeast, Midwest, South, and West. Although the samples for the two measures of LGBT attitudes do not include all of the same individuals, the similar demographic makeup of the two samples suggests that the findings are representative of similar target populations (see Table 7.2).

Table 7.2 Weighted distributions of independent variables across samples

	Same-sex relations sample		Same-sex marriage sample	
	Freq.	*%*	*Freq.*	*%*
Sex				
Female	2,636	53.0	2,936	53.8
Male	2,186	47.0	2,364	46.2
Race				
White	3,712	76.8	4,091	77.2
Black	654	12.5	714	12.4
Other	456	10.7	495	10.5
Age				
18–29	829	19.5	910	19.4
30–44	1,421	29.3	1,556	29.3
45–59	1,368	29.1	1,517	29.4
60+	1,204	22.0	1,317	21.8
Socioeconomic index				
Bottom quartile	1,168	24.5	1,260	23.9
Second quartile	1,245	25.7	1,363	25.2
Third quartile	1,036	22.4	1,151	22.5
Top quartile	1,373	27.5	1,526	28.5
Religion				
Mainline Christian/Catholic	2,087	43.9	2,280	43.8
Conservative Christian	1,728	35.5	1,880	34.9
Other/No religion	1,007	20.7	1,140	21.3
Political affiliation				
Democrat	1,635	33.3	1,792	33.3
Independent	1,868	38.7	2,060	38.7
Republican	1,319	28.0	1,448	27.9
Region				
Northeast	763	15.6	828	15.7
Midwest	1,168	23.0	1,317	23.5
South	1,842	38.9	1,980	37.9
West	1,049	22.5	1,175	22.8
N	4,822	100.0	5,300	100.0

The likelihood of having negative LGBT attitudes is presented in the form of predicted probabilities, which allows us to compare the likelihood or probability of a certain outcome for various race and class subgroups. In Figures 7.3 and 7.4, we present mean predicted probabilities of having negative attitudes toward same-sex sexual relations and same-sex marriage, which were modeled using interaction effects. These predicted probabilities are estimated for males, ages 30–44, who are mainline Christian or Catholic, independent, and from the South. Although variation in these characteristics could collectively increase or decrease predicted probabilities, the differences between race and class subgroups would not vary substantially.

Regarding negative attitudes toward same-sex sexual relations, we predict that for whites, class works as expected, with lower-class whites being the most likely to believe that same-sex relations are always or almost always wrong (at 70%), followed by the second (61%), third (46%), and fourth (40%) quartile groups. The results for African Americans, which do not mirror those of whites, merit further explication. As expected, collectively, the predicted probabilities of blacks are higher than for other racial groups. Furthermore, as with whites, the bottom

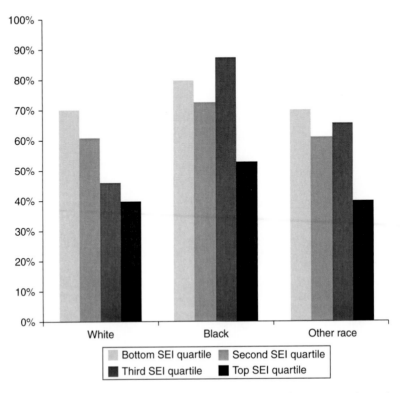

Figure 7.3   Predicted probabilities of believing that same-sex sexual relations are almost always wrong or always wrong by race and socioeconomic index quartiles

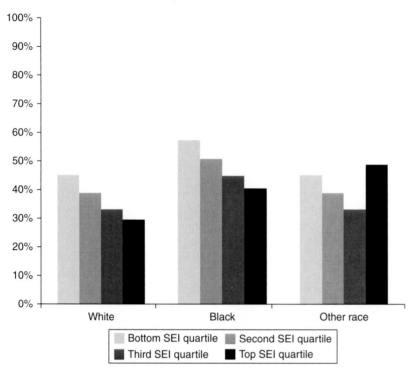

Figure 7.4 Predicted probabilities of disagreeing that same-sex couples should have the right to marry by race and socioeconomic index quartiles

two black SEI quartiles show a similar pattern, with the predicted likelihood for the lowest SEI quartile at 80% and the second quartile at 72%. This similarity continues for the top black SEI quartile as well at 53%. However, the third SEI quartile for blacks, a presumably middle- to upper-income bracket, does not follow the same trend. In fact, we predict that they have a nearly 90% likelihood (despite their class status) of believing that same-sex sexual relations are always or almost always wrong. Interestingly, we also find a similar but less substantial bump in negative attitudes in the third SEI quartile for other-race individuals; however, overall, the probabilities of other race individuals regarding same-sex sexual relations mirror those of whites.

These findings are instructive as they indicate that class-based trends in the white community do not mirror those in the black community, with respect to views of homosexual sex as measured by what is right and wrong. For African Americans, a higher class position does not necessarily indicate a shift in positive attitudes toward homosexual sex, but suggests the opposite instead, at least for middle- and upper-middle-class blacks. While trends for individuals from other racial groups mirror that of African Americans, given the obvious diversity and nonspecific racial and ethnic categorization within that grouping, and given that the trend effect is not nearly as large vis-à-vis the black community, the source of this trend is more difficult to interpret.

Meanwhile, findings from analysis of attitudes regarding same-sex marriage rights tell a different story for blacks. As Figure 7.4 indicates, African Americans remain more conservative than whites on the question of the right to marry; however, the class-based trends are the same for both racial groups. Additionally, differences in predicted probabilities across SEI quartiles are much smaller. For example, whites in the lowest SEI quartile have a 45% likelihood of disagreeing with same-sex marriage rights. This likelihood continues a downward trend in the second (39%), third (33%), and top (30%) SEI quartiles, but the difference between those in the lower- and upper-class quartiles is only 15%, which is only half the size of the difference between these same groups regarding negative attitudes about same-sex relations. Blacks show a similar pattern, with lower-class blacks (bottom SEI quartile) having a 57% likelihood of disagreeing with same-sex marriage rights compared to upper-class blacks at 41%. The only subgroup that did not follow this overall pattern was upper-class other-race individuals; however, given the racial and ethnic diversity of this group, it is difficult to identify the source of this trend.

Altogether, these findings suggest that although an overwhelming majority of middle-class African Americans perceive same-sex sexual relations as always or almost always wrong, they are much less likely to disagree with homosexual couples having the right to marry. Furthermore, it is very likely that a near majority of blacks do not disagree with same-sex marriage, despite personal reservations about same-sex relations, because they view marriage as a civil right. Interestingly, these attitudes existed before the alleged Obama effect—including President Obama's pro-same-sex marriage announcement, the Democratic Party's 2012 platform position in favor of same-sex marriage rights, and the NAACP's resolution in support of same-sex marriage—which many pundits argue is the main reason for decreasing negative perceptions of LGBT issues in the black community.

Implications: Homosexual Action versus Homosexual Rights

Findings from the General Social Survey regarding the black middle class are striking. The interactive effects of race and class indicate that when it comes to attitudes about same-sex sexual relations, a significant portion of middle-class blacks contradict trends set by whites as well as their own opinions regarding the rights for those same individuals to marry. The reasons for this disparate relationship are presumably manifold and strongly suggestive of how black middle-class status may actually limit blacks' increasing support of LGBT issues.

On the one hand, the data might suggest, as many speculated with Proposition 8, that blacks' conservative religious attitudes are closely tied to their attitudes toward same-sex relations. Subsequent analyses show that for the sample of African Americans in the GSS, age, political affiliation, and regional location do not seem to be driving the black middle-class effect, because the trends for these subcategories of blacks mirror those of whites for the same question—a downward trend in the belief that same-sex sexual relations are wrong as SES increases. While it remains accurate that older African Americans (and Americans generally) are more conservative on questions of LGBT issues, over the six-year period of the GSS data studied herein, the trend continues in the same downward direction despite there being little change in religious affiliation across groups. Finally, alleged black religious conservative attitudes fail to adequately explain the trends in Figure 7.3 because although there are clear class differences in African Americans' perceptions of same-sex sexual relations, there is very little variation in the distribution of religious affiliation across black SEI quartiles (see Figure 7.5), which means that the religious affiliation of middle-class blacks is not substantially different compared to lower- and upper-class blacks.

Another plausible argument centers on the linked fate hypothesis and politics of respectability argument.[37] The vast majority of the respondents in the GSS surveys who were asked their sexual orientation indicate they are heterosexual— upwards of 96% for African Americans. As such, black respondents may hold negative views toward homosexual sex because they worry about how others may react to blacks, as a group, if they support it. In Dawson's linked fate argument, "the historical experiences of African Americans have resulted in a situation in

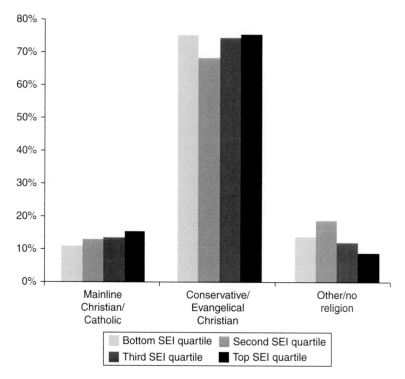

Figure 7.5 Weighted percentage of religious affiliation for black respondents by socioeconomic index quartiles

which group interests have served as a useful proxy for self-interest."[38] However, since blacks, particularly middle-class blacks, view same-sex relations so negatively, if this were due to linked fate, we would expect these negative attitudes to also hold for same-sex marriage rights. Yet, this is not the case, because although an overwhelming majority of middle-class blacks believe same-sex sexual relations are wrong, a much smaller proportion of middle-class blacks actually disagree with giving homosexual couples the right to marry. Moreover, as SES increases, there is a clear downward trend in negative attitudes toward same-sex marriage, with middle- and upper-class blacks being significantly less likely to disagree with same-sex marriage than lower-class blacks.

A third possibility is that blacks are making a sophisticated distinction between homosexual sex and the right to marry. For many blacks, religious upbringing and conservative social values may explain Figure 7.3; however, these same values may also help explain Figure 7.4, especially if blacks are viewing the two issues through different lenses. Blacks may differentiate between homosexual sex (e.g., as deviant) and marriage (e.g., as traditional), resulting in increasingly positive attitudes toward same-sex marriage, while still maintaining negative attitudes toward same-sex sexual relations (perhaps because it is presumed to occur outside of marriage). But why do middle-class blacks perceive same-sex relations more negatively than blacks from other class groups? Particularly for blacks, being middle class comes with a level of uncertainty, because many middle-class blacks lack the wealth necessary to maintain their middle-class status were it to be challenged.[39] This instability may be motivation for middle-class blacks to present the African American community as respectable with regard to what they perceive to be deviant behaviors, thus the greater perception of same-sex sexual relations as wrong. However, if they equate marriage with stability and traditional values, and come to view same-sex marriage as a civil right, they could at the same time show increasing support for same-sex marriage. We suggest that this argument is stronger than the previous two for understanding middle-class blacks' LGBT attitudes, because it acknowledges the role of religion and identity politics, while at the same time recognizing that blacks have the ability to differentiate between homosexual actions and homosexual rights.

Ultimately, we find the large divide between middle-class blacks' attitudes regarding homosexual sex being wrong and their attitudes regarding homosexual couples having the right to marry very puzzling and intriguing at the same time. The disparate relationships, regardless of the ability to situate the results in pre-existing theories neatly, suggest that higher-SES African Americans are not necessarily becoming more liberal on all LGBT issues. While for marriage, which has received the largest media attention, blacks' attitudinal trends are congruent with other major social groups, for other LGBT issues, this may not always be the case.[40] As such, scholars, pundits, and advocates should be careful not to assume that broader trends are always reflective of trends in the African American community.

The other major finding is that African Americans in higher-SES groups are not necessarily more supportive of LGBT issues. Hence, theories that suggest one's higher income, greater educational attainment, diverse social networks, etc., improve social attitudes might not account for the limited changes in attitudinal beliefs for all groups. Hence, when class is interacted with other social demographics, shifts that seem consistent in the aggregate may not be consistent for various subgroups.

Class still impacts how blacks think about LGBT persons and issues, but more research is needed on the class-based interactive effects within minority communities concerning their attitudes on shifting social questions in 21st century, particularly as it concerns LGBT issues beyond the marriage question.[41] Data largely reported in the aggregate may be excluding the in-group differences necessary for a robust discussion on the status of attitudes toward LGBT-related issues in the black community. The reality that SES status does not necessarily lead to changes in political behavior or attitudes for African Americans in terms of homosexual sex suggests sweeping theories that report the influence of higher SES on those social positions need further explication in the disaggregate.[42] The result: negative perceptions of LGBT-presumed behavioral choices (i.e., sex) remain firm among higher-SES African Americans, despite their greater support for same-sex marriage. Additionally, negative attitudes regarding same-sex sexual relations are not always isolated to the lowest classes, and, at times, subgroup trends are not consistent with main effects, which are often driven by the dominant group.

Notes

1. Ravi K. Perry is assistant professor of political science; Yasmiyn Irizarry is assistant professor of sociology; and Timothy J. Fair is a PhD student in the Department of Political Science and Public Administration—each at Mississippi State University. Correspondence may be directed to rperry@pspa.msstate.edu, 105 Bowen Hall, PO Box PC, Mississippi State University, Mississippi State, MS, 39762.
2. Baunach (2011, 2012).
3. Hazeldean and Betz (2003), Kumar (2012).
4. Connelly (2012), Page (2012), Saad (2007).
5. Baunach (2012), Boykin (2012), Brownstein (2012), Hicks (2012), McCollum (2012), Pew (2012).
6. See, e.g., Byers (2012).
7. NAACP (2012).
8. Clement and Somashekhar (2012), Jensen (2012), Sides (2012), Vavreck and Enos (2012).
9. Boykin (2012).
10. Mach (2012), Pew (2012), Vick and Surdin (2008).
11. Biewen (2012), Curtis (2012), Newsome (2012).
12. Merica (2012).
13. Shimron (2012).
14. Blake (2012), Pattillo (2005), Richen (2012), Wiggins et al. (2011).
15. Johnson (2002), Semuels (2012).
16. Baunach (2012).
17. Franklin (2000).

18. Gordon and Snyder (1989).
19. Berrill and Herek (1992), D'augellei and Grossman (2001), Hesson-McInnis and Daugelli (1998), Rose and Mechani (2002).
20. McNaron (1997).
21. Yang (1997).
22. Brooks (2000), Hicks and Lee (2006), Loftus (2001).
23. McNaught (1993).
24. Flax (1990).
25. Jones (2007).
26. Hansen (1982), Herek (2000), Larsen, Reed, and Hoffman (1980).
27. Wood and Bartkowski (2004).
28. Gates (1999).
29. Gates (1999), Hudson and Ricketts (1980), Levitt and Klassen (1976), Tiemeyer (1993).
30. Perry (2013).
31. Cohen (2013), Curry (2013).
32. Abrajano (2010).
33. Davis, Smith, and Marsden (2013).
34. Subgroup sample sizes for respondents who were asked the same-sex sexual relations question and the homosexual marriage question varied in 2004 ($N = 898$ and $N = 1,216$, respectively), 2006 ($N = 2,003$), 2008 ($N = 1,352$), and 2010 ($N = 1,281$).
35. Nakao and Treas (1992).
36. Steensland et al. (2000).
37. Dawson (1994), Higginbotham (1994).
38. Dawson (1994), pp. 77.
39. Bullard (2007), Cashin (2004).
40. Cohen (2012).
41. Cohen (2012).
42. See, e.g., Knoke (1979).

Works Cited

Abrajano, Marisa. "Are Blacks and Latinos Responsible for the Passage of Proposition 8? Analyzing Voter Attitudes on California's Proposal to Ban Same-Sex Marriage in 2008." *Political Research Quarterly* 63 (2009): 922–32.

Baunach, Dawn Michelle. "Decomposing Trends in Attitudes toward Gay Marriage, 1988–2006." *Social Science Quarterly* 92 (2011): 346–63.

Baunach, Dawn Michelle. "Changing Same-Sex Marriage Attitudes in America from 1988 through 2010." *Public Opinion Quarterly* 76 (2012): 364–78.

Berrill, Kevin T., and Gregory M. Herek. "Primary and Secondary Victimization in Anti-Gay Hate Crimes: Official Response and Public Policy." *Journal of Interpersonal Violence* 28 (2013): 401–13.

Biewen, John. "Black Christians Struggle over NC Gay Marriage Ban." *NPR*, May 6, 2012.

Blake, Aaron. "African Americans and Latinos Spur Gay Marriage Revolution." *Washington Post*, November 12, 2012.

Boykin, Keith. "Why Blacks Evolved So 'Quickly' on Gay Marriage." *Huffington Post*, June 5, 2012.

Brooks, Clem. "Civil Rights Liberalism and the Suppression of a Republican Political Realignment in the United States, 1972 to 1996." *American Sociological Review* 65 (2000): 483–505.

Brownstein, Ronald. "Minorities and Gay Marriage: It's Evolving." *National Journal*, May 11, 2012.

Bullard, Robert D., editor. *The Black Metropolis in the Twenty-First Century*. Lanham, MD: Rowman and Littlefield, 2007.

Byers, Dylan. "Gay Marriage: Why Robin Roberts Got the Exclusive." *Politico*, May 9, 2012.

Cashin, Sheryll. *The Failures of Integration: How Race and Class Are Undermining the American Dream*. New York: Public Affairs, 2004.

Clement, Scott, and Sandhya Somashekhar. "After President Obama's Announcement, Opposition to Same-Sex Marriage Hits Record Low." *Washington Post*, May 23, 2012.

Cohen, Andrew. "After Cautious Argument, Don't Look for Historic Ruling on Same-Sex Marriage." *Atlantic*, March 26, 2013.

Cohen, Cathy J. "Obama, Neoliberalism and the 2012 Election: Why We Want More Than Same-Sex Marriage." *Souls* 14 (2012): 19–27.

Connelly, Marjorie. "Support for Gay Marriage Growing, but US Remains Divided." *New York Times*, December 7, 2012.

Curry, Tom. "Supreme Court Hints That It Won't Issue Sweeping Ruling on Same-Sex Marriage." *NBC News*, March 26, 2013.

Curtis, Mary C. "Black North Carolina Voters and Gay Marriage: Will the Issue Affect Obama's Chances?" *Washington Post*, May 3, 2012.

Davis, James A., Tom W. Smith, and Peter V. Marsden. General Social Surveys 1972–2012 (Data file). http://www3.norc.org/GSS+Website/Download. Accessed March 10, 2013.

Dawson, Michael. *Behind the Mule: Race and Class in African American Politics*. Princeton, NJ: Princeton University Press, 1994.

Franklin, Karen. "Antigay Behaviors among Young Adults Prevalence, Patterns, and Motivators in a Noncriminal Population." *Journal of Interpersonal Violence* 15 (2000): 339–62.

Gates, Henry Louis, Jr. "Blacklash?" In *Dangerous Liaisons: Blacks, Gays, and the Struggle for Equality*, edited by Eric Brandt, 25–30. New York: New Press, 1999.

Gordon, Sol, and Craig W. Snyder. *Personal Issues in Human Sexuality: A Guidebook for Better Sexual Health*. Boston: Allyn and Bacon, 1989.

Hansen, Gary L. "Measuring Prejudice against Homosexuality (Homosexism) among College Students: A New Scale." *Journal of Social Psychology* 117 (1982): 233–36.

Hazeldean, Susan, and Heather Betz. "Years Behind: What the United States Must Learn about Immigration Law and Same-Sex Couple." *Human Rights*, June 2003.

Herek, Gregory M. "The Psychology of Sexual Prejudice." *Current Directions in Psychological Science* 9 (2000): 19–22.

Hicks, Jonathan P. "Black Support for Same-Sex Marriage Seems to Increase." *BET News*, December 10, 2012.

Higginbotham, Evelyn Brooks. *Righteous Discontent: The Women's Movement in the Black Baptist Church, 1880–1920*. Harvard University Press: Cambridge, 1994.

Hudson, Walter W., and Wendell A. Ricketts. "A Strategy for the Measurement of Homophobia." *Journal of Homosexuality* 5 (1980): 357–72.

Jensen, Tom. "Maryland Same-Sex Marriage Referendum." *Public Policy Polling*, May 24, 2012.

Johnson, Valerie C. *Black Power in the Suburbs*. Albany, NY: SUNY Press, 2002.

Jones, Jeffrey M. "Some Americans Reluctant to Vote for Mormon, 72-Year-Old Presidential Candidates." *Gallup News Service*, February 20, 2007. Retrieved from http://www.gallup.com/poll/26611/some-americans-reluctant-vote-mormon-72yearold-presidential-candidates.aspx.

Knoke, David. "Stratification and the Dimensions of American Political Orientations." *American Journal of Political Science* 23 (1979): 772–91.

Kumar, Anugrah. "Polls Show Sudden Increase in Black Support for Gay Marriage." *Christian Post*, November 10, 2012.

Larsen, Knud S., Michael Reed, and Susan Hoffman. "Attitudes of Heterosexuals toward Homosexuality: A Likert-Type Scale and Construct Validity." *Journal of Sex Research* 16 (1980): 245–57.

Levitt, Eugene E., and Albert D. Klassen, Jr. "Public Attitudes toward Homosexuality: Part of the 1970 National Survey by the Institute for Sex Research." *Journal of Homosexuality* 1 (1976): 29–43.

Loftus, Jeni. "America's Liberalization in Attitudes toward Homosexuality, 1973 to 1998." *American Sociological Review* 66 (2001): 762–82.

Mach, Andrew. "Black Pastors Group: Obama's Support for Gay Marriage 'Might Cost Him the Election'." *NBC News*, July 31, 2012.

McCullom, Rod. "Obama's 'Halo Effect': Black Support for Gay Marriage Exceeds the General Population." *Ebony Magazine*, May 24, 2012.

McNaron, Toni AH. *Poisoned Ivy: Lesbian and Gay Academics Confronting Homophobia.* Philadelphia: Temple University Press, 1997.

McNaught, Brian. *Gay Issues in the Workplace.* New York: St Martin's Press, 1993.

Merica, Dan. "Black Pastors Launches Anti-Obama Campaign around Gay Marriage." *CNN*, July 31, 2012.

NAACP. "NAACP Passes Resolution in Support of Marriage Equality." May 19, 2012. Retrieved from http://www.naacp.org/press/entry/naacp-passes-resolution-in-support-of-marriage-equalit.

Nakao, Keiko and Judith Treas. "The 1989 Socioeconomic Index of Occupations: Construction from the 1989 Occupational Prestige Scores," *GSS Methodological Report No. 74.* Chicago: National Opinion Research Center, 1992.

Newsome, Melba. "Anti-Gay Marriage Amendment Divides North Carolina African-Americans." *The Grio*, May 7, 2012.

Page, Susan. "Poll: Attitudes toward Gays Changing Fast." *USA Today*, December 5, 2012.

Pattillo, Mary. "Black Middle-Class Neighborhoods." *Annual Review of Sociology* 31 (2005): 305–29.

Perry, Ravi. "Crafting an Agenda for the Black LGBT Community." Paper presented at the 25th National Conference on LGBT Equality: Creating Change, Atlanta, Georgia, January 25–29, 2013.

Pew. "Two-Thirds of Democrats Now Support Gay Marriage." *Forum on Religion and Public Life,* July 31, 2012.

Pew. "Behind Gay Marriage Momentum, Regional Gaps Persist." Pew Research Center for the People and the Press, November 9, 2012.

Richen, Yoruba. "The Black Vote for Gay Marriage." *New York Times*, November 1, 2012.

Saad, Lydia. "Tolerance for Gay Rights at High-Water Mark." *Gallup News Service*, May 29, 2007.

Semuels, Alana. "Voters Approve Gay Marriage in Maine, Maryland." *Los Angeles Times,* November 7, 2012.

Shimron, Yonat. "N.C. Black Pastor Treads Carefully on Gay Marriage." *Washington Post*, May 3, 2012.

Sides, John. "New Data on Obama's Endorsement of Same-Sex Marriage." *Monkey Cage*, May 18, 2012.

Steensland, Brian, Jerry Z. Park, Mark D. Regnerus, Lynn D. Robinson, W. Bradford Wilcox, and Robert D. Woodberry. "The Measure of American Religion: Toward Improving the State of the Art." *Social Forces* 79 (2000): 291–318.

Tiemeyer, Peter E. "Relevant Public Opinion." In *Sexual Orientation and US Military Personnel Policy: Options and Assessments*. National Defense Research Institute, pp. 191–208. RAND Corporation, 1993.

Vick, Karl, and Ashley Surdin. "Most of California's Black Voters Backed Gay Marriage Ban." *Washington Post*, November 7, 2008.

Wiggins, Ovetta, Carol Morello, and Dan Keating. "Prince George's County: Growing, and Growing More Segregated, Census Shows." *Washington Post*, October 30, 2011.

Wood, Peter B., and John P. Bartkowski. "Attribution Style and Public Policy Attitudes toward Gay Rights." *Social Science Quarterly* 85 (2004): 58–74.

Yang, Alan S. "Trends: Attitudes toward Homosexuality." *Public Opinion Quarterly* 61 (1997): 477–507.

CHAPTER 8

Democracy without Class: Investigating the Political Unconscious of the United States

M. Lane Bruner

Using the United States as a yardstick by which to measure attempts by governments to ameliorate the more egregious consequences of class differences is perhaps unfair for any number of reasons, but it is a telling measure nonetheless. After all, as the most powerful economic and military force in the world, and as a country that consistently sees itself as a beacon for freedom and democracy, the United States currently displays many of the worst characteristics when it comes to class disparities.[1] Since the end of the Second World War, but especially since the administration of Ronald Reagan, any dispassionate observer can see that citizens of the United States have been subjected to an upper-class revolt against the "socialist" legacy of the New Deal, primarily though not exclusively through the mechanisms of McCarthyism and economic neo-liberalism.[2] As a result of that revolt, not since the age of the Robber Barons in the nineteenth century has the divide between the rich and the poor been greater in the United States.[3] While it is true, as Peter Sloterdijk acknowledges in *You Must Change Your Life*, that "any member of a non-utopian left secretly knows all too well that the 'classless society' cannot exist for a number of convincing reasons,"[4] this is no reason not to explore some of the key factors that exacerbate class conflict. Such explorations are all the more pressing in the wake of the patent failures of communism and neo-liberalism, and in a world where even a "communist" state like China has become a neo-liberal state (where "economic liberty" is combined with political repression). Such explorations are also important because history shows that any attempt to impose large-scale equality by law eventually results in widespread violence.[5] After all, no matter what system of law individuals find themselves in, some people will be more or less ethical, more or less intelligent, more or less competitive, more or less motivated, more or less empathic, and so on. So much is obvious. Nevertheless, few would or should deny that one of the primary functions of law, when sufficiently attuned to changing historical circumstances, is to ensure a certain quality of life and equal *opportunity* for everyone.[6] Therefore, understanding what processes lead to greater class conflict and human unhappiness versus those that lead elsewhere remains among humankind's most pressing tasks.

To explore such processes, this chapter investigates the political unconscious of failed republics, which historically have repressed their working classes both materially and ideologically, with a focus on the United States. The political unconscious of the United States, I argue, is a recent instance of the general historical failure of Western countries to create sound republican forms of government. This helps to explain why so many citizens in the United States, which is obviously divided by tremendous class disparities, imagine their country otherwise.[7]

Confronting why the United States falsely imagines itself to be a "democracy without class" requires investigations into what I have discussed elsewhere as a repressive state's "fields of the unspeakable."[8] Through such investigations, one can trace the contours of the political unconscious by identifying the outlines of what is true that "cannot be said." Exemplifying such fields, and as a sign of the repression of class issues in the United States, James W. Loewen, in his survey of the most popular high school history textbooks in the United States, noted the following:

> Six of the dozen high school American history textbooks . . . contains no index listing at all for "social class," "social stratification," "class structure," "income distribution," "inequality," or any conceivably related topic. Not one book lists "upper class," "working class," or "lower class." Two of the textbooks list "middle class," but to assure students [falsely] that America is a middle class country.[9]

Such discursive erasures in history textbooks, of course, are only the tip of the unconscious iceberg when it comes to class-related issues in the United States, though they are among the more obvious signs that class itself is an "unspeakable" element in a country characterized, at least since the economic victories of Alexander Hamilton and the takeover of the courts by the Federalists in the early history of the United States, by oligarchic rule by the rich.[10]

The political unconscious has been theorized by thinkers as diverse as Sigmund Freud, Karl Marx, Louis Althusser, Frederic Jameson, and others, and it is a crucial notion for those interested in statecraft. In *Civilization and Its Discontents*, Freud, for example, argued that all of civilization is based on the sublimation of repressed desires.[11] William C. Dowling, in summarizing the thinking of Marx, Althusser, and Jameson, more specifically maintains that the political unconscious of any political community is based on the fact that "the collective consciousness represses historical contradictions."[12] That is, "historically speaking we 'hear' only one voice because a hegemonic ideology suppresses or marginalizes all antagonistic class voices," but critiques of the political unconscious are possible because "the hegemonic discourse remains locked into a dialogue with the discourse it has suppressed."[13]

Arguably one of the most powerful analysts of the political unconscious today is Slavoj Žižek.[14] In one of his many explications of Lacan's psychoanalytical account of "the Real," Žižek maintains that we humans exist discursively within a "distorting screen which always 'falsifies' our access to external reality . . . [and] which gives a pathological twist to every symbolization, that is to say, on account of which every symbolization misses its object."[15] To name only a few such "pathological twists" in the United States, a country seemingly incapable of confronting directly its (unnecessarily) extractive capitalist core, note how the party spearheading the attack on the New Deal, the Republican Party, is supported not only by the wealthy, which is understandable, since more fully informed Republicans are unashamedly the party of the rich, but equally by lower-class and middle-class individuals who mistakenly see Republicans as being "on their side."[16] Also, when one looks at the "blue" (Democratic) and the "red" (Republican) states, one cannot help but be struck by how the color distribution in national elections defies political logic. The Republicans, the predominantly white bourgeois party that supports "free" trade, international banking, the decimation of the tax base, privatization and deregulation, transnational corporations, and the upper class, dominate politically in poorer, largely rural, states in the middle and southern portions of the country. Conversely, Democrats, the party that usually supports the lower and middle classes, farmers, small businesses, and social safety nets for the poor, dominate politically in the wealthier states, predominantly on the coasts, where most of the upper class live, and where banking, international trade, and high finance flourish.[17] As yet another "pathological twist" reflective of the political unconscious of the United States, while people have been increasingly turned into things since the beginning of the slave trade, US Supreme Court decisions in the wake of the passage of the 14th Amendment, and even more intensely since the George W. Bush administration, have increasingly sought to turn things, especially corporations, into increasingly powerful "artificial persons" with far greater political power than "natural" persons.[18]

To illuminate one of the primary sources of such "pathological" manifestations of the political unconscious in the United States, and the fields of the unspeakable that unconsciousness requires, what follows is a cursory review of the historical failure of republicanism in general. I will then turn back to the United States, reflecting on the contemporary situation that resonates with my larger argument.

I should emphasize at the outset, however, my staunch advocacy for basic republican principles (obviously with a small r) that political theorists have defended across the millennia, which again are *radically* anti-Republican principles. My ultimate goal, therefore, is markedly "conservative," despite how it might be read by individuals on the political right. Healthy (and happy!) states are indeed states that protect the interests of all classes, and we cannot understand the "workings" of class outside of basic republican principles.

Classical Republican Principles: Ideals versus Realities

Well over two millennia ago, Aristotle argued in his *Politics* that the best possible form of government is a mixed form combining rule by the just one (the monarch), the just few (the meritocratic aristocracy), and the just many (a polity of informed and reasonable citizens). Problems occur in polities when tyrants, oligarchs, or mob rule interferes with the ideal political mix of sufficient representation for the rich, the middle class, and the poor. The primary obstacle to maintaining healthy republican states is factional self-interest, for whenever an unwise person (a tyrant), or a few unwise people (oligarchs), or the mob (the unreasonable poor) take power, history repeatedly reveals that political crisis soon follows.[19] Later scholars augmented this notion of mixed government by stressing the additional importance of "checks and balances" and "separations of powers," as well as the importance of the rule of law, public education, critical citizenship, and responsible forms of mass media. Unfortunately, history shows that meeting such ideal requirements has proven anything but easy.

When we look closely at almost any of the actually existing republics in history, we quickly discover that they have tended ultimately toward oligarchies of the rich, becoming imbalanced by failing to protect adequately the interests of the poor or to ensure that the rule of law was directed toward the common good.[20] Examples of such tendencies are easy enough to find. In Rome, for example, more ideal republican constitutional arrangements, temporarily achieved through mass strikes on the part of the plebs, were disrupted by military leaders cum emperors who crushed the Republic by destroying the power of the Senate, humiliating the aristocrats, and diverting the masses with spectacular diversions.[21] The experiments with republicanism in the Renaissance Italian city-states, enabled by a temporary balance of power between the Holy Roman Empire and the papacy, were eventually brought to an end by the rise of banking families such as the Medicis and invasion by the French.[22] France witnessed a series of revolutions in 1789, 1830, 1848, and 1871, which each failed to create a republic capable of protecting the interests of all classes, especially the poor, who were ultimately repressed both materially and aesthetically in order to maintain the fantasy of just government.[23] In Great Britain, the policies of Walpole, later to be praised and emulated by Hamilton, where "economic rationality" would take precedence over "less predictable" dependence on anything as fickle as public reason or civic virtue, worked to ensure that debt relations and raw money power would replace the quickly dying cries from Old Whigs for more classical forms of republicanism.[24] In the United States, the defeat of the Anti-Federalists and the Federalist takeover of the judiciary aided early attacks against republicanism and policies favoring empire. Later, corporate control of the Supreme Court (especially during the Nixon, Reagan, and George W. Bush administrations), coupled with communist witch hunts and neo-liberal policies after the Second World War, would slowly but inexorably chip away at the "socialist" gains of the New Deal and the so-called "welfare" state, even as the increasingly consolidated corporate media came to focus on their own version of profitable spectacular diversion instead of complementing such diversions with critical public information and reasoned debate on issues of common concern, even as public education turned toward information memorization instead of humanistic training in the arts of debate and critical citizenship.[25]

In sum, while admittedly only a sampling of the more well-known attempts among the more powerful states in Western history to create republican forms of government ostensibly based on classical principles, the pattern is rather clear: temporary achievement of an artful balance of relatively equal constitutional protection for the upper, middle, and lower classes has consistently been undermined by wealth and/or brute power. As a result of the plain fact that the poor are persistently repressed, it follows that, in order to maintain the illusion that governments are there to protect all of the people, which they plainly are not, that very repression itself has to be repressed in the political imaginary.[26]

Characterizing the Political Unconscious of the United States Today

This brings us, admittedly all too quickly, back to the failed republicanism of the United States, whose citizens from all the available evidence seem blissfully unaware of its failures when it comes to the working class. Like other historically important republican state experiments, the United States has also undergone its own transformations. Early in its history, only the richer citizens could vote or run for office, and slaves, women, and the poor were excluded from the "republic." From the administration of Andrew Jackson forward, the franchise slowly expanded, first to include poorer white males, then black males, then women, and then citizens between 18 and 21 years of age. There were both good and bad effects as the franchise expanded. On the positive side of the ledger, public education, social security, civil rights, and other government policies served to strengthen meritocracy while providing more equal opportunity for all classes. On the negative side, the corporate takeover of the press, the relative lack of oversight over corporations, coupled with their ever-increasing legal protections, and the very expansion of the franchise itself led to politics blending with spectacle. Since the Reagan administration, followed by three other neo-liberal administrations (Bush I, Clinton, and Bush II), we have seen the crippling of the tax base, the steady erosion of public education, the decimation of the middle and lower classes, an explosion of upper-class wealth, and an even more consolidated corporate mass media. In balance, therefore, the republic has become considerably weakened.

However, to diagnose the situation, it is useful to at least briefly touch on the aesthetics/politics relation in the United States today, and what it has to say about the political unconscious as we more fully enter the twenty-first century. Therefore, I shall turn to one representative example of that relation: the media battle between Jon Stewart and Glenn Beck.[27] As is well known, Stewart is the host of the highly popular *The Daily Show* on the Comedy Central network, which of course is part of the for-profit corporate media. Nevertheless, while Stewart repeatedly stresses that his show is "just comedy," it is actually much more. In a world where corporate news is increasingly a joke (focusing, for example, on who won a recent competitive television show, or focusing on sex and violence instead of issues of broader social concern), Stewart's show has received two prestigious Peabody Awards for journalistic excellence and 11 Emmy Awards.[28] Conversely, Glenn Beck is a dangerous demagogue with tremendous influence on lower- and middle-class individuals who vote Republican. He enjoyed a very popular show on Fox News (a Republican mouthpiece) for several years, he has a highly popular radio show, and he is consistently a best-selling author. Even as I type, Glenn Beck's newest book, *Control: Exposing the Truth about Guns*, is the seventh best-selling book in the United States. Furthermore, in the ratings games, there is no doubt whose discourse has the largest reach: Glenn Beck.[29]

Jon Stewart constantly satirizes Beck, along with the corporate media in general, which is in fact the pro-bourgeois and anti-worker media, and there are also other sources of aesthetic resistance that are a glimmer of republican promise in a media landscape generally overwhelmed by demagoguery. One of particular interest, as it reveals the new direction aesthetic resistance can take in the new media age, is a "mash-up" video called *Right Wing Radio Duck*, which mixes old Disney Donald Duck cartoons with audio taken from Beck's radio programs.[30] In the video, we find Donald Duck as a window washer, overhearing Glenn Beck on a radio, asking if his listeners are angry that the rich are getting richer and the poor are getting poorer, and announcing (correctly) that the divide between the rich and poor has not been greater since just before the Great Depression. As Donald listens, he sees a literal "fat cat" smoking a cigar and laughing at the radio. Angry, Donald frightens the cat, who then has Donald fired. Unable to find work, a newspaper hits him in the face with headlines that read "Obama Bails Out Wall Street," "Unemployment Reaches 20%," and "Record Profits for Wall Street" as we hear Beck say (correctly) that "Wall Street owns government." Back in his now foreclosed home, Donald listens to his radio, where Beck's voice turns more obviously demagogic: Beck ominously asks his listeners if they know any Nazis, Marxists, communists, or anti-capitalists. Donald peers through binoculars at other Disney characters saying "1, 2, 3." Beck then provides a list of people and things to fear, suggesting his listeners may soon be sent to concentration camps. Grabbing a gun, Donald runs outside, only to find the streets empty and bucolic. Back inside, Beck assures Donald that "Obama is doing this to us," and that if people will send Beck money, then a device will be delivered to their homes that will "explain everything." Though almost penniless, Donald scrapes together the money, and when the device arrives, it consists of a large fist that comes out of a machine and repeatedly hits Donald over the head. When Donald, confused, asks the machine why he cannot find work, and what he should do about his house, the machine, speaking in Beck's voice, says that Donald is lazy, that he took a gamble when taking out the loan, and that he should go out and get a job! Of course, Donald is not lazy, and there are no jobs, so he takes out a gun and blows the machine to smithereens.

What is especially telling about the political unconscious is that at the end of the video you can click on a link that takes you to Glenn Beck's (now cancelled) Fox television response to this mash-up. Beck wants his listeners to know there is "an amazing piece of propaganda" that has been produced by an artist who teaches "digital resistance" to "youth in Chicago" (he says ominously). He claims, without evidence, that projects like this are "funded by the White House," adding that Walt Disney hated unions because he hated the "communists, socialists, union organizers, and, dare I say, progressives," noting in passing how ironic it is that the Disney corporation apparently "does not mind" this flagrant misuse of their art. He then concludes by saying he has nothing to fear because "the truth will set you free," and that people who tell lies "will destroy themselves through their lies." Then, with even greater cynicism, as if that were possible, he calls upon Gandhi, playing sitar music, reassuring his listeners he is telling the truth and nothing but the truth.

Ultimately, therefore, we see a total blurring of the fictional and the real. There is no distinction between the actual political malfeasance that led to the 2008 financial meltdown, primarily through radical neo-liberal policies such as deregulation of the financial industries, and Obama's fictional "socialism." Notice how communists, socialists, union organizers, and progressives are all blurred together, magically blending Obama's "socialism" and "Wall Street bailouts." Here, a propagandist *par excellence* is "teaching" his susceptible listeners, who have legitimate grievances about unemployment, foreclosures, and Wall Street bailout, about propaganda, all the while completely deceiving them about the source of their suffering. Because Beck's listeners are predominantly lower- and middle-class (white) citizens who consistently vote Republican, and because of the significant influence demagogues such as Beck have in the United States today over (false) public memory, there is a significant threat to republicanism.

Perhaps, however, despite the dangerous power of demagogues in the United States, the neo-Hegelians are correct. Perhaps the excesses and stupidities of the corrupt oligarchs and their media minions will eventually come back to bite them. Perhaps Obama's reelection, despite the grotesque obstructionism of the Republican Party and the cynical stalling of the economy through "debt reduction measures"—when the debt burden exploded under the administration of George W. Bush—is a positive sign. Perhaps the shifting demographics in the United States will derail the upper-class revolt. Perhaps. Still, one could hardly claim that "the United States is a healthy republic." The tax base remains eviscerated, corporate power is at an all time high, the corporate media is "amusing us to death," the divide between rich and poor is an embarrassment, public education is being defunded, and everything and everyone is subject to "market" pressures, where profits consistently are placed above people. These, however, are the very facts that remain largely repressed among those in the lower and middle classes who continue, in their naïve but honorable patriotism, to listen to demagogues, misunderstand history, and fail to resist on their own long-term behalf.

Regardless of the future of republicanism in the United States and elsewhere, we shall always find ourselves having to "work" on class. Exploring the political unconscious and fields of the unspeakable, I have argued, however cursorily, is one fruitful way for doing that "work." The question, ultimately, is how actually to work on class, not simply identify the problems caused by class conflicts, since many popular alternative approaches have not helped us with this work. For example, when looking at influential post-Marxist thinking on the failures of capitalist societies, one is anything but reassured. Hardt and Negri, for example, conclude their otherwise impressive work, where they outline our current global predicament with great precision, by listing a completely lame set of ideal expectations without giving us any clue whatsoever as to how to achieve those expectations. They are not alone. In contemporary critical theological studies, such as Mark Taylor's *After God*, we once again see an excellent explication of the various discursive and material tensions that lead to many of the intellectual stalemates that stand in the way of making the world a more reasonable place, but Taylor too concludes with a list of idealistic demands that are completely unreasonable given the very stalemates he outlines.

As Jean Baudrillard observes in *Simulacra and Simulation*, we "postmoderns" live in a world of the "hyper-real," where parsing out the differences between fact and fiction has become next to impossible. This is much to our peril. When Franklin Roosevelt was attempting to bring the United States out of the Great Depression, and seeing how the excesses of unchecked capitalism were largely to blame, and how the poor in the country were largely without protection, he championed what he called a "New Deal." That deal was thoroughly republican, inasmuch as he sought to ensure that the government of the United States protected the interests of the rich, the middle class, *and the poor*. Then, from around 1950 to 1970, the entire country prospered, not only because of victory in the Second World War but because of a sound tax base, a strong social safety net for the poor, sufficient expenditures for public education, and so on. With the onset of the globalization of capitalism in the 1970s, and with the efforts of the Republicans from 1945 onward (including McCarthyism, packing the Supreme Court with pro-corporate supporters under Nixon, neo-liberalism from Reagan to George W. Bush, and so on), most of those republican benefits have been lost. Only time will tell if they can be regained.

The pressing question, therefore, for public intellectuals and political activists who truly care about the future of the United States as a republic, and the future of public reason in general, is to discover mechanisms for reversing the political trends that have undermined protections for the poor and middle classes. Discovering as many means as possible for exposing fields of the unspeakable, and in so doing engaging in collective political psychoanalysis, is one such means. Many more, undoubtedly, are necessary.

Notes

1. Hope Yen, "Income Gap Widens: Census Finds Record Gap between Rich and Poor," *Huffington Post* (September 28, 2010), http://www.huffingtonpost.com/2010/09/28/income-gap-widens-census-_n_741386.html (accessed May 26, 2012). In 2011, an OECD report showed that the United States ranked fourth worst in global

income equality. See Harry Bradford, "10 Countries with the Worst Income Inequality: OECD," *Huffington Post*, http://www.huffingtonpost.com/2011/05/23/10-countries-with-worst-income-inequality_n_865869.html#s278234&title=10_New_Zealand (accessed May 5, 2013).

2. This despite the fact of the gross incompatibility between McCarthyism, which associated any sympathy for workers and the poor with "communism" as a form of economic determinism, and the "reverse" economic determinism of neo-liberalism. The source of the incompatibility is as follows: whereas "vulgar" communists foolishly argued that the base of production determined the superstructure, neo-liberals foolishly argue that if markets are freed from government intervention then "freedom and liberty" will "naturally" follow.

3. Robert Reich discusses how real wages grew across class sectors from 1945 to 1973, mainly as the result of New Deal policies, but from 1973 to 1991 the income gap between the rich and poor steadily widened. See *The Work of Nations* (New York: Vintage Books, 1992). The trend has since steadily worsened.

4. Peter Sloterdijk, *You Must Change Your Life: On Anthropotechnics*, trans. Wieland Hoban (Malden, MA: Polity Press, 2013), p. 185.

5. Walter Benjamin, "Critique of Violence," in *Reflections*, ed. P. Demetz (New York: Schocken Press, 1921/1978), pp. 277–300.

6. For measures of happiness across states, see Valentina Pasquali and Tina Aridas, "The Happiest Countries in the World," http://www.gfmag.com/tools/global-database/ne-data/11940-happiest-countries.html#axzz2LEPMyPEN (accessed February 18, 2013). In the "Happy Planet Index," which measures how well states create "happy and healthy lives for their citizens," the United States ranks toward the bottom (105 out of 151), while "The Better Life Index" of the Organisation for Economic Co-Operation and Development, looking at different factors among a more limited set of states, places the United States at 12 out of 36, with social democracies consistently ranking higher (e.g., Denmark, Norway, Austria, the Netherlands, Switzerland, Australia, Canada, and Finland comprising the top eight states).

7. For a video summarizing a Harvard study mapping the disparities between actual and imagined income disparities in the United States, see Makini Brice, "These Three Charts Sum Up Income Inequality in America Perfectly," http://eunoic.com/2013/03/04/these-three-charts-sum-up-income-inequality-in-america-perfectly (accessed May 4, 2013).

8. See M. Lane Bruner, *Repressive Regimes, Aesthetic States, and Arts of Resistance* (Berlin: Peter Lang Press, 2012); see also William C. Dowling, *Jameson, Althusser, Marx: An Introduction to the Political Unconscious* (Ithaca, NY: Cornell University Press, 1984).

9. James W. Loewen, *Lies My Teacher Told Me* (New York: Simon and Schuster, 1995), p. 202.

10. On the victory of the Federalists over the anti-Federalists, and the consequences of that pyrrhic victory for republicanism in the United States, see M. Lane Bruner, *Democracy's Debt: The Historical Tensions between Political and Economic Liberty* (Amherst, NY: Humanity Books, 2009), pp. 237–73.

11. Sigmund Freud, *Civilization and Its Discontents* (New York: W. W. Norton, 1962).

12. Dowling, p. 115.

13. Dowling, p. 131. Such a perspective can be usefully compared with Friedrich Nietzsche's *On the Advantage and Disadvantage of History for Life*, trans. Peter Preuss (Indianapolis, IN: Hackett Publishing Company, 1980); and Michel Foucault,

"Nietzsche, Genealogy, History," in *The Foucault Reader*, ed. Paul Rabinow (New York: Pantheon, 1984), pp. 76–100.

14. See, for example, Slavoj Žižek, *The Sublime Object of Ideology* (New York: Verso, 1989); and Slavoj Žižek, *Welcome to the Desert of the Real* (New York: Verso, 2002).

15. Slavoj Žižek, *The Puppet and the Dwarf: The Perverse Core of Christianity* (Cambridge, MA: The MIT Press, 2003), pp. 66–67.

16. In May 2012, the incumbent Democratic President Barack Obama had the support of only 34–40% of whites without college degrees, while the numbers only significantly improved among whites with postgraduate degrees. Racism, of course, accounts for much of these numbers, but poor whites in general tend to think of themselves as "conservatives." See, for example, Ronald Brownstein, "Obama's Last Line of Defense," *National Journal*, http://decoded.nationaljournal.com/2012/05/obamas-last-line-of-defense.php (accessed May 26, 2012); and Frank Newport, Jeffrey M. Jones, and Lydia Saad, "In Tight Race, Both Obama, Romney Have Core Support Groups: Obama's Solid Support from Nonwhites Is Offset by Romney's Advantages within the White Vote," http://www.gallup.com/poll/154568/tight-race-obama-romney-core-support-groups.aspx (accessed May 26, 2012); and "GOP Makes Big Gains among White Voters: Especially among the Young and Poor," Pew Research Center Publications (July 22, 2011), http://pewresearch.org/pubs/2067/2012-electorate-partisan-affiliations-gop-gains-white-voters (accessed May 26, 2012).

17. Superficially, this "photographic negative" of the electoral map can be explained by the fact that those living on the coasts tend to be more educated and cosmopolitan, and thus they vote for the political party most likely to secure sound government over the long term. Correspondingly, one might associate such disparities between actual interests and fantasized political affiliation with the cynical machinations of those running the two parties' rhetorical machines. For a fascinating discussion of such machinations, see George Lakoff, *Don't Think of an Elephant* (White River Junction, VT: Chelsea Green Publishing Company, 2004), which reveals how the framing of issues is far more important than facts in political campaigns.

18. For an introduction to the relationship between slavery and early capitalism, see Stephen M. Best, *The Fugitive's Properties: Law and the Poetics of Possession* (Chicago: University of Chicago Press, 2004). For a broader perspective on the "ontological scandal" whereby people are turned into things and things into people, see Nneka Logan, "The Ontological Scandal of Corporate Personhood and Speech: A Rhetorical Analysis of Key Supreme Court Decisions" (unpublished dissertation, Georgia State University, 2013).

19. See Aristotle's *Politics*, trans. Trevor J. Saunders (New York: Penguin Books, 1982), esp. pp. 235–72. On ancient Western political theory and its influence on republicanism across the ages, see J. G. A. Pocock, *The Machiavellian Moment* (Princeton, NJ: Princeton University Press, 1975); and Gordon S. Wood, *The Creation of the American Republic 1776–1787* (Chapel Hill, NC: University of North Carolina Press, 1998).

20. The Roman philosopher Polybius maintained that all political systems are doomed to decay because of their inability to maintain the proper balance between the rich, the middle class, and the poor. Polybius, *The Histories of Polybius, Book Six*, trans. Evelyn S. Schuckburgh (Cambridge, ON: In Parentheses Publications, 2002).

21. On the public humiliation of the Roman aristocrats and the political use of spectacle in ancient Rome, see Richard C. Beacham, *Spectacle Entertainments of Early Imperial Rome* (New Haven, CT: Yale University Press, 1999).

22. On the rise and fall of the "oligarchic republics" of Renaissance Italy, see Lauro Martines, *Power and Imagination: City-States in Renaissance Italy* (Baltimore, MD: The Johns Hopkins University Press, 1988), esp. pp. 45–61 and 130–61.

23. On the widespread alienation caused by the bourgeois takeover of the state, especially during and after the July Monarchy between 1830 and 1848, see Ellie Nower Schamber, *The Artist as Politician: The Relationship between the Arts and the Politics of the French Romantics* (Lanham, MD: University Press of America, 1984); and F. W. J. Hemmings, *Culture and Society in France: 1789–1845* (Leicester, UK: Leicester University Press, 1987). On the alienation caused by the emergence of consumer culture between the failed workers' rebellions of 1848 and the aftermath of the First World War, see Jerrold Seigel, *Bohemian Paris: Culture, Politics, and the Boundaries of Bourgeois Life, 1830–1930* (Baltimore, MD: The Johns Hopkins University Press, 1986).

24. See, for example, Richard Carruthers, *City of Capital: Politics and Markets in the English Financial Revolution* (Princeton, NJ: Princeton University Press, 1996); J. G. A. Pocock, "Virtue and Commerce in the Eighteenth Century," *Journal of Interdisciplinary History* 3, no. 1 (1972): 119–34; and P. G. M. Dickson, *The Financial Revolution in England: A Study in the Development of Public Credit 1688–1756* (New York: St Martin's Press, 1967).

25. On media consolidation, see Herbert Schiller, *Culture Inc.: The Corporate Takeover of Public Expression* (New York: Oxford University Press, 1991). On corporate influence in the destruction of republicanism, see the first five chapters of Alex Carey, *Taking the Risk out of Democracy: Corporate Propaganda versus Freedom and Liberty* (Carbondale: University of Illinois Press, 1996); and Ted Nace, *Gangs of America: The Rise of Corporate Power and the Disabling of Democracy* (San Francisco, CA: Berrett-Koehler Publishers, Inc., 2005).

26. The classic text on national imaginaries is Benedict Anderson's *Imagined Communities* (New York: Verso, 1991). On the relationship between national imaginaries and fields of the unspeakable, see M. Lane Bruner, *Strategies of Remembrance: The Rhetorical Dimensions of National Identity Construction* (Columbia: University of South Carolina Press, 2002).

27. One could just as easily look at popular comedies across the decades, from *The Andy Griffith Show* to *Two Broke Girls*, or "reality" television, or other popular televisual texts to read the political unconscious. Also, as Žižek has shown, reviews of popular movies can do the same work. See, for example, his *Welcome to the Desert of the Real*, where he considers why *The Truman Show* and *The Matrix* were the top box office hits in the years prior to the terrorist attacks on September 11, 2013. Today, however, widespread public controversy over the arts are often difficult to detect because of the "privatization" of aesthetic consumption.

28. "Jon Stewart Biography," http://www.thedailyshow.com/news-team/jon-stewart (accessed May 9, 2013).

29. Demagogues on radio reach far more people than Stewart does on television. In 2010, three demagogues topped radio ratings. Rush Limbaugh drew over 15 million a week, Sean Hannity 14 million, and Glenn Beck 9 million. See Rodney Ho, "Rush Limbaugh Tops Talk Radio Rankings as Usual, Glenn Beck Moves

Up," http://blogs.ajc.com/radio-tv-talk/2010/03/03/rush-limbaugh-tops-talk-radio-rankings-as-usual-glenn-beck-moves-up (accessed May 9, 2013). In 2011, Stewart only reached approximately 2.3 million viewers a week. See David Ferguson, "Jon Stewart's the Daily Show Ratings Soar, Fox News Slumps in May Numbers," http://www.rawstory.com/rs/2011/06/05/daily-show-ratings-soar-fox-slumps-in-may-numbers (accessed May 9, 2013).

30. Mash-ups are interesting postmodern aesthetic forms where fragments from disparate but culturally significant texts are remixed, oftentimes to make critical political statements. "Donald Duck Meets Glenn Beck in Right Wing Radio Duck," http://www.rebelliouspixels.com/2010/right-wing-radio-duck-donald-discovers-glenn-beck (accessed May 1, 2013).

CHAPTER 9

Re-Forming Class: Identity, Wealth, and Cultural Transformation in South Africa

Lisa Nel

This discussion about "Living with Class" in contemporary South Africa contains a less subtle correlative about the dismantling of its cultures and death of its diversity. These processes are irreversible. They are being steadily and systematically controlled by Western economic policies—between Wall Street and the Johannesburg Stock Exchange—which, while inscrutable to the vapidly poor and uneducated, are both mercilessly challenging the cultural viability of an African way of life and subsidizing the affluence of a narrow margin of politicians and entrepreneurs.

South Africa's cultures have undergone a myriad of historically transformative events; the most recent being Apartheid. These cultures are inextricably linked to specific ethnic groups, many of which are desperately trying to preserve their own identities, which they have fought for centuries to establish.

The "Coloreds," for instance, have their own ancestry derived from the Khoisan as well as mixtures of Bantu African, North European, Pilipino, Dutch, and Huguenot settlers. They have classified themselves as "Coloreds" not pejoratively but proudly. They speak their own Afrikaans dialect and have distinctive traditions particular to their culture. The Malays, while also part of the Colored culture, to some extent share similar ancestry. All the Cape Malays are Muslim and trace their lineage back to people brought over as slaves from Indonesia some of whom were political exiles. Many of these people brought over by the Dutch were skilled artisans such as silversmiths, cobblers, singers, and tailors. The "Cape Malay" (as they are still called) have their own traditional cuisine and customs that separate them from other Colored groups. Yet while the origins of this class of people are widely diverse, their confluence resides in their common language of

Afrikaans as well as in a history of experiences they shared that transformed them into their own distinctive entity. Some of the Cape Coloreds share their ancestry with Indians, while some Malays also descend from Indian lines. Although Muslim Malays can marry into different Colored Christian families, many do not, and they prefer to marry within their own specific sect. And although all of these groups contain their own distinctive traditions, customs, and food, they share a broad denomination as Cape Coloreds.

In addition to the Coloreds, South Africa is home to the Afrikaners, Xhosas, Zulus, Tswanas, Vendas, and Indians, to name the most palpable. For an outsider to try and understand the intricate but tenuous relationships that bind these distinctive ethnic groups together is an exercise in futility. Equally futile is the assumption that a Western consummate view of delineating ethnicity can be supplanted (effectively) onto this society. For instance, there are no such distinctively inclusive terms such as "ethnic Xhosa," "ethnic Tswana," or "ethnic Afrikaner."

The American codified version of class is the great equalizer that seeks to incorporate its ethnic cultures into the latest homogenized edition of the modern success story of the "land of immigrants," a story that, in its "second coming," venerates the rapid accumulation of wealth as the ultimate fulfillment of democracy: that equal opportunity to join the consumer class trumps the necessary quotient of its affordability. It wasn't always like this. In America, from the early philanthropic steel magnets like Carnegie to the elite southern gentry of Virginia tobacco farmers, the socioeconomic hierarchy that emerged was an inevitable outcome of a Protestant ethic and opportunism, both of which were afforded them by the preexistence of a Western democratic process. This process was fomented out of the melting pot of a unified belief in equality, religious freedom, and vindication from monarchical tyranny.

The American experience has been ingrained into the very fabric of semantic and episodic events in the lives of its people. Americans are defined as a nation by their collective and collected, cognitive and historical development. The process is particular to itself and can neither be exported as a conceptual framework in which other cultures can be perceived to exist, nor be exported particularly in a commoditized form.

The doctrine of the American dream, (theoretically) accessible to all who apply themselves, cannot exist in developing countries, in which freedom and equality for the majority of people is still associated with the right to vote. Hard work in the gold mines of Johannesburg in the 1950s only just put food on a miner's table with never even a suggestive whisper that he could become either a shareholder or a CEO in one of these companies.

During the first half of the twentieth century, Africa and its people were leased out to the major colonial powers. Neo-colonials still lurk in the monolithic remnants of their grandfather's successes, as for instance colonial officers, in the pseudo-exotic fringes of the now-gated communities still dominated by whites whose perceptions of the "natives" are more primitive than patronizing.

In South Africa, the advent of this "second coming" in this century has heralded the denunciation of a traditional lifestyle, forcing people to become deracinated from the safety of customs, beliefs, practices, and ways of life to which they can never return.

South Africa, with its "unofficial" unemployment rate of 40%, cannot afford to be addicted to even the images of luxury imported items, let alone be encouraged to believe that they are readily available to them. But it is too late to stymie the flow of a need that has been created. Township tours. Are they sympathy runs, are people setting up endowment funds, or are these tours advertising more inaccessibility to the people in the SUVs, the clothes they are wearing, the cameras they are taking pictures with, and the sterile digital lives they are living? Realigning people's perspectives is a dangerous road trip to take when these communities are easily enticed to spend their meager earnings on the newest BlackBerry rather than putting food on their tables.

Feeding one's family in these impoverished and at times violent communities is not based upon bringing home the paycheck. An "earned" reward, rather than being awarded a medical scheme or down payment on a car, is being asked to work for another day as a builder, gardener, or domestic worker. And the only subsidized food these families receive (ANC members only) is that which is doled out by the ruling party just before election day. The care packages arrive with promises of better housing, subsidized electricity and water, and of course eventual employment, all provided by the state.

State officials, however, having exacted unconditional party loyalty, do not feel unconditionally morally obligated toward their people. These spokesmen know the price for freedom requires no dividend for people, who after years of marginalization associate freedom with the right to vote.

Being an elected leader, a Member of Parliament, or a civil servant has come with its own pre-packed designer bonuses. They are in a class of their own: a new genre that has been validated by the pirated ethos of Western success and fueled by the global machinery of greed, which has delivered no handbook on ethics for South Africa's leaders to follow. America took awhile to become greedy. Africa has become instantly and desperately greedy to become beneficiaries of global economic hegemonic policies that have been forced upon them. Unfortunately, modern greed is poor compensation for the loss of its entire cultural wealth with its reservoir of irreplaceable diversity. But the new class, which has been created in part by default, has had little incentive to seek an alternate path.

This is the genre in which material wealth is the defining criterion for global accessibility and socioeconomic respectability. It is the postmodern affirmation of success. Academic qualifications are often eschewed in the wake of democratization of business transactions by BEE (Black Economic Empowerment) entrepreneurs. These successful businessmen further endorse the enlistment of countless friends, cronies, and residual connections from their days of the struggle. Handpicked ministers and individuals in the civil services, department heads, and CEOs of state-owned enterprises also slide beneath the academic radar of qualifications and seem not to need even a high school diploma to get appointed.

The "horror" has reemerged by the formation of this class whose totemic hall pass is an extension of their membership to the elite revolutionary cadres of the ANC in exile. The reopening of South Africa's jewelry box to the global economy in 1994 ushered in extended amnesty transactions like missing diamond digging contracts as a means of evading unethical economic privileges, which guaranteed its new curators a piece of the shiny rock in the bottomless pit. As recompense for business deals done that had benefited the previous elite, the contents of the box are auctioned off (again) with impunity to the highest bidder. Everyone is contentedly indefensible but rich and equal in the ledgers of offshore accounts.

Unfortunately, wealth accrued without any semblance of a hard-earned reward has destroyed the cultural scaffolding upon which so many people still rely on to restructure their lives. Unearned profit has no traditional talisman. The adoption of the concept of instantly gratified entitlement is problematic for other reasons: It assumes that South Africa, with its lingering ethnic and racial cleavages, has lowered the bar of corruption to the point where vast accumulation of wealth by any means is (and historically has been) more important than equalizing the bandwidth of the Rainbow Nation. In reality, however, racial and ethnic issues are deliberately exploited to determine financial benefit and to divide and ensure political loyalties.

More importantly, party loyalty has sabotaged the ANC's own fundamental promise to educate and enlighten its people. While high school students in the Eastern Cape waited for over six months to receive their textbooks in 2012, the tragic resultant trajectory was the exposure of incompetent and insouciant leadership, desperately clinging to colonial-era excuses for poor service delivery as a scapegoat for the ANC's "oversight." As education is hailed as the gateway to secular knowledge, the convenience of keeping (especially) students in ignorance seems distinctly advantageous to leaders who are themselves uneducated and unqualified. Any belief to the contrary is just another brick in the wall of deception.

Deceiving the uninformed also guarantees that rural people are easily induced to toyi-toyi (a demonstration in the form of a dance of protest with specific chants and slogans to protest government or authoritative policies), toward a redirected resentment of "whites."

The class or group of people most susceptible to the grand deception is the quasi-militant youth: the followers of Julius Malema, previously president of the Youth League but recently fallen into disgrace for tax evasion, racketeering, and tender fraud.

The apotheosis of Malema was an indictment of the seriousness of how the perception of class entitlement has deleteriously affected people in this group. And the youth (in any country) are the future. Malema's followers tend to be extremists and he urges them to react with violence. His message has continually been to provoke the discussion about nationalization of mines and forced seizure of white-owned farms. He has unequivocally supported the genocidal policies of Robert Mugabe, indicating that such "reforms" should be implemented in South Africa. Malema does not dress in the modest style of one who is representative of social equality and equal opportunity; instead, while organizing marches for reform, he brandishes a Rolex watch and designer clothing and drives away in either a Range Rover Sport or Aston Martin. He has personal investments worth millions, yet he is able to seduce his followers with promises of the "white man's" wealth as their right...a right that was taken away from them and to which they now (should) have unmitigated entitlement. Ironic perhaps that many in the Youth League either were not born until *after* Apartheid was dissolved or were too young to have been directly affected by its policies. Malema tried to further the racial divide, tactically demonizing the trappings of Western materialism yet encouraging the masses to embrace the very things he displayed. He was able to instigate strikes and incite violence directed upon riot police and reporters with sublime ease. Because the Youth League members are already angry, indoctrinating his followers with a cult mentality that rekindles racism in songs like "Kill the Boer," and calling President Ian Khama (President of Botswana who is of mixed race) an "imperialist puppet" are readily absorbed deliberate distortions whose only purpose is to foster antagonistic beliefs about whites.

At the presidential level, racist comments are interspersed to remind the people that they are continually "owed." That it is a "right" to frequent expensive restaurants and drive expensive cars while patronizing whites, suggestively implying that they are still fortunate to be "allowed" to own farms. The emphasis on payback and unmitigated compensation, rather than on hard work, education, and incorporation of different skills and ideas from different ethnic backgrounds, serves to polarize people with revolutionary propaganda. Using words like "comrade" and "struggle" conjures passions and imposes ideologies suggestive of a freedom fight that is not yet won. If the president of South Africa has been reported to have made reference to the fact that owning and walking a dog is part of the "white culture," what kind of mixed message is being conveyed? And he further (purportedly) commented that even if blacks do straighten their hair (as people of all races do!), they can never be "white." What is taking place among Africans is cultural suicide.

The Afrikaner, on the other hand, has its own culture which to this day remains coherent and venerable. They are not easily displaced ideologically. The original Afrikaners who colonized the Cape in 1652 were recolonized in their own country by the British in 1815. The combination of this internal annexation as well as the inevitable two Boer Wars that ensued created the milieu in which the "*volk*," the Afrikaner identity, began to germinate. An Afrikaner ethnic identity became crucial for these early Dutch settlers to distinguish and appreciably separate themselves from the English oppressors. The British considered themselves culturally and racially superior and looked down upon the Afrikaner as a lowly hybrid.

These "hybrids," however, were undeterred in their mission to form an Afrikaner culture, which found expression in the development of a common vernacular, customs, and traditions that became consolidated as an independent identity. This identity eventually took on mythological overtones with glorified stories of the Voortrekkers, which have been immortalized in Homeric tales of adventures, adventures in which the conquest of a hostile land by the perseverance and suffering of a handful of pioneers in ox wagons resonate with elegiac legends.

In addition to their conquest over the African veldt, these Afrikaners were able to extend this nascent penumbra of a chosen *volk* because the Pact government in 1924 was determined to create a unified Afrikaner society, which had been forced into stratification during industrialization. The early settlers had been predominantly involved in farming and husbandry but soon found themselves with limited skills, as the rapid growth of cities and the discovery of gold in 1886 attracted businesses for which their agricultural background had no use.

The Afrikaners knew that preservation and future sustainability of their people meant that they had to reeducate the unskilled, find employment, and create housing for the poor and essentially reconstruct their entire social order and economic system. Engineering a system of social integration by uplifting the status of the less educated by creating opportunities like subsidizing investments in farms and implementing a network of community services not only ensured the survival but also guaranteed the success of a people, a *volk*, and an ideology.

Although the Afrikaners have emerged as a recognized unified culture, they have yet to extricate themselves from the ignominy of Apartheid. The racial and ethnic divisions implemented during those years, far from being displaced by Mandela's vision of a multi-ethno-racial utopian precedent for a collective social imperative of a new South African identity, have again been subdivided and reclassified. Rather than our ethnic groups celebrating their recrudescence and empowering themselves to regain the spirit of their traditions, most have succumbed to contaminated images of material idealism. Beneath the shroud of newfound moral superiority, traditional values and customs are laid to rest.

University students, those for whom "Apartheid" is just a term, represent a class who are victims of cultural decimation, and, more disturbingly, they have freely and consciously made this choice. These are the students who are hard-pressed to visit their villages on holidays. They are embarrassed. Many adopt European Christian names, preferring anything other than their "tribal" name, which traditionally had spiritual and historical significance for the family and the community. For example, in many African cultures, the paternal grandparents will choose a name for the first-born grandchild. The name is special and usually relates to an event or experience. "Dikeledi" (pronounced dee-ka-lay-dee) means tears, while "Boitumelo" (pronounced boy-ee-too-mellow) means joy or happiness. These grandparents (those that remain) despairingly cling to their dying pride, immortalizing their name and culture by hand-weaving baskets with special symbolic patterns intricately woven into artifacts, which to tourists and shop owners are sold for a profit into insignificance. In their "commoditized" form, the craft will become prolifically nameless as will the traditions from which it came.

Traditional practices run into more pungent polemics when Western moral superiority, in its postmodern haze of rhetorical righteousness, lobbies for the eradication of traditional circumcision, while paradoxically supporting a country's genocidal leaders. Subsuming Africa's diverse and ethically challenging practices, from a Eurocentric lens of acceptability, reaches a dangerous fork in the road over issues such as FGM (female genital mutilation), which rather ironically is practiced by several immigrant groups in the United States.

The perception that is created in this country over these Western "enlightened" ambivalences has provoked a useful paradigm shift among its leaders. In the murky waters of ethical admissibility, politicians have no problem re-lining their postcolonial pockets as gratuities for embracing a Western lifestyle. They have reclassified themselves and their ethic priorities, justifying blatant disregard for addressing morally contravening practices because they have been issued with a hall pass from the world's undisputed leaders: leaders who bleakly close their in-country manuals on cultural etiquette as they board their private jets to the next multinational meeting at an undisclosed safari lodge.

The purchasing power of South Africa's resources has fixed its interest rate on its certainty that the country's leaders will be prepared to accept a decorative democracy in exchange for the guarantee that the international conglomerates remain their service providers. These service providers were put into place when the dollar provided developing countries with a guaranteed loan agreement.

During the Nixon administration, the dollar emerged as a free floating agent, released from its bondage of being pegged to gold as the international standard of currency. Once developing countries (a tenuous label ascribed to South Africa in the 1970s during the hiatus of Apartheid) were able to borrow dollars to finance their business, not only did the World Bank become a super-factory for a worldwide dollar-based recycling plant, not only did the dollar become the new global foreign secretary, but an entire ethos made a cataclysmic turn down the rabbit hole.

This was a drop into a chasm where ideological canons of belief, like the egalitarianism of the freedom struggle of the ANC, were instantly and effortlessly replaced with an effigy of belief. American greed and economic hegemony gripped the ANC in the twilight of its ideology, with the implacable surrender to the dollar as the supreme commander of unquestionable success and the irrepressible measure of modernization.

This new agency opened the door for elite economic entrepreneurs to prosper unconditionally, giving them their own distorted lens from which they could view saliently unethical policies of governance with impunity.

The morally bereft racial war of Apartheid transformed under the ANC into a different brand of social war, one dominated by a rapacious class of leaders more interested in their newly emerged hierarchical global stature than any form of good governance that would benefit the country with its fractured social and economic policies. For this class, accountability has been as easily replaced as rearranging the seating plan in the boardroom to suit the new order. The new order is the members-only club, the inner circle of trust whose collective sympathies for the people who voted them into power changes "our turn to eat" into a metaphor for "let them eat cake."

Unfortunately the cake is indivisible. The layering has been outsourced and the people who have labored to make the ingredients again find themselves not morally but economically marginalized. There is no such thing as "an equal piece of the pie" or, in South Africa's case, an equal share in the gold mine. People who with faithful ignorance surrendered their souls and truncated earnings to leaders and politicians had (until recently as evidenced in the Marikana massacre) no idea that the ANC had drifted so irretrievably far away from the common workers' struggle for a better life.

What now are we confronted with but the ineluctable modality of change by default rather than progressive, collective, and nonpartisan involvement in choosing a common path toward a progressively modernizing society?

The democratic South African narrative displays an unassailable message to the people who helped transform this country whichever ethnic class, culture, or group to which they belong. The leadership in this country is not only bought and paid for, but they have sold their cultural souls to the devil of global economic hegemony. But hegemony, which has spread into a virus, causes not just a cascading of cultural infrastructures but also the dissolution of a way of thinking, a way of life, and most importantly has caused the annihilation of a value structure whose demise is now dissected and reassigned to academics, journalists, and policy-makers in air-conditioned lecture rooms and editor's lounges.

Our new ruling elite has deliberately fragmented its own precious resources, the cultures, and the ethnic variety that have made this country not only incomparable but unique in its (former) ability to retain, celebrate, and be proud of its diversity. This fragmenting has trickled down into the very soil of its rural people, separating them even further from their own more prosperous people.

Although Western media and marketing campaigns expostulate laboriously on images of universal African successes, their conclusions are at best anecdotal. The well-dressed designer TV anchors and actors displayed on beer or car commercials not only speak in accents of those well schooled in English or American universities, but have also adopted a form of acceptance to comply with a global standard.

Many of these middle-class and prosperous Africans have consciously drifted as far away from their "roots" as African Americans. This class of people, well educated and well on their way to becoming successful signature models of a bourgeois African society, reinforces the imported side effects of homogenizing culture, which dismissively watches the descent of its own death. What reemerges is the birth of a belief in a merciless commercial Leviathan, which has mutated cultures to fit into an incorporated amorphous ideal of owning a fast food chain, mass-producing pottery, baskets, or carvings, all as a guarantee of keeping up with the pace of the global economy.

The descent into mediocrity is everywhere. On the streets of Johannesburg or Durban, the Apple coterie represents the converts: those to whom any connection to their ethnicity is as removed as their understanding of Apartheid. The young aspiring executives of South Africa have emulated Americans in this same category to perfection. They too have joined the ranks as the progeny of the money-eyed elite trust fund club who roam the sterile corridors of private institutions clutching skinny lattes while wired to the latest iPhone.

What have we done? Modern choice or its ruthless imposition is no longer liberation from a repressive way of life; it has created a new bondage to Western socioeconomic convention, which has only served to decimate difference. In the words of Edward Wilson, "Culture is a product; is historical; includes ideas, patterns, and values; is selective; is learned; is based upon symbols; and is an abstraction from behavior and the products of behavior."[1] The next Rubicon to be crossed will be for South Africans to reestablish themselves in the globalized social order, independent of any lease agreement to which it has been historically and is presently bound.

Note

1. Edward O. Wilson, *Consilience* (New York: Alfred A. Knopf, 1998): 142.

Bibliography

Baggini, Julian. *Philosophy.* London: Hodder Education, 2012
Bottomley, Edward-John. *Poor White.* Cape Town: Tafelberg, 2012
Chopra, Deepak, Mlodinov, Leonard. *War of the World Views.* New York: Rider, 2011
Giliomee, Hermann. *The Last Afrikaner Leaders.* Cape Town: Tafelberg, 2012
Mills, Greg, Herbst, Jeffrey. *Africa's Third Liberation.* London: Penguin, 2012
Plaut, Martin, Holden, Paul. *Who Rules South Africa?* Cape Town: Jonathan Ball, 2012
Ramadan, Tariq. *The Quest for Meaning.* London: Penguin, 2012
Russel, Alec. *After Mandela.* London: Hutchinson, 2009
Twineyo-Kamugisha, Elly. *Why Africa Fails.* Cape Town: Tafelberg, 2012
Wilson, Edward O. *Consilience.* New York: Alfred A. Knopf, 1998

CHAPTER 10

Whiteness as Currency: Rethinking the Exchange Rate

Emily M. Drew

For societies in which racism is an operating system, whiteness is a form of currency with a significantly high exchange rate. Its value is so meaningful, George Lipsitz argues, that it produces a false group solidarity and possessive investment[1] in its continuation. For many white people in the United States, whiteness has provided a pathway to opportunities for acquiring society's transformative assets: land, housing, jobs, and education. In this way, whiteness has been a tool for social mobility and intergenerational economic security.[2] Put simply, it has material benefits that can pay a high economic yield. Yet, for *most* white people in the United States, the real dividend of whiteness comes in its symbolic value: its deeply felt power in shaping social status, group membership, and identity. In this way, whiteness provides a well-documented identity to buy into, one that promises a placement in the social hierarchy higher than people of color. For whites, who become what Charles Mills calls "signatories" in a racial contract, they will "live in an invented delusional world, a racial fantasyland, a 'consensual hallucination.'"[3]

Therefore, it is impossible to imagine a world without class without understanding how race and class operate together, without disentangling the complex ways in which whiteness functions as currency. Understanding whiteness as material and symbolic, the "entangled relationship between race and property [reveals how] historical forms of domination have evolved to reproduce subordination in the present."[4] Reducing or eliminating the tremendous disparities between classes could have significant implications for racial identities, particularly for whiteness in the United States. Beyond eliminating economic disparities, imagining a world without class itself requires also an imagining of a de-racialized society. It requires a complete rebuilding of a society in which race and class do not aid and abet one another in shaping people's worldview, self-concept, and conceptions of the Other.

Economic and Symbolic Currency

A significant feature of a racialized society is that individuals get socialized into the dominant ideology of white supremacy, one that creates and maintains a pro-white/anti-Other logic. As with other forms of social stratification, racial groups get created and ranked in a hierarchy, and society's rewards and punishments get unequally distributed based upon that group membership. Members of the dominant group—white people, in the United States—get inculcated with false notions of superiority, coming to believe that their social status was earned and that they are in fact entitled to superior access to society's resources. As it has been noted by numerous critical race theorists ad antiracism activists, membership in the dominant group—whiteness—has its privileges. Those privileges are awarded as white people enter into a social contract in which they agree to participate in the system of white supremacy, in exchange for becoming white, and, thus, beneficiaries of society's resources. In fact, as Harris argues, "Whites have come to expect and rely upon these benefits and over time, these expectations have been affirmed, legitimated, and protected by the law."[5]

Racial status does not stand as a pillar on its own; it is maintained by an economic system that stresses competition and pits groups against one another for social and economic rewards. Class disparities amplify the significance of racial identity to and for white people. Under an imposed class system, poor and working class white people scapegoat people of color, blaming these communities (not the power elite nor our economic system) for the lack of available jobs, dysfunctional public systems, and the violence in our cities. McKinney notes that most whites even go so far as to conceive of their group status as a social liability,[6] working as a "reverse racism" that limits mobility and success.

A classed society is both the product of and fuel for a racialized society. Historian David Roediger documents the historical processes through which white people gave up class-based solidarity with people of color in order to buy into whiteness.[7] He argues that throughout history, whites have sold themselves short, giving up their economic self-interest, in order to become white, and reap its benefits of superior *social* status. This trend continues as white people vote against their own economic self-interest in order to gain symbolic rewards associated with a superior group status.[8] Many note the profound costliness of this commitment to whiteness over people's movements for social and economic justice.

And working class white people are not alone in a socialization that deludes them into choosing racial status over concrete material benefits. White feminist movements continue narrowly defining an agenda for reproductive rights instead of reproductive justice,[9] demanding tougher sentencing for domestic violence perpetrators instead of restorative justice models,[10] and "reclaiming" hyper-sexualized identities (e.g., "the SlutWalk"[11]) in ways that completely ignore the racialized sexualization of women of color's bodies. In this way, white women continue settling for the "wages of whiteness," selling themselves short of the potential for gender solidarity that could lead to more effectively challenging the conditions of patriarchy.

While whiteness affords its possessors a heightened sense of worth, an identity rooted in false notions of superiority, whiteness also has concrete economic benefit. Organizers like Meizhu Lui at Boston's "United for a Fair Economy" have documented the economic benefit of being white for entire generations of white people. In *The Color of Wealth*, she and her coauthors argue that whiteness has allowed white people far greater access to transformative assets that result in cross-generational social mobility, including land, housing, education, and taxing income instead of wealth. White individuals, not just entire generations of white people, receive economic benefits from racial group membership through— to name only a few—access to jobs based upon white-sounding names[12] and assumptions about lack of criminality.[13]

A Case Study: The Value of Whiteness

In my own case, spending my childhood amid the working poor, my whiteness acted as literal currency, shielding me from many of the assumptions made about people of color (both poor and not). For example, teachers did not assume I came from a single-parent home. I imagine that they had little idea that my mom and I lived in a Section 8 housing complex, struggled to pay bills, or the frequency at which clean clothes were scarce because they were often stolen from the laundry mat. And when my mom was the last parent to arrive at day care to pick me up from the day, that was attributed to her hard work, not poor parenting.

In school, my whiteness had teachers select me to be in-charge of the classroom when they had to step out, and hailed me as "a good example" to my peers of color. And in a classic form of liberal racism, my whiteness had me receive praise by being named "citizen of the month" for playing with students of color at recess (a praise that my mother rewarded me with by taking a trip to Patsy's, a local ice-cream store). When I behaved as a loud or unruly student, rather than being tracked for discipline as my peers of color were, I was tracked into "gifted and talented." I recall to this day my teacher's explanation to my mother at parent–teacher conferences: "it is obvious that the curriculum is not stimulating your daughter and this boredom is causing her classroom disruptiveness." So, while my peers of color's disruptions began their educational record of behavioral problems, my white disruptions placed me on a path to advanced and honors classes that created countless opportunities in the 20 years of education that followed.

Although I almost always worked hard for my education, doing so behind the armor of whiteness allowed me opportunities that I watched my peers of color be denied. It gave me the opportunity to exchange my currency for opportunity. It was certainly easier to be "successful" when teachers assumed my honesty, always thought of me for income-earning opportunities, and clamored to mentor me. Unlike my peers of color, every time I selected a History Day project on civil rights leaders, wrote an editorial or bill for Mock Congress supporting affirmative action, or did a research paper on racism, I was praised, both socially and through concrete awards and honors. I was never charged with being self-interested, biased, too political, or a one-trick pony. In fact, my city's newspaper named me as one of that year's "best and brightest" high school graduates for my commitment to racial justice, an honor that was also appealing to several nonprofit organizations that later helped subsidize my college education through scholarships.

Outside of school, my extracurricular activities reinforced the supremacy of whiteness through promoting a liberal racism that allowed me to continue my currency exchange of whiteness for distance from my working poor roots. The activities we often engaged in provided my white peers and me with a sense of superiority, rooted in whiteness and increasingly class *un*conscious. For example, through my Catholic youth group, one of the sources of my deeply held values in social justice, we organized an "urban plunge" (mission trip) in which we thought it our place to "bring God to the ghetto" and we made tee shirts that said as much. Through Girl Scouts, we earned merit badges about Native Americans while recreating powwows at camp "Indian Village." And through volunteer work we determined the needs of poor communities (which our minds determined to be recycling bins) without ever asking the people themselves. These programs were identity shaping, reaffirming my whiteness while slowly distancing me from "the poor" and learning to associate poverty with people of color.

Together, these examples added up to assert the primacy and currency of whiteness in my life, and the power of race to diminish the ability to see and think clearly about social class. While class consciousness would have been a logical framework to make sense of the oppression all around us, my peers and I banked upon the currency of our whiteness, as it was the source of social and economic status. In my case, racism was a currency that bought me *out* of negative assumptions about my inferiority as a "poor kid from a broken home," and bought me into educational opportunity, social praise, and tangible economic reward.

Today, as a sociologist who studies institutionalized racism and an antiracism activist increasingly committed to economic justice, there is a shameful part of me that is thankful for racism. My racial identity afforded me economic, social, and symbolic rewards. Without racism, I could not have enjoyed class mobility. Such class transition has not come without its challenges, mostly a psychosocial cost that comes from leaving others behind, from rarely celebrating successes (which often feel unearned), and from being unable to unlearn and ignore that there is still not economic or social justice. Imagining a world without class would require looking to its racialized source in my life. Such an examination is likely to produce relief: not just in the lifting of an oppressive economic system, but also of the racism that is both its fuel and outcome.

Living without Racialized Class: Destablizing Whiteness

What becomes of whiteness if its possessors are "living without class"? Does it open the potential for cross-racial, multigenerational movements for economic and social justice? If the philosophers of "human nature" are correct, then the disappearance of class could indeed amplify racial identity. This is a cautionary tale, if, after all, without class distinctions determining our self-worth and the value of Others, people might embrace more deeply other identities for distinction. After all, whiteness is guaranteed; living without poverty feels like so much more precarious of a proposition. However, imagining life without social class is asking us to consider the possible.

Without poverty, without a condition that inspires people to seek scapegoats and place blame, there may be little need to differentiate one's self from an Other; in fact, without class, we open up the potential for a society without hierarchy in all of its forms. If people of all races have their basic needs met, have access to opportunity, and thrive, the incentivized need to root one's worth in an "us" and demonize a "them" serves little function. Without class, a window opens up for a new whiteness to emerge, one no longer about delusion and fantasy. Without class, and thus with a destabilized meaning of whiteness, we make far more possible our potential to live in community.

Notes

1. George Lipsitz, *The Possessive Investment in Whiteness: How White People Profit from Identity Politics* (Philadelphia: Temple University Press, 1998), 18.
2. Meizhu Liu, "Climbing the Up Escalator: White Advantages in Wealth Accumulation," in *The Color of Wealth*, eds Meizhu Liu, et al. (New York: The New Press, 2005), 225–266.
3. Charles Mills, *The Racial Contract* (New York: Cornell University, 1997), 18.
4. Cheryl Harris, "Whiteness as Property," *Harvard Law Review* 106 (1993): 1714.
5. Ibid., 1713.
6. Karyn McKinney, "Confronting Young People's Perceptions of Whiteness: Privilege or Liability," *Sociology Compass* 2:4 (2009): 1303–1330.
7. David Roediger, *The Wages of Whiteness: Race and the Making of the American Working Class* (New York: New Left Books, 1991).
8. Joan Walsh, *What's the Matter with White People: Why We Long for a Golden Age That Never Was* (Hoboken, NJ: Wiley & Sons, 2012).
9. Robin West, "From Choice to Reproductive Justice," *Yale Law Journal* 118 (2009): 1394–1432.
10. INCITE: Women of Color against Violence, *The Color of Violence* (Cambridge, MA: South End Press, 2006).
11. Abka Soloman, "Is the SlutWalk Movement Relevant for a Black Feminist," *Colorlines* (2011), accessed May 15, 2013, doi: http://colorlines.com/archives/2011/08/since_late_may_various_people.html
12. Marianne Bertrand and Sendhil Mullainathan, "Are Emily and Greg More Employable Than Lakisha and Jamal? A Field Experiment on Labor Market Discrimination," *The American Economic Review* 94:4 (2004): 991–1013.
13. Devah Pager, "The Mark of a Criminal Record," *American Journal of Sociology* 108:5 (2003): 937–975.

CHAPTER 11

Dying with Class: Race, Religion, and the Commodification of a Good Death

Ann Neumann[1]

"Evelyn's never had a Twinkie." That's the first thing Marvin[2] says to me when I answer the phone late one November night. "She'd like to try one." Before she dies, we both think. I spent most of the next morning, my birthday, visiting every deli in three neighborhoods looking for a last, discontinued Twinkie[3] on the shelves, but found none. Finally I searched eBay and slapped down $25 for the odd, dying wish of a very wealthy woman, perhaps the last American to never have a Twinkie cross her palate.

When I get there, Evelyn is neatly arranged on the sprawling divan in the front room, like an antique doll. Her long, gray hair, slightly mussed, is pinned up on the back of her petite head giving her the appearance of casual permanence, as if she'd been there since I had last kissed her papery cheek goodbye two days before. Her thin legs, bones really, with folds of pale skin hanging in tidy rows, are tucked up under her, cross-legged. The bare, neat toes at their ends are wiggling constantly with an energy that contradicts her limited mobility. She wears wide linen pants and a men's collared shirt with the sleeves rolled up. It's a shirt I know well, plaid and peach, soft as a rag, from having sewn the pockets back onto its threadbare front panels myself. I sew for Evelyn, in what is our assumed generational roles. She tells me stories as I sit at her knee, a thread and needle in my hand, stitching her life together even as it falls away. Evelyn's eyesight is quickly going now, though it still returns unexpectedly to let her read the name of a Russian opera singer on the muted TV screen behind me or the title on the cover of a book sticking out of my bag. Losing her sight is the greatest difficulty for Evelyn, who is now struggling with a large number of difficulties. Death being the big one.

Evelyn is rare in that she's been enrolled in that "six months or less" club, hospice, for two years now. Over the years I've met her family, heard her life history, cried with her over the harrowing stories of her difficult mother; she's counseled me on my career, my writing, and my relationships. She's dying now, which is a strange thing to say about someone who's 80 years old and in hospice. But I've done this often enough to see that death is closer to her, that her dying has quickened. She is much less collected, her mind wanders, the oxygen tube is in her nose full time, and she sleeps longer and longer hours. Evelyn has lung cancer, which she acknowledges she brought on herself from sucking down a pack of cigarettes a day for well more than half a century. She's nonetheless had a good run of it by most accounts, including her own.

In a number of striking ways, how Evelyn is dying, at home and not in a hospital, is also rare. About 80% of Americans say they want to die at home (which is a service that hospice provides) yet only 20% of us—who look a lot like Evelyn—do. Like most other hospice patients she is female (56%), white (72%), over 65 (80%), on Medicare (83%), and dying of cancer (40%).[4] Why so few poor or minority Americans die a prolonged death is a question with a lot of speculative answers including: fears of the medical community among minorities, enforced by historic bias and exploitation; our cultural disinclination to discuss death and dying—which overlaps with religious faith in God's miracles; doctors' inability to discuss end-of-life decision-making, preferring to continue a quest for cure long after a cure is possible and the community's lack of training in how to alleviate pain; and the challenge of facilitating the agency of patients who have no idea what's coming—and often look to authority for answers.

A series of small tables are arranged around Evelyn, crowded with necessary things—scraps of paper with jagged notes scratched on them in blue ink, a half-drained glass of Bushmills whiskey, a cordless phone, the TV remote, a full, clear cap of anti-diarrhea medicine, the used metal filters of her e-cigarette—in an order she can easily interpret and reach, despite her failing eyesight, despite being tethered to a humming oxygen machine by a floating plastic tube. The placement of these items is very important to a woman who has always been in control of her surroundings, her family, her career, her life. If I touch anything on her tables, I tell her what I'm doing to quell her anxiety.

Evelyn will be my fourth death, unless her husband Marvin beats her to it. He's been in and out of the hospital over the past year. When he's in, I count out the cash for the women who work in shifts to care for Evelyn, responding to the whistle she blows to call them because she doesn't have the breath to raise her voice. They're all women of color, paid in cash "under the table," making less than $15 an hour to keep Evelyn clean and fed. Like many domestic workers, they take care of the dying because it pays cash, because they're undocumented, because it's the work they can get. Even at this rate, 24-hour care is beyond the means of most hospice patients. Medicare pays for only a few hours a day.

I first met Evelyn and Marvin when my exasperated hospice coordinator, Catherine, called to see if I would take another home patient. I told her I didn't want to. Volunteering to fall in love with a person who is about to die is a dry kind of masochism, though in the world of hospice platitudes, you're not supposed to say so. But to be honest, as much as I love Evelyn, and I do love Evelyn, I didn't agree to meet her because I wanted to appreciate living.

"She wants someone to help her write her memoir," Catherine had told me on the phone, "And she's very particular. We can't find anyone she likes." Evelyn had been a medical doctor and a practicing psychiatrist. If anyone might be willing to talk about their own dying, I thought, it would be a doctor and psychiatrist. Doctors don't die the way the rest of us do. They know too much about the small return of aggressive treatment to put themselves through it. Writes Ken Murray, a doctor, in a 2011 article[5] that was widely circulated among caregivers and the end of life community:

> Almost all medical professionals have seen what we call "futile care" being performed on people. That's when doctors bring the cutting edge of technology to bear on a grievously ill person near the end of life. The patient will get cut open, perforated with tubes, hooked up to machines, and assaulted with drugs. All of this occurs in the Intensive Care Unit at a cost of tens of thousands of dollars a day. What it buys is misery we would not inflict on a terrorist. I cannot count the number of times fellow physicians have told me, in words that vary only slightly, "Promise me if you find me like this that you'll kill me."

Doctors have witnessed enough to know how the end of life can go down. And they intimately know what a hospital environment is like; they get themselves out of it when they can, to go home for that final rest in their own beds. I wanted to know how Evelyn would die. It was dead summer, a stifling June day, when I made my first trip to Evelyn and Marvin's apartment on Central Park West.

Evelyn comes from what you might call old New York money and was raised and educated in a way that Americans no longer are, according to the expectations of a bygone aristocratic class, with maids and butlers, summers abroad, boarding schools, Greek and Latin and etiquette classes. After a few late-adolescent years living on an allowance in Paris and Italy, she returned to the States for medical school. It was the end of the 1950s; she was one of a few women in her medical class. With the help of Evelyn's mother, the young couple moved to a 3,000 square foot flat in what was then—and remains—an immaculately kept deco-era building with one of the best addresses in the city, with a fleet of attentive doormen and a constant display of fresh flowers in the lobby. Evelyn's apartment has parquet flooring, sprawling rooms full of books, art, and antiques, maids' quarters, and a history of famous, well-heeled neighbors who practiced psychoanalysis at a time when it made celebrities.

Evelyn, Marvin, and I got on like a house on fire. I stayed two hours on my first visit, charmed by the perfectly arranged woman on the divan, entertained by her knowledge of current politics, intermittent recitations of poetry, and tales of her days as a child psychiatrist in Harlem. Evelyn liked my summer dress and my deference. We decided I should visit any time I liked.

* * *

Hospice is an old idea. During the High Middle Ages, the Catholic Church established hospices, or shelters, for soldiers returning home from the Crusades. Modern hospice, however, wasn't established until 1967 when Cicely Saunders, a British nurse and a devout Catholic, opened St Christopher's Hospice in the United Kingdom. After falling in love with a Polish Jew who was dying of cancer on her ward, Saunders became determined to help dying patients—often in extreme pain and abandoned by doctors when the possibility of cure is gone—to die more peacefully. Until that time, the practice was to call for the priest or opioids to relieve pain. Two years after Saunders opened St Christopher's, Elisabeth Kübler-Ross published her groundbreaking study on the five stages of grief, *On Death and Dying*. Saunders and Kübler-Ross revolutionized an area of medicine that had been largely ignored until that time; in an odd turn of medical history, how to relieve pain is relatively new. In 1971 the first modern hospice was established in the United States. More than 1 million Americans now die in hospice care (out of a total of 2.5 million deaths per year), although many enter with less than two weeks to live. More than a third die after only seven days in the program.

Hospice care can be provided at home, as in Evelyn's case, or in a medical institution like elder homes, hospice facilities, or hospitals. When I don't have a home hospice patient, I volunteer at the hospice ward of my local hospital. It's an 18-bed facility; patients' stays are often very short, less than a week. Most often, they or their families didn't anticipate or accept their impending death, didn't know they could stop treatment earlier, didn't know they could die at home or don't have the resources to die at home. While the in-hospital hospice ward, appropriately on the same floor as the maternity ward, is an excellent facility with talented and respectful staff, I don't like volunteering there. Hospitals are dangerous places; home patients, better oriented in familiar surroundings, tend to live longer. As much as patients and families can prepare for death, the people in the hospital are often just beginning to reckon with its immediate certainty, sideswiped by a reality their culture has taught them to ignore. It's difficult to watch the hopeful abandon hope.

The desperate need for a program that addresses end-of-life comfort, pain, and dignity—frustratingly unquantifiable terms—has in large part been exacerbated by the way medicine has evolved over the past 50 years. We don't die like we used to. Death, throughout history, has meant the almost simultaneous cessation of three bodily functions: heartbeat, breathing, and brain activity. But a series of relatively recent medical advancements has changed the way we define death and has hence opened up a new legal and bioethical terrain. Defibrillators and respirators, which reached wide use in the 1970s and have since saved millions of lives, can keep the heart and lungs going indefinitely. But they have also complicated the decision-making role of patients and doctors. "Death" can now be a medical decision. When does a family remove their father from a respirator? When is a pacemaker turned off? How can such decisions be made when brain activity is difficult, at best, to measure and qualify? What does an alive brain do? What functions can an impaired brain recover? Does consciousness—a state with a strongly disputed definition—mean that someone is alive? And why do we describe those who come out of comas as miracles? What role does hope play in recovery? In comfort? When should we give up hoping? As difficult as these questions are, they lead to a second set of questions: Who makes such decisions? The patient via a legal document like a living will or advanced directive? The spouse, the children, the estranged sibling, the hospital? The courts? And yet a third level of questions: How are patients and their families educated about dying?

Increasingly, a comfortable death depends one one's race and class, and, by extension, religion. Because patients and their families look to the authority of doctors to guide their medical decisions and because doctors have been focused on curing illness rather than easing patients into death, those with lesser resources and knowledge wind up on a path of successive treatments in an institution. Our political dialogue about rationing of health care isn't helping.

The medical "path" that has been established at hospitals now for nearly a half century is to save lives, to do whatever is necessary to keep a patient's body functioning. "I want you to do everything you can to save my mother." For patients, their families, and their doctors, denying possible treatments goes against the emotional desire to keep a loved one alive, present. As a result, studies show that "futile care," the use of invasive treatments that do not actually save lives but often prolong death, is at epidemic proportions. For families and patients with little knowledge of the medical system and the dying process, it is difficult or impossible to understand that there are some things worse than death, to understand that medical treatments, while developed to save lives, can also be a kind of emotional and physical torture. Often, the nature of end-of-life decisions—by patients, their families, and doctors—is determined by social factors, including class and race.

To die at home or as one wishes is practically a luxury today, a commoditized "treatment" that involves insurance complications, state laws, religious mores, and the assistance of a medical industry that, in the face of our nation's increasing elder population, is woefully unprepared for the escalating need for end-of-life care. A few decades ago, dying was not something that had to be explained and chaperoned by specialists. It was the realm of the family pastor, witnessed by even the youngest members of a family, gathered around the sick bed to watch, wait, pray, and care. But the disintegration of the nuclear family, the prevalence of 911 lines (which can result in resuscitations that provide a patient only a few days or weeks more and can break ribs and cause other painful complications) and for-profit medicine, the social taboo against talking about death, the increase of medical procedures that are devoted to curing illnesses rather than caring for patients have all intersected with class in such a way that has created a dying crisis.

This crisis is evidenced by: 45 million Americans uninsured; an unwieldy national health-care bill that addresses the current hemorrhage of resources; two-thirds of Medicare and Medicaid spent on "waste"; an inestimable number of Terri Schiavos hooked up to machines across the nation; rampant lawsuits over what plugs to pull; chemotherapy doled out like a panacea to patients who won't live long enough to finish the course; ineffective legal documents that protect no one, not even the patient; and a war in a dozen states of what right a terminal (as in less than six months to live) patient has to medically end their life.

Evelyn's ability to go at dying on her own terms is made possible by a number of social factors, but also by knowledge, because she was a doctor, of how death comes. Not like a dramatic closing of the eyes but a slow loss of dignity and increased disability. "I'm done," she told the doctor during her hospital stay two years ago. She didn't want more chemotherapy, more tests, a respirator. She wanted to go home to her own bed, her family, and enough morphine to keep her comfortable. In his 1993 bestseller, *How We Die: Reflections on Life's Final Chapter*, Dr Sherwin Nuland writes:

> Poets, essayists, chroniclers, wags, and wise men write often about death but have rarely seen it. Physicians and nurses, who see it often, rarely write about it. Most people see it once or twice in a lifetime, in situations where they are too entangled in its emotional significance to retain dependable memories.

In addition to having little experience with death, Nuland writes, "We compose scenarios that we yearn to see enacted by our mortally ill beloved, and the performances are successful just often enough to sustain our expectations." These scenarios, or "mythologies" of a beautiful death, prevent us from better preparing for it. We think death will gracefully crawl into bed with us, embrace us into that good night. Sometimes it does. But more often than not we get talked into tubes and machines, we're propped unconscious in some pale blue room of the ICU.

How all these factors play across racial and class lines is no surprise. The nature of the inequality, however, is counterintuitive. Because care is often wrongly equated with expensive and invasive treatments, those receiving the most "care" are suffering longer, inside institutions instead of at home, removed from family, hooked up to machines. It's a torture of excess, a funneling of unnecessary resources to those without the knowledge or ability to say no.

* * *

Marshall was awake when I entered his room; the small flat-screen TV reached from the wall like a dentist's lamp and hovered about 18 inches from his head. His face was contorted, his hand across his small black and distended belly. He had pushed the white blanket down to his waist, showing the top gathered edges of his adult diaper. He brightened when he saw me and I gave him a smile to show how happy I was to see him. This was my fourth visit to Hamilton Health Care Facility in Lower Manhattan, established for the care of HIV/AIDS patients.

"Shall I read to you?" I asked him. I walked to the window side of the room, passing by a curtain that divided Marshall's space from his neighbor's. Timothy was bent over his bed with two disposable cups of cereal in front of him on the sheet, their foil labels curled back like eyelashes.

"Hi Timothy," I said, watching him dig his stiff and dirty fingers through the small cups. And after a pause, "What are you doing?"

"Can't chew the raisins," he said, pointing to a pile of small, white-dusted lumps on his bedspread. He smiled and turned back to his bran; I borrowed his *New York Post* and returned to Marshall. But the paper offered nothing to lift Marshall out of his pain.

He finally drifted off to sleep and I sat looking, in turns, at the rise and fall of his wheezing chest and the celebrity gossip page, too distracted by his restlessness to sit still myself. During my prior visits, he had been dressed in gray or forest green sweatpants and a matching sweatshirt. Today he was in a hospital gown and his wasted arms and legs were clearly visible, almost painful to look at. He seemed smaller today. In time the attending nurse brought him Maalox in a small plastic cup. He opened his eyes and, grimacing, downed it with one swig, wiping an escaped chalky-white drop from his lower lip with the edge of the blanket. He pushed the blanket back down to his waist to show us his discomfort. The upper quilted edge of his Depends encircled his bloated belly, the top of his penis pressed in the elastic. Marshall's body was a dying body. It had already surrendered all pride by dragging him to this bed, by becoming inept at caring for itself. The nurse left. In a convulsion of nausea, Marshall flung his head over the bed railing and puked the Maalox into the trash can; I wiped his chin and rested my hand on his shoulder. "I just want to die," he whispered to me. Exhausted, he laid back on the pillow and dozed again.

"Brother Marshall," a man bellowed from the doorway. "How you doin' today?" Marshall's face remained slack, his eyes heavy. He shook his head.

"You know, Marshall, you are in the palm of God's hand and He can heal you whenever He wants to. Cancer ain't no big deal for God. You just need to keep on praying that He save your soul and He can wipe that cancer right away, Marshall. Praise God, He can heal you today." This was said in a long string of unbroken words, like a greeting or a song. Sonny smiled through a crooked and incomplete set of teeth. Marshall nodded his head. I watched his eyes wander over the collage of get-well cards on the wall at the foot of his bed. Hope for the hopeless.

"You belong to the Lord for more 'an two weeks now, ain't that right Marshall?" Marshall nodded again, then dropped his head back on his pillow. "Give God your problems and worries," Sonny said looking at me. I really wanted to.

I looked at Marshall, dying of lung cancer and AIDS. He had been a welder, a husband, and a father before he came to this bed. His wife Rose visited him every other week, though his son lived in New Jersey, too far away for a visit, Marshall had explained. Less than 9% of hospice patients are black;[6] Marshall had probably been enrolled by the facility where he was being treated. His wife worked during the day and was unable to keep him at home. There are really only two ways that people get HIV: drug use and sex. I never asked Marshall how he got it and he never offered me details, but I was certain that some "sin" had pushed him to become born again. Sin and a desire to make the pain go away.

During my next visit, I leveraged my feet, one behind the other, to lift Marshall up off his bed, spin 90 degrees, and sit him back down in his wheelchair. It was a simple maneuver. He weighed very little now and he was specific with his instructions. I had finally convinced him that it was a beautiful day and that getting outside would cheer him up. And maybe make his bowels move. When we reached the first floor, I turned left toward the patio but Marshall stopped me. "Go in there," he said in a small voice, pointing to two large sliding glass doors.

"And thank you great Lord for bringing us Brother Marshall today. Welcome Brother Marshall!" All the attendees, about 25 black people of every age, disability, and gender, hailed Marshall, and he grinned sheepishly, glancing at me to see if I saw how they, his ramshackle family, doted on him. I hunched down in my seat, half behind a pillar, trying not to stand out in my relative health and whiteness. The pastor stood before a modest wooden pulpit, performing a story of Jesus moving through the streets of a city healing people. "I don't care if you can't walk, brother. I'm telling you to get up and dance with me! And the man took Jesus' hand and he stood!"

> Cause you see, Jesus don't care if you can't walk, He don't care if you got AIDS, He don't care if you're poor or if you're sick. He don't care what the doctor tell you 'cause He knows all you need is Him; He will cast off your sickness, He will defy the germs and the viruses. If He wants to heal you and make you walk, He will take your hand. He will heal your body and your soul. He will take you right to the end of this life and beyond. Alpha and Omega! He will heal your soul! And that cripple man took Jesus' hand and stood up with Him and he said, "Even me, Lord! Even me!"

The preacher rhythmically banged his closed fist on his chest and bobbed on bended legs with the words.

The next time I visited I found Marshall doubled over in pain. He had been sending Thomas out for Advil instead of telling the nurses how bad the pain was, perhaps because he distrusted them or was ashamed of his pain. His dosage of medicine was too low or too infrequent to keep him comfortable and the "break through" pain between doses was excruciating. I found a nurse who had no authority to change his current regimen. I found the head doctor and we all gathered around Marshall's bed, the staff looking to me instead of Marshall to make any decisions, like he was a wayward child whose behavior we were brought together to discuss.

> "Please do something for his pain," I pleaded.
> "He doesn't want to be groggy," they told me.
> "He doesn't want to suffer," I said. "What about Methadone?"
> "It's addictive," they told me. "There are side effects."

"He's in hospice!" I wanted to say, he's dying! Give him whatever it takes! I leaned down to Marshall's ear and asked him which was worse, some grogginess or the pain he had now.

"The pain," he mouthed. Without an advocate, someone with him regularly, Marshall had no way to communicate what he was going through. The staff, surrounded by patients suffering the direct damages of drug addiction, defaulted to, in any other situation but Marshall's terminal one, a healthy fear of the addictive properties of pain medication. Also, they all lacked the language to frankly discuss his impending death. Finally, the doctor consented to switch to Methadone. He applied a small square patch with rounded corners to Marshall's belly. However far I had overstepped the boundary of my role as a volunteer, within half an hour Marshall had relaxed, then dozed comfortably.

I began to visit more often than my scheduled weekly visits. I would sit in the chair by Marshall's bed, his hand in mine, leaning on the railing by his head, watching TV. For hours at a time. I'd get there in time for *Judge Mathis* or *House of Payne*, shows that I had never seen before. Sometimes I'd stay to catch Oprah. Marshall and I would talk little but he'd hold tight onto my hand. Before I left I would ask him if it was OK if I came back the next day or the day after. "I'm not going anywhere," he'd whisper, looking at his withered legs. It was weeks since he'd gotten dressed. His lower legs were constantly elevated, his feet in special slippers to prevent heel sores. The nurses had begun turning him to prevent bed sores. He had lost power over his legs; his arms now tired easily and his hands were shaky. He was scared.

I read to Marshall from the book of Psalms during my next visit. "For in death there is no remembrance of thee: in the grave who shall give thee thanks?"[7] My voice in the fluorescent-lit room mixed with noises from the hallway, my hand grasped tightly in his. I couldn't sleep that night. I thought I could smell the scent of his skin on my hands. I hoped that the nurses were close; he hated to be alone and yet all his days now were lonely. The next morning Catherine from hospice called. Marshall had died a few hours after I left him. Two weeks later, Catherine called to see if I would meet Evelyn, the dying doctor.

* * *

"Do you think marijuana would help me?" Evelyn asked me one Friday night. I was sitting on a tan leather footstool at her knees, like I usually do. Her toes wiggled. She gracefully took a long drag from her e-cigarette, looking more like a society girl than a stoner, all chic and no shabby.

"It might," I answered. "Do you want me to get you some?"

The next visit I sat on the floor at the foot of her overstuffed leather chair and rolled her a slim joint—a pinner—from the contents of my ziplock. I found her an ashtray, reminded her to remove her oxygen, placed the joint in her mouth, lit it, and watched her get stoned. "Magic stuff," she eventually said.

In her professional life she had only seen the negative effects of marijuana. The invariably black kids in hospitals or jails, paying for their magic. But here she was at 80 asking me what the big deal was. "Magic" became our habit. I'd light up for Evelyn and as I watched her relax, her anxiety slip away, I'd read through the old files she had stored in a cabinet. I could only read the ones that were public, affidavits to courts on hunger-striking prisoners, strip-searched high schoolers, and mentally ill petty thieves caught in the belly of the incarceration beast. The irony of these stoned evenings wasn't lost on either of us.

Notes

1. Research for this article was funded by a Knight Grant for Religion in American Public Life by the Annenberg School for Communication and Journalism at the University of Southern California.
2. The names of all patients, family members, and institutions have been changed for privacy.
3. Twinkies are now back. http://www.nbcnews.com/business/twinkies-real-ones-back-store-shelves-july-6C9590050.
4. "Hospice Care in America: National Hospice and Palliative Care Facts and Figures," January 2012, http://www.nhpco.org/files/public/Statistics_Research/2011_Facts_Figures.pdf.
5. "How Doctors Die: It's Not Like the Rest of Us But It Should Be," Ken Murray, November 2011, http://www.zocalopublicsquare.org/2011/11/30/how-doctors-die/ideas/nexus/.
6. "Hospice Care in America."
7. Psalms 6:5, King James Version.

CHAPTER 12

New Materialisms and Digital Culture: Productive Labor and the Software Wars

Ted Kafala

Software production is perhaps the epitome of a labor practice that exists in a decentered and placeless space throughout our increasingly shared and global information society. Through the Open Source Initiative, its practitioners have found a powerful voice in support of creativity, the sharing and free redistribution of resources, open legal licenses, and a structure of constraints on the oligopolistic growth of large software firms. As players in the increasingly heated and competitive "software wars," coders engage in daily resistance to the control of capital by the very few, and struggle for greater control and community sharing of their abstract labor power. New materialisms have emerged that offer renewed explanations of the quasi-material, ephemeral nature of "infoware" and Web 2.0 applications in computer environments—on our pads, laptops, screens, and wireless devices. These materialist philosophies help conceptualize the ontology of information objects and practices that are based on coding and programming practices. To theorize about the nature of software objects is also to promote a continued discussion and debate about the increasingly displaced nodal connections between authors, artists, educators, users, and consumers. Returning science to its practitioners is a force behind the recent reconsideration of the ontology of objects in reference to materiality. Both the coders and users of the Open Source Initiative software are in many ways participants in a diffuse and fluid "class war" against proprietary software platforms and the conventional Microsoft .NET model.

The Open Source Initiative and Decentered Capital

The Open Source Initiative software movement requires a needed autonomy from both private and public control in order to continue its cooperative pattern of building an open community of practitioners and users. Geert Lovink writes, "Creating new connections is pivotal in a political-artistic process. It is the moment of 'change' when the desert of consent turns into a blossoming oasis."[1] By 1997, programmer Bruce Perens had established the groundwork for the Open Source Definition, the goals of which include a freely available operating system that could serve as the platform for running GNU software, greater liberties with software licensing, and an increasing indiscrimination when mixing proprietary and open-source software. As a consequence, many open-source licenses permit the use and redistribution of software without compensation. This movement largely began with the free distribution of the Netscape browser source code and the ability to mix and distribute it with other, open and quasi-proprietary software. Such actions create a larger market share for client code, which in turn creates demand for a platform and its free and open standards. The ability to build new platforms for distribution helps in the dissemination of open knowledge and educational technology.

This chapter emphasizes the mediation of science by creativity as a generator of the open-source movement and a point of resistance to oligopolistic forms of capital. The shift to knowledge-based economies involves new ways of creating surplus value and accumulating capital that are moving away in postindustrial economies from industrial labor to more communicative, cooperative, and affective forms of labor in distributed networks. The more recent forms of exploitative capital as epitomized by the upper 10 percent of wealth in both postindustrial macro- and microeconomic pockets throughout every hemisphere embody, following Hardt and Negri, a "decentered and deterritorializing apparatus of rule" that increasingly envelopes both online and offline habitats in its ever-expanding frontiers.[2] Hardt and Negri's notion of capitalist domination as "Empire" establishes no "terri-tonal center of power" and does not rely on fixed boundaries or barriers: "Capital seems to be faced with a smooth world—or really, a world defined by new and complex regimes of differentiation and homogenization, deterritorialization and reterritorialization."[3]

The production of software and "cultural capital" is part of the new productive practices, which concentrate productive labor on the plastic and fluid terrain of the new communicative, biological, and mechanical technologies. Hardt and Negri explain that the spatial configuration of what is inside and outside of capital has led to many political positions surrounding and affirming the place of "use value," pure and separate from "exchange value" and the relations that surround the accumulation of capital. In the contemporary world, this spatial configuration has changed. We find software production in the fragile and contradictory position of existing as both an art and commodity, and helping to ossify the development where creative arts are now regarded as commodities and where proprietary software are sold by corporations, such as Microsoft and

Oracle, themselves driven by profits and determining the exchange value and consumption trends.

Hardt and Negri observe that the relations of capitalist exploitation are expanding everywhere, not limited to the factory but tending to occupy the entire social terrain that includes Web 2.0 cultural products. They discuss the changing nature of abstract labor, from which derives the amorphous and quasi-organic surplus value of labor, as a comprehensive power which has not only been hijacked by corporatist oligopolies, but wields a placeless comprehensive power. They contend that this "abstract labor" is an activity without place that also retains a special power: "It is the cooperating set of brains and hands, minds and bodies; it is both the non-belonging and the creative social diffusion of living labor; it is the desire and the striving of the multitude of mobile and flexible workers."[4] Hardt and Negri locate the initial definition for placeless abstract labor in Marx's analyses of capital's constant need for expansion, first by focusing on the process of realization and thus on the unequal quantitative relationship between the worker as producer and the worker as consumer of commodities. Of course we observe historically since Marx's time that this realization is a major factor that drives capital beyond its boundaries and has created the continuing problems surrounding globalization and universal markets. This is an old story that takes on new dimensions, and Hardt and Negri insist on that, in order to trace the problem from its roots in industrial exploitation and early class relations. "To begin with," we read in the *Grundrisse*, "capital forces the workers beyond necessary labour to surplus labour. Only in this way does it realize itself, and create surplus value."[5]

Perhaps there's an even more salient and materialist reading of capitalist relations schematized in the *Grundrisse* that surrounds the redistribution of labor power in variable forms. We find in its text Marx's predictions for the circulation and distribution of capitalist forms. We read in the *Grundrisse* how capital is posited doubly both as an agent of production and as a "source of income," or, in other words, a determinant of specific forms of distribution.[6] Exchange and consumption are reciprocal sides of the same coin: Distribution of products is related to the distribution of the agents of production as itself a moment of production. In an almost Nietzchean passage, Marx describes how "definite production" thus determines a "definite consumption," and describes how distribution and exchange are simply the same process in different moments in time.[7] As Hardt and Negri observe today, variable capital based on wage labor constitutes an increasingly small part of the total value of the commodities and so the workers' power of consumption is increasingly small with respect to the commodities produced. Expansion of the sphere of circulation outside the capitalist realm continues to spread out and displace the destabilizing inequality.

No longer requiring a territorial or physical center, the production of software is also subject to this fragmented and dispersive condition that includes the offshoring of coding practices. Each segment of this environment is transformed differently while simultaneously being integrated organically into the expanding body of capital and wealth among the very few. As the astute cultural observer

Geert Lovink remarks, "the medium is the mind. It shapes what we see and how we see it. With the Internet's stress on speed, we become the Web's neurons: The more links we click, pages we view, and transactions we make, the more intelligence the Web makes, the more economic value it gains, and the more profit it throws off... With the miniaturization of hardware combined with wireless connectivity, technology becomes an invisible part of everyday life."[8] Web 2.0 applications and infoware respond to this trend and attempt to extract value from our every situation. The data-mining machines constantly probe and survey us to know our tastes, purchase habits, social media contacts, and preferences for entertainment and virtual spaces. Echoing Lyotard's early observations from 1984 in *The Postmodern Condition*,[9] Hardt and Negri discuss more broadly how information technologies tend to make distances less relevant, forcing the tendency toward the deterritorialization of production to become more pronounced through the processes of immaterial labor, or in other words through "the new productive processes," or the enterprises that infuse capital globally and manipulate knowledge and information. At the pinnacle of contemporary production, information and communication are the very commodities produced.[10]

In contrast to dispersive, oligopolistic forms of capitalization, the Open Source Initiative advocates "Creative Commons," open content, free software, and open access as part of a larger movement that experiments with (alternative) revenue models and includes activities such as "unconferencing," kickstarters, hackathons, bricolabs, and other anarcho-creative enterprises. The original impulse behind the Open Source Initiative before the dot-com bubble deflated was an extension of the scientific method, because computer science resides at the center of programming and coding practices, and computer science has only one means of enabling peers to replicate results: "Share the source code!"[11] So, we cannot consider the implications of Web 2.0 culture on our daily lives and practices without redefining the ontological nature of science itself.

The open-source development model does not just mean access to the source code, but rather implies that sharing source code facilitates creativity. Programmers working on complementary projects can each leverage the results of the other, combine resources into a single project, test in a wider variety of contexts than one coder could generate alone, debug in a distributed manner, and invest and expand in a broadly accepted platform. Of course, the Internet and the nature of virtual environments and spaces for work and sharing information make this possible, through technologies such as GitHub, which has transformed the Open Source Initiative into a vital and burgeoning alternative over the past three decades.

New Media, New Materialisms

The expansion of information industries and practices has spurred the transformation of the material conditions of work and production and the associated ontological mechanisms or apparatuses that define the software object, media object, and modular code. For Hardt and Negri, the nature of this transformation in technoscience and capitalist enterprise takes on a Nietzschean conception: The circulation and distribution of capitalist objects as well as their exchange value have their ontological basis in "trans-valuation," that is, in the capacity to often arbitrarily create, or destroy the prices and values on the global markets. New media requires new materialisms to conceptualize the ontology of information objects and practices that are based on coding practices and the production of object-oriented software. Reminiscent of what Jacques Rancière describes as the French intellectual reaction to the co-option of science by Gaullist and pseudo-proletarian politics in the 1950s and 1960s, it is most accurate to relinquish the determination of value, and the whole process of valuation of new media objects to the practitioners, who understand their use value and can build on advances in coding and software to build free redistributions of open systems and platforms and their derivations. Rancière and Battista write, "We found this power in 'science', and it was from within science that we tried to undercut every attempt to contest the authority of knowledge (savoir). Contrary to what the critiques—superficial or interested—of 'theoreticism' might suggest, it was the desire to act that spurred us on to the defense of the hierarchies of knowledge (savoir)."[12]

The rejuvenation of science as an information praxis is intertwined with the reconceptualization of the ontology of objects and their material "thingness" and objecthood, without regressing into naïve realism, but rather with a fresh look at the interconnectedness and relations between objects in the world. This has led to a number of variants in speculative metaphysics and contemporary continental materialism and realism, which correspond to the decentered and deterritorialized nature of work and its capitalist exploitation. Naïve realism takes the ontological assumption that the world is a closed set containing classes of entities and objects, which are pregiven and correspond to absolute facts and essential truths about those objects.[13] This "principle of sufficient reason" at work in Cartesian metaphysics was actually formulated by Leibniz, who postulated that every entity, thing, and event must have a cause, and consequently every entity is absolutely necessary, so that we can reason the world to infinite regress if we can furnish, or reveal the global law for it. This makes the immanence, or emergence of new and novel objects impossible, the converse of a constructivism. This obsolete stance also obviates any continuity of creative processes.

The schools and variants of thought surrounding speculative materialist and realist currents include the ideas of Whitehead, Deleuze, Bergson, and Simondon from decades past, and the recent thought of Manuel De Landa, Bruno Latour, Graham Harman, Michel Serres, Quentin Meillassoux, Isabelle Stengers, Iain Hamilton Grant, and others (this list is not mutually exclusive). These currents invoke new critical directions, beginning with a dissatisfaction with the limited critique of late-twentieth-century cultural criticism and continuing by applying a critical lens on object-based philosophies, object and surface topologies, embodied and carnal phenomenologies, and other types of immanent-emergent, spatiotemporal, evolutionary-processual approaches to the software, or media object. Hopefully these ideas shed light on the autonomy of the object generally, and the nature of the computer object more specifically.

With wider acceptance of this critique, contemporary variants of speculative materialism and realism have tended to unite around the publication of French philosopher Quentin Meillassoux' book, *After Finitude*, which, while it calls for the acknowledgment of empirical access to objects and entities that exist before and outside human thought and history, also resists devolving into a variety of naïve realism: Meillassoux defers from dismissing relational and phenomenological theories outright in lieu of his radicalization of what he calls "correlationism" from within itself.[14] In fact, defying accusations of a resurrected Lockean empiricism and realism, Bryant, Srnicek, and Harman (2011) suggest that many of the ideas from speculative materialism, triggered in part by *After Finitude*, endeavor to undertake a "sweeping critique" of the self-enclosed, dual-nature Cartesian subject. They draw attention to the contemporary "speculative turn" in continental materialism and realism, which shifts attention toward reality itself, puts forward notions of nominal objects, and speculates on the nature of reality independent of human thought more generally.[15]

Moving beyond the seminal texts of Deleuze and Guattari, which set forth an ontological vision of a "subjective realm of becoming, where subject and thought are only the final, residual product," the speculative materialists attempt to correct and/or invert the "correlationism" and antirealism that finds its source in Kant's Copernican revolution of metaphysics. Kant's transcendental thought is deepened by Hegel's critique of nominal objects, which reduces them to phenomenal illusion in service of an absolute idealism, and subsumes all ontology into the phenomenal world.[16] Meillassoux's identification of time as the condition in which empirical objects and bodies exist and perish is of concern here: The transcendental-empirical idea that the "condition of temporality entails that every entity can be destroyed"[17] may comprise the basis for a post-relational object-based philosophy and a theory of autonomous, software, and media objects.

New approaches to the materiality of the new media object come from theorists and practitioners in the new media field, an interdisciplinary offshoot of communication theory. New media studies is no longer "new" and has morphed and diverged into innumerable branches, such as software studies, cyberspace studies (also no longer new), code studies, digital humanities, network studies, video game studies, information aesthetics, webware and infoware studies, ubiquitous computing, and many others. A general knowledge of new media theory in some recent historical context, and relating to the idea of materiality in computer arts and media, may help enable a better understanding of the new "object-based" thought. Research in networked cyberspace studies came on the heels of critical studies of technolibertarian culture. Donna Haraway, McKenzie Wark, Sadie Plant, Sandy Stone, Hakim Bey, and others have contributed to this critique. Technolibertarian discourse is partly premised on the idea that the analog relationship between the image and the real referent that exists in photography is broken when the image is approximated to a symbolic number, or integer value in the process of digitization.

In contrast, for Lev Manovich (2002), the "new media object" is a more empirical combination of data and code, but the actual way that data are stored in the object takes the form of the code, that is, the set of instructions associated with that object.[18] The bitmapped images that form the visual dimension of new media objects are epitomes of the symbolism, Boolean algebra, and operational logic of switching associated with rudimentary computer operations. As a basis of a semiotic theory, any rigid dichotomy between meaning and form, code and surface, it is not difficult to undermine as a false dichotomy, including the binaries signified and signifier, *langue* and *parole*, deep and surface structure, competence and performance, and periphery and core grammar. On the level of binary code, all digital images are organized by the indexical logic of the computer database: The logical architecture of computers processes the real world to a high level of formality, less through indexical figuration than through simple index, or catalog.

As Manovich discusses at some length in *The Language of New Media*, object-oriented programming involves small and autonomously functioning modules and subroutines, and then assembling these into larger programs that enable complex behaviors. Subroutines may also be called procedures, functions, or scripts, depending on the computer language. The modular parts of a structured program may be accessed, modified, substituted, and sometimes moved around without destroying the overall structure of the program. "New media objects" take on the more fluid qualities of "variability" when they are related to each other in the recursive programming associated with high-level computer languages and scripts. Manovich defines this "variability" as the ability of the computer object to exist in different, discrete, and numerous versions, which is another consequence of its coded, algorithmic, and modular structure.[19]

Manovich's approach rethinks the historical convergence between the material medium and the computer object during the last few decades of the twentieth century. His most recent work, *Software Takes Command* (2013), is kind of an expansion, if not a kind of reversal, which takes on software studies through media history and in its much broader cultural contexts. Here Manovich suggests that "cultural software" does not merely consist of things such as programming practices, values, and ideologies of programmers, but also our current culture of remixology, including motion graphics, media authoring software, and editing software.[20]

Whereas critics have been skeptical of Manovich's (2002) empirical and reductive notion of code, or his way of spatializing code, whether pixel based, data based, or culture based, other theorists may be accused of essentializing the database form as a means to arrive at a more convergent "intermediality." As Lyotard puts forward the symptom of postmodern media, media art begins with a general crisis in representation where both art and commodity are coded into generic and incommensurable information. These phenomena create a damaging rupture in realistic ways of knowing that continually makes us question the construction of knowledge.[21] Information is a pattern perceived in the data, or in the binary stream, after the data have been seen through the expectations of an imaging scheme, form, or code. Following Lyotard's reluctant recognition of the database as the quintessential albeit problematic postmodern form, media theorists from Henry Jenkins to Friedrich Kittler have fetishized the database as an artistic form. The result has been to collapse all computer media into database technologies.

The post-hermeneutic concept of intermediality is one such recent notion that theoretically embraces and encompasses all media as the simplest binary information. Kittler does much to demonstrate how human experience is mediated by the computer and information technology generally, one of the first to discuss historically how human imagination is limited by microchip architecture design and capacity, while also acknowledging the pervasiveness of Leibniz's binary symbolism and mathematics in contemporary applications.[22]

More recently cultural critics have pushed the relational-nexus and antirealist perspectives further away from both Marxian and materialist approaches: From these premises, computer arts and media embody a "materiality"—and the term is used loosely—on social and global levels both in the social exchange and material enterprises that encompass e-business and in the Net art that parodies and makes alternative uses of those commercial practices. A less convincing argument comes from theorists who profess that computer media is a new communication medium based on its properties of "interactivity," "interface," and "display," which may or may not be meaningful and descriptive of an aesthetic practice.[23]

Accepting the important notion of "computational discreteness" as a principal property of contemporary computer science, Ian Bogost attempts to correct the more "rigid structuralism" he says is promoted by Manovich and Kittler in reference to the expansion of digitality into human culture. In his book *Unit Operations*, Bogost presents his model of "unit operations," which he claims can account for computer-programmable environments and our broader narrative culture, many things and events ranging from anthropological accounts of myth to the plots of video games. Bogost contends that information technology and "literary theory" have much in common in their endeavor to reveal shifting relationships between "discrete units": Drawing on Alain Badiou's interpretation of Cantor's transfinite set theory as an important method for configuration,[24] Bogost suggests that his open and expansive system called "unit operations and analysis" provides the discrete, encapsulated logics needed to "understand the world."[25]

At the root of this approach, with large caveats and reservations, is Aristotle's object ontology, which fundamentally ties form and matter in the experience of object in the material world, and creates a tension between the teleological procession of matter/substance through categories of "things" and "species," and the realization of abstract form in the laws of final causality. Bogost suggests that the long tradition of Aristotelian formalism continues to inform system and unit operations, but he is careful to move beyond a formal tool set of abstractions, including object-oriented programming concepts such as "encapsulation" and "polymorphism," to promote the understanding of cultural products and phenomena as open sets, structures, or configurations of constituent objects that are continually in flux within a larger pool of an ontological multiplicity.[26]

Bogost is careful to distinguish object technology (OT) and object-oriented programming (OOP), the innovative use of autonomously functioning modules and subroutines, from the areas of computer science and software systems with Graham Harman's "object-oriented philosophy" (also OOP), which discusses the universe of self-referential and -contained objects and how they form linkages and relations beyond themselves. Sometimes in his books and blogs, however, particularly when discussing the contributions of Spinoza, Leibniz, Žižek, Badiou, and others to unit operations, both the ideas and jargon of OT and OOP are conveniently conflated. Despite Bogost's creative intentions to avoid the pitfalls of the precritical nominalists and to encourage the application of a fluid and flexible "unit operations" and "unit analysis" to concrete examples and practices, emphasizing strategic processes and "praxis" over structures, Bogost acknowledges his allegiance to the idea of object *substance, or essence*, particularly Spinozan substance.[27] Apparent in Bogost's writings and online debates, it is easy to notice a particular type of materialism at work, which is often attributed to Spinoza, Badiou, and Harman, albeit with some significant differences between them. Nevertheless, Bogost makes a contribution to the discussion of object autonomy (for more or less intelligent agents, bots, and avatars) and the idea of a materialized "thingness" in software objects.

The difficulty in grasping the notion of materiality in digital and electronic realms continues to be a research focus. In some very interesting work, Wendy Hui Kyong Chun's research on software as metaphor, amalgamation, "neighborhood of relations," "programmed visions," and "things that always seem to be disappearing" moves away from the analysis of specific content and technologies to software as an elusively intangible "visible essence" through its interfaces and virtual objects by which the we navigate the world. In Chun's view, software take on a "vapory materialization" through their ghostly interfaces that assemble, dismantle, or disperse power relations, but even more importantly encompass temporal and spatial processes while simultaneously refusing to be reduced to codes and algorithms.[28] By interacting with interfaces (in some ways visible, other ways invisible—an "odd combination"), we are mapped as data, or, in other words, data-driven machine learning algorithms process our collective data traces in order to discover underlying patterns.[29]

Chun's most recent unpublished research in progress heralds back to Haraway and Latour and Serres,[30] in its concern with networks as biological-technological-social mergings that are self-generating and spread through a kind of promiscuous exchange, or viral contagion, referencing Manuel Castells's swarm theory as well as the contemporary media archeology of Jussi Parikka.[31] Rather than deal with the conceptual content and motivations of the various computer objects themselves, Chun attempts to tackle the hard work of understanding broadly their quasi-material manifestations and relational effects as she seems to acknowledge computer software as a kind of ether, with a nod to its "thingness."

How can something be both ethereal and distributed and take an autonomous object form? Chun evokes Latour, who follows Whitehead in his theory of "object concrescence," which insists that an object's flux and perpetual perishing does not preclude, or undermine its endurance, or permanence. Against all forms of reductionism regarding physical objects, Latour and Serres (1994) championed the idea of irreductionism in which all corporeal and incorporeal beings are equally real and capable of having effects on the world,[32] and by which, following Whitehead, an ontology of entities coexists and changes with the flux of time, evolving and perishing.[33] Bruno Latour's writing of later decades casts a critical eye on the anthropomorphic perspective on natural objects, objects of science, and the corresponding knowledge as preexistent, independent of thought and human access. Similarly, Whitehead's temporal asymmetry in *Process and Reality* puts forward the organic interrelatedness of events of the determinate past and the dynamic present, so that, and in other words, creative elements of the past are made available to derivative, creative events in the present.[34] To understand the nature of software artifacts that encapsulate abstract labor but are simultaneously distributed and reusable systems and platforms, we need a doctrine of reproduction, or reflective autopoesis as repetition with a sense of difference, but not duplication. Bruno Latour and Manuel De Landa's careful delineation of a flat ontology of objects, for example, avoids the pitfalls of essences and embraces a repetition of generative patterns and forms within the flux and flow of experience.[35] The decentered nature of mobile and flexible workers in the information sciences dictates that abstract labor cannot be quantified or localized, but continues on through the redistribution and effusiveness of their creative cultural products, specifically software and infoware applications.

Open-Source versus Proprietary Software: Which Will Win Out?

The Open Source Initiative has had a profound and energizing impact on the software industry, steering it toward more innovation and larger cooperative communities and away from proprietary exclusions. The malleable and ephemeral nature of software makes this possible, contradictorily increasingly complex and yet so ubiquitous in everyday life. Even the difficult design patterns are being widely shared while the elitism and isolationism of the programmer are simultaneously being eroded. In an environment of increasing convergence, the boundaries between mobile devices, wirelessly connected laptops, broadband and entertainment delivery, and consumer devices like the iPod and TiVO are all blurring.

> The central idea of "copyleft" is that we give everyone permission to run the program, copy the program, modify the program, and distribute modified versions— but not permission to add restrictions of their own. Thus, the crucial freedoms that define "free software" are guaranteed to everyone who has a copy; they become inalienable rights.[36]

The DMCA (Digital Millennium Copyright Act) of 1998 has already rendered itself obsolete and counterproductive, rendering criminal what copyright law would otherwise overlook, or forgive. It encourages continued corporatist control over the direction of technological determination, and interferes and oftentimes prohibits our own ability to "tinker" with and adapt software products to suit our own desires. Many traditional software oligarchs continue to their long-term detriment to focus on purely proprietary solutions, but as open-source technology "guru" Tim O'Reilly suggests,

> To really take advantage of Open Source, you need to value ubiquity in your marketplace at least as much as you value scarcity in your product portfolio. In fact, your smartest move may be to take some of the products you're selling, and make them ubiquitous by moving them from proprietary/closed to open/public domain—literally, from scarcity to ubiquity.[37]

Ubiquity drives standardization, and any innovation in defense of monopoly is looked upon askance by the Internet community. In fact, most software is distributed these days through Web portals, and most Web-based applications are built on open-source materials and infoware. Most software objects, including those provided by Sun, Oracle, Novell, and RealNetworks and a multitude of small companies and start-ups, are built on open-source JavaScript platforms, such as "barebones.js" and "node.js." As O'Reilly explains, "the GPL's protections are triggered by the act of software distribution, yet web-based application vendors never distribute any software: It is simply performed on the Internet's global stage, delivered as a service rather than as a packaged software application."[38] Dispersed communications systems, such as the Internet, are based on widely accepted standards and protocols that encourage swappable software. Amazon and Google are large platform businesses constructed largely on shared open-source building materials, such as in-house versions of Apache servers and the BSD-based operating systems projects.

Many large and medium-sized firms are engaged in cooperative open-source initiatives to prevent Microsoft-like oligarchic configurations from reemerging and to open up market categories where once only proprietary platforms and silos existed. Thousands of software platforms that are globally useful and without a proprietary agenda serve the well-being of the many producers and consumers over the very few. Mozilla Public License (MPL) developed by the Netscape Mozilla team has remained a standard for BSD-style licenses in the spectrum of open-source software licenses over the past decade. It has two key differences: It mandates that changes to the "distribution" in source code also be released under the same copyright as the MPL, which thus makes it available back to the project. Google has joined Mozilla as a trendsetter in a number of arenas, such as the development of open-source end-user products like Web GL and HTML games, combining volunteer and commercial activity in open-source projects, and providing employment for a huge number of developers and programmers.

Even Apple, which assiduously guards its intellectual property, is seeking its own unique strategies for participating in open-source development projects, exhibiting an acceptance of open source as foundational infrastructure albeit based on their often shared usage of Objective-C code with a large community of developers. Apple's strategies have been complex and multiform; for example, Apple has kept QuickTime and its growing portfolio of "i" applications on the proprietary side, even while opening them to free usage. As Lovink observes,

> Companies no longer profit at the level of production, but through the control of distribution channels, and users do not immediately realize how their free labor is being exploited. Apple, Amazon, eBay and Google are the biggest winners in this game. Google's late public offering in August 2004, six years after its founding, is the symbolic launch of Web 2.0: a comprehensive set of web applications driven by the rapid growth of users with access to broadband.[39]

Consequently, the Open Source Initiative places constraints on the Microsoft .NET model of proprietary software platforms, enabling new pathways and limits on the new global flows of capital that have been accompanied by a radical transformation of the dominant productive processes themselves. As Hardt and Negri predict, "capital" seems to be faced with a smooth world defined by new and complex regimes of differentiation and homogenization, deterritorialization and reterritorialization. Programming is largely regarded as a creative gift by those who are skilled enough to possess it, and we need new concepts to understand the ongoing struggle of software and media practitioners, mobile and transnational workers, to wield control over their labor power in a growingly complex, decentered, and treacherous international environment. Likewise, new media theories will emerge and mature which better explain the quasi-material, ephemeral, and spatiotemporally transcendent nature of software objects that are now ubiquitous in our world.

Notes

1. Geert Lovink, "Unlike Us: Web 2.0 Culture" (unpublished manuscript), 135. Later published as *Networks without a Cause: A Critique of Social Media* (London: Polity Press, 2012).
2. Michael Hardt and Antonio Negri, *Empire* (Cambridge, MA: Harvard University Press, 2001), iii–iv.
3. Ibid.
4. Ibid., 401.
5. Ibid., 421.
6. Karl Marx, *The Grundrisse* (New York: Harper and Row, 1972), 27.
7. Ibid., 29.
8. Lovink, "Unlike Us," 8.
9. Jean-Francois Lyotard, *The Postmodern Condition: A Report on Knowledge*. G. Bennington and B. Massumi (trans.) (Minneapolis: University of Minnesota Press, 1984).
10. Hardt and Negri, *Empire*, 430.
11. Chris DiBona, Sam Ockman, et al. *Open Sources: Voices from the Open Source Revolution* (Sebastopol, CA: O'Reilly Media, 2005), 7.

12. Jacques Rancière and Emiliano Battista, *Althusser's Lesson* (London: Continuum Press, 2011), 43.
13. Manuel De Landa, *Intensive Science & Virtual Philosophy* (New York and London: Continuum Press, 2005), v. See also Gilbert Simondon, *Du mode d'existence des objets techniques* (Paris: Presse de Aubrier, 2001).
14. Quentin Meillassoux, *After Finitude: An Essay on the Necessity of Contingency* (London: Continuum Press, 2006).
15. Levi Bryant, Nick Srnicek, and Graham Harman, eds, *The Speculative Turn: Continental Materialism and Realism* (Melbourne: re.press, 2011), 3.
16. Ibid., 4.
17. Ibid., 115.
18. Lev Manovich, *The Language of New Media* (Cambridge, MA: The MIT Press, 2002).
19. Ibid., 18–45.
20. Lev Manovich, *Software Takes Command: Extending the Language of New Media* (London and New York: Bloomsbury Academic Press, 2013).
21. Lyotard, *The Postmodern Condition*, xxv.
22. Friedrich Kittler, *Gramophone, Film, Typewriter* (Berlin: Brinkmann & Bose, 1986), 20–46.
23. Dominic McIver Lopes, *A Philosophy of Computer Art* (London: Routledge, 2009).
24. Alain Badiou, *Being and Event* (London: Continuum Press, 2007).
25. Ian Bogost, *Unit Operations: An Approach to Videogame Criticism* (Cambridge, MA: The MIT Press, 2008), 30–31.
26. Ibid., 13, 23.
27. Ibid., 8–9.
28. Wendy Hui Kyong Chun, *Programmed Visions: Software and Memory (Software Studies)* (Cambridge, MA: The MIT Press, 2011), 2–3.
29. Ibid., 9.
30. See Donna Haraway, *Modest_Witness@ Second_Millennium.FemaleMan_Meets_Onco Mouse: Feminism and Technoscience*, 1st edn (New York: Routlege, 1997); and Bruno Latour and Michel Serres, *Éclaircissements* (Paris: Flammarion, 1994).
31. See Manuel Castells, *Communication Power* (Oxford and New York: Oxford University Press, 2009); and Jussi Parikka, *What Is Media Archaeology?* (London: Polity Press, 2012).
32. Latour and Serres, *Éclaircissements*.
33. Bryant, Srnicek, and Harman, *The Speculative Turn*, 5.
34. See Alfred North Whitehead, *Process and Reality* (New York: Free Press, 1978); and Steven Shaviro, *Without Criteria: Kant, Whitehead, Deleuze, and Aesthetics* (Cambridge, MA: The MIT Press, 2012).
35. De Landa, *Intensive Science*, 3.
36. DiBona, Ockman, et al. *Open Sources: Voices from the Open Source Revolution*, 59.
37. Chris DiBona, Mark Stone, Tim O'Reilly, and Danese Cooper, *Open Sources 2.0: The Continuing Evolution*, Kindle edn (Sebastopol, CA: O'Reilly Media, 2008), loc. 7652–54.
38. Ibid.
39. Lovink, "Unlike Us," 6.

CHAPTER 13

Feminist Theory and the Critique of Class

Robin Truth Goodman

From the mid-1970s to the mid-1980s, there was a vibrant debate within feminist scholarship in both the humanities and the social sciences about the relationship between Marxist theory and feminism. Following on Juliet Mitchell's call in the late 1960s for a socialist criticism that took seriously "the subordination of women and the need for their liberation,"[1] feminists tried to grapple with concepts like ideology, exchange, labor, and class struggle, and ask if and when they could be applied to oppressions in women's social conditions, collected under the umbrella term of *patriarchy*, or if women's forms of subordination were so culturally specific that they needed their own, independent rubric.[2] Feminists also contested that the capitalist–proletariat relationship posed by Marx made class into a singular, overriding, and abstract concept for identity that wiped out both difference and experience. Heidi Hartmann, for example, famously reproves, "the categories of Marxism are sex-blind."[3] In about 1985, such inquiry lost its fervor.

At the same time, more women than ever were entering the global workforce while economic polarization was on the increase both nationally and internationally, and women's impoverishment was on the upswing.[4] In other words, the more the number of women who worked, the poorer laboring people got globally, and the larger the percentage of wealth was accumulated by the wealthy. The end of a heated discussion about feminism, class, and Marxism therefore coincided with a rise in an expanded corporate profiting from women's work.[5] The discussion about class was buried under the linguistic turn of postmodernism. Feminism developed a really lively debate around the Symbolic and how meaning was produced in reference to gender without easily being able to connect this discussion to economic thinking and changes in the nature of work. As Kathi Weeks has remarked, "[T]he gendering of work is not just a matter of . . . institutionalized tendencies to distinguish various forms of men's work and women's work, but a consequence of the ways that workers are often expected to do gender at work."[6] This chapter first considers the implications for feminism of the separation of the category of gender from its imbrication within a class system. It ultimately argues that as labor is becoming newly politicized and newly gendered both nationally and internationally, feminism needs to reconsider the relationship between gender and new regimes of profit and exploitation.

The symbolic of femininity is expanding as the new economy focuses increasingly on the work of reproduction: service labor, nurturing labor, part-time labor, the production of language and ideas. The extension of femininity across the workforce accounts for the deepening of exploitation and the cheapening of wages and leads to the capture of class conflict within the symbolic of femininity. In effect, the media uses gender to talk about class while displacing it, a displacement that serves to give a positive moral gloss to capital's side in its struggle against labor. In a 2012 *New York Times* article, "Two Classes, Divided by 'I Do,'" Jason DeParle blames changes in gendered lifestyles for (women's) wage depression. "College-educated Americans," DeParle specifies,

> are increasingly likely to marry one another, compounding their growing advantages in pay. Less-educated women . . ., who left college without finishing [a] degree, are growing less likely to marry at all, raising children on pinched paychecks that come in ones, not twos . . . Changes in marriage patterns—as opposed to changes in individual earnings—may account for as much as 40 percent of the growth in certain measures of inequality.

"The middle is shifting to the bottom," DeParle further explains, and the reason is "not the impact of globalization on their wages but a 6-foot-8-inch man named Kevin." In other words, women themselves are responsible for the impoverishment of the middle class by choosing a particular gendered demographic life pattern, a home life without men.

For *The New York Times*, women's entry into the paid workforce at the expense of married life has negative effects on children. Whereas conventionally married parents have the time (as well as the money) to send their kids to Boy Scouts as well as summer camp, karate lessons, Disney, and sing-along, for single mothers—who are "more likely to have children with more than one man"— "[t]ime away [from work] is money lost." Whereas children of conventionally married parents can overcome obstacles, succeed, and move up, according to the Brookings Institution, "there are suggestions that the absence of a father in the house makes it harder for children to climb the economic ladder." The effects of single mothering, as presented in DeParle's anecdotal evidence with the appropriate level of pathos and "end of the world" sensationalism, are economic but also physical, spiritual, and psychological, ranging from hunger to problems in school, including autism. Though statistics are given that demonstrate the relative hardship of children growing up in homes with single mothers rather than married ones, no comparative data are presented for children growing up in households with single fathers (or any other arrangements). The article refuses to consider that absent fathers may influence their offspring's economic future and instead insists that only mothers are to blame (in the example given, the mother is to blame for a pregnancy during college where the father is African American, though racial designations are not otherwise assigned, marking the act even further—the article seems to suggest—with a sense of failure, depravity, and wrongdoing, even maybe deserving of such dire economic punishment).

According to "Two Classes," the growing economic polarization between children of families with single mothers and children of families with married mothers (a disparity that extends even to adulthood, according to studies) can be said to result from many different historical factors, though marriage for women is touted as the most significant parameter. Less significant are: "the growing premium a college education commands, technological change that favors mind over muscle, the growth of the financial sector, the loss of manufacturing jobs to automation and foreign competitors, and the decline of labor unions." The influence such factors play on the economic standing of women and their jobs is not explained because the article funnels all such causes into the higher potential of women's marriage to elevate, and of women's non-marriage to denigrate, regardless of the broader structural frame. Women's decision to marry or not to marry is the primary catalyst toward economic dissolution, the cause for which these other factors are but effects.

Additionally, as women and their work stand in for the failed economy (because of their moral failing), they also are positioned as exhibiting the failure of public supports for work: "After Ms. Schairer [the unmarried example] had an operation for cervical cancer last summer, the surgeon told her to take six weeks off. She went back to work five weeks early . . . 'I can't have six weeks with no pay.'" As a descent into the depravity of the working class, "women's work" indicates not only a lapse in the public obligation of supporting workers through, for example, health care, sick leave, and child care but also a lapse in the politicization of work that collective bargaining might ensure. Instead, as a model of the impoverishment of workers through work, "women's work" is plotted through an assumption that protective rights are not even thinkable, let alone negotiable.

Patriarchy, the Autonomy of Culture, and the Critique of Ideology

The relationship of women's work to the category of productive labor can be said to be a question that governed the development of feminist theory from the late 1960s on. The trajectory of feminist thought went from asserting, on the one hand, that women's oppression could not be explained as class exploitation and wage exploitation and trying to understand its own specific dynamics, to, on the other, rejecting the category of class in favor of the categories of culture, language signification, and variability. In the former case, women's oppression appeared excessive to capitalism, and therefore existed as pure ideology, disconnected from an analysis of production. The premise of a separate space and status for women's oppression, outside of the social relations of production in a sphere of reproduction, was adopted by feminists from Marx's indication, in "The German Ideology," that all ideology—as the reproduction of social relations— seemed independent from the material base: "Thus all collisions in history have their origin, according to our view, in the contradiction between the productive forces and the form of intercourse,"[7] including the family, the law, and civil society. In fact, Marx identifies the family here as the first instance of a social stage or superstructure, as divorced from practical activity, set apart from productive forces, even outside the time of production. Feminism interpreted this cut as the split between men's paid work in industrial social relations and women's unpaid exchange in excess of capital.

In the 1970s, when feminism was bursting onto the theoretical scene, many critics were interested in understanding the psychic relationship that informed patriarchy, but still had to contend with a strong leftist tradition that explained social forms through means of production theses. Such feminist critics, however, were becoming increasingly impatient with the determining primacy that means of production explanations seemed to hold on formative theories of the subject. Theories of ideology envisioned the family, for example, as Annette Kuhn remarks, as "simply a vehicle for the transmission of representations of those relations [of production],"[8] that is, as a transparent or functional lever for the transmission of ideas already established elsewhere (e.g., in production) in the interests of the ruling class. There was a growing tendency to separate out the critique of patriarchy—defining culture as what was outside of production—in order to free considerations of the subject from its role as a reflection of a history managed solely through economic processes.

Many here came to appreciate Engels more than Marx, since Engels—in *Origin of the Family, Private Property, and the State*—took seriously his assertion that the division between men and women in the household was the first class division, and granted analytic primacy to the patriarchal household as a precapitalist social arrangement. For Engels, the oppression of women was based in a residual family form, where the father controlled the tools of production and wanted to transmit them to his legitimate offspring, meaning that household production lost its formative collective character, or "Mother Right." Because family nuclearization was becoming inessential to a working class without property to transfer, it would, according to Engels, eventually disappear, as "no basis for any kind of male supremacy is left in the proletariat household,"[9] except as a brutality left over from the old practices of monogamy. The offshoot was that women's oppression was made to have a narrative of causality divorced from considerations of labor or labor time under industrial capitalism.

Gayle Rubin's 1976 essay "The Traffic in Women" exposes the muscular analytic efforts feminists exerted to think of a platform for subjectivity outside of capitalism and its modes of production. This canonical piece inaugurated a set of inquiries into what Rubin first labeled as the "sex/gender system"—the mutual indeterminacy between the material world of bodies and the cultural world of symbols that would open up into post-structuralist interest in the arbitrariness of signification, the signifier–signified split, that is, in difference. Rubin was following in the footsteps of Juliet Mitchell, who, for example, proposed that "The working class has the power to take back to itself (for mankind) the products of the labour which are now taken from it; but no simple extension of this position can be taken to apply to patriarchal ideology,"[10] arguing that the patriarchal psyche no longer matches the realities of the base material structures of modern society and therefore belongs to an archaic residue within ideology.

Rubin starts out thinking about the "genesis of women's oppression"[11] that, she says, cannot be rooted within the classical categories of Marxist historicism because women's oppression existed before capitalism began. She grants that Marx is able to elucidate more aspects of women's oppression than other theories—for example, the relationship between production and reproduction, the role of women in producing surplus value by contributing unpaid labor. Yet, "to explain women's usefulness to capitalism," she continues, "is one thing. To argue that this usefulness explains the genesis of the oppression of women is quite another."[12] Sifting through the ethnographic record, Rubin observes instances of patriarchal power that exceed women's induction into industrial capitalism. Therefore, she concludes, one needs to find a "historical and moral element"[13] that is the key to explaining the cultural heritage of sexism. Rubin never defines the "oppression of women," nor catalogues what types of behavior, institutions, or social routines might fall under that term, but instead merges all its instances into one arching problem to be resolved by one arching solution. For Rubin, since the oppression of women is so all-pervasive in time and space, there must be a singular cause of patriarchy, and since the oppression of women cannot be totally subsumed within the Marxist political-economic critique of capitalism, the singular cause of patriarchy had to reside not there at all but totally elsewhere, within an autonomous cultural structure.

As is well known, Rubin locates the cause of the oppression of women in the incest taboo and, in particular, following Freud, Lacan, and Lévi-Strauss, in the exchange of woman that the incest taboo incites. In this, women communicate alliances. The exchange of women sets the social world of gender apart from the material world of sex, thus establishing the social as symbolic: women are symbols that communicate between men. Rubin uses the instance of the "primitive tribe" to illustrate the formative moment of the exchange of women as also the moment of the birth of the human and its culture, using anthropological retrieval as the point of identification of the universal, even while citing contemporary exemplars. The shift to culture here, however, does not absolutely escape economic determinants (only relatively), but rather separates out a critique of production as value creation in order to devise an alternative place of "gift exchange," or exchange before money, defined as culture, symbolic circulation, or reproduction—or ideology. Contrary to Marx, who understands circulation as the realization of the surplus money and capital that eventually passes back into production (and thus is sutured to it), Rubin ascribes the archaic and the tribal to a past and estranges the perfectly contemporary event of exchange and circulation from contemporary production, calling it "gift-giving" to present it as the universal, beyond labor's present and not historically bound by it.

Division of Labor

Perspectives such as Juliet Mitchell's and Gayle Rubin's were adapting to feminist analysis the methods of ideological critique, such as Louis Althusser's, where mental (superstructural) and manual (infrastructural) forces operated effectively in "relatively autonomous" but reciprocally interactive levels of a singular edifice erected on a singular base (production). For Althusser, this descriptive view allowed Marxism to illuminate the ways that the superstructure interacted with the base *on the basis of reproduction*[14] (emphasis in original), within an overall effective structure. Given this separation, one area, for example, that seemed particularly difficult to broach with women's oppression positioned outside of production was why women's productive wages were lower than men's. "[N]othing about capital itself," writes, for example, Heidi Hartmann, "determines who (that is, which individuals with which ascriptive characteristics) shall occupy the higher, and who the lower rungs of the wage labor force."[15]

The theoretical split between patriarchy and capitalism within feminism was partly grounded in an interpretation of Marx that projected production and reproduction (or, circulation) into relatively disparate, noncommunicating, and incompatible conceptual spheres, even different historical stages. This perceived rift between women and productive forces (or, class) limited feminist inquiry, as women's subordination had to be articulated as predominantly cultural, within a separate sphere of exchange and consumption. Feminist theory became very concerned with the Symbolic: how it is formed through an originary loss and a demand; what relation it has to the formation of the subject; how does it articulate and move through chains of desire, signification, and difference; and what mechanisms exist for the Symbolic of "man" and "woman" to be exposed as shams and failures and, finally, changed.

By placing the circulation of gender, symbols, and culture in a precapitalism, before production was oriented around paid labor, feminist theory was not recognizing that women's unpaid labor time was already a constitutive ingredient in paid labor's profits. In order to resituate women as agents of production and not just objects of culture, some trends in feminism therefore insisted that women's work had to be considered inside of the productive process and that their involvement in these processes accounted at least in part for their relation to the Symbolic. These trends did not consider women workers as abstracted into a universal equivalence defined singularly as the seller of labor power, devoid of bodies and differences, and neither did they see women as within a sphere of ideology that contrasted with the way value was created in production. Rather, they aimed to explain the division of labor as integral to the Symbolic. This would indicate how class itself was culturally multiple rather than singularly motivated, and that cultural differences were not economically insignificant, inelastic, or superfluous.

In response to this stalemate, feminist theorists questioned the dichotomous view of class that Marxist historicism offered. Feminists identified a need to develop analytical categories that could account for women's separate status inside the productive apparatus. Instead of a history that progressed through the dualism of class struggle, where women's reproductive work would be described on the outside—in the "ancient" or "primitive" world, for example, or in the home, as distinct and independent from the means of production—feminists like Iris Marion Young proposed a model where the family would no longer be considered as a separate sphere from capital or as a primary place of socialization or consumption. Instead, patriarchy would be examined as internal to productive processes. This would mean a breaking apart of class as a singular conflicting force, and substituting more various, concrete, specific accounts of the "*activity* of labor itself"[16] (emphasis in original) and the specific, multiple forms of cooperation, consciousness, and institutions that such activity demanded. A division-of-labor thesis would not assume that all women fell under a unified situation of oppression but would be able to notice how diverse, variable tasks, values, and functions were assigned usually, within a particular society, to a particular gender, for structural reasons, according to the demands of the means of production.

In response to the premises of ideology critique, the division-of-labor thesis merged cultural circulation into production, made them seem interchangeable, or revealed them as overlapping instances of a process (as they are in Marx). "In my research," begins French sociologist Christine Delphy, for example, in her groundbreaking study *Close to Home*, "I discovered first what a huge quantity of goods change hands without passing through the market. These goods change hands through the family—as gifts or inheritance."[17] For Delphy, the types of exchange systems in which women circulate are not to be differentiated from productive exchange circuits but rather explain its internal hierarchies. She uses Engels to skip over the centrality of industrialization in Marx's descriptions of modernization, where the Symbolic of money circulates often outside of production but also within it. Because transmission precedes production, the hierarchy between paid and unpaid labor came first, and then gendered was produced by gathering together disparate traits of the "unpaid" into a particular vision of the sexed body. In Delphy's understanding, production and reproduction are both modes of production: "In the traditional peasant farm economy, the family produces a large part of the goods which it consumes... The product which is consumed by the family, and thereby has a use-value, also has an exchange value, since it could have been sold on the market."[18] Delphy shows statistically that domestic production is only different in content from other types of commodity production in that it is unpaid: that use value cannot be distinguished in content from exchange value, that services provided by wives are not distinct in content from services provided by markets, and that producing for personal consumption is really "on a continuum"[19] with production for a wage. "In our society," she explains,

> it is not a case of certain tasks being forbidden to women, but of our being allowed to do them only in certain conditions. It is not that women may not act diplomatically, but that we may not be diplomats; it is not that women may not drive a tractor, but that we may not get one to own as the boss, nor even as a *paid* worker, etc.[20]

Intending to show that the Symbolic of gender is not relatively autonomous from the class structure but fundamentally integral to it, Delphy sets out to show that the Symbolic of gender comes first as the expression of hierarchy between paid and unpaid labor in its particular historical form: "men" and "women" are the bodies that get captured in different positions of the hierarchy leading into industrial capitalism; before then, the hierarchy designated only the primogenitor in the position of paid labor, where wives', younger siblings', and children's productivities were gathered into the subordinated position of the unpaid. She thus refutes feminist analysis based on the idea that sex is the ground of gender and challenges feminist perspectives that place domestic life in its own alienated category with women at its center, not only removed from production but also irrelevant to the money form and inconsequential to the commodity. Though focused on production in the agricultural setting, Delphy contests that the relations of the farming family parallel all modern forms of kinship and family nuclearization where the labor of the housewife is expropriated.

Delphy does not escape from the problem in Marxism that envisions the singular conflict between capital and labor as the singular motivating force of history, even as she allows a diversity of types of labor as reproductive or unpaid labor at different stages of history. She also is unable to resolve the critique of Marxism as economically deterministic—the Symbolic can only function in the service of capital and cannot, as later feminist perspectives like Kristeva's and Butler's allowed, unleash creativity, changing institutions by making them unstable: for Delphy, only capital can be creative or set the Symbolic in motion. As feminism dismissed the idea of work as the socialized overcoming of nature, the integration of the Symbolic of gender into the class conflict forced work to become uncreative, as it was not for Marx. However, the important question that Delphy does ask is about the relationship between the Symbolic—the social production of gender in circulation—and class conflict, that is, how the Symbolic of gender is needed by capitalism to produce creatively a sphere of unpaid labor as pure surplus. This line of inquiry took a backseat to the line of inquiry that tended, following Rubin, to think of the Symbolic as relatively autonomous from the means of production.

As the division-of-labor thesis opened up the category of work to diversification, class would become one instance of a wide array of symbolic divisions, each contingent and replaceable by other links in the chain of difference. Feminist theorists like Ernesto Laclau and Chantal Mouffe would then be able to generate a concept of civil society—"the political"—modeled on the structure of work in the division-of-labor thesis though without work at its center. Laclau and Mouffe attest that even at the time of Marx's writing, class and class antagonism were not the principal divisions demarcating historical action: they reject "the vanity of the aspiration that the 'class struggle' should constitute itself, *in an automatic and a priori manner,* in the foundation of this principle [of social division]"[21] (emphasis in original). The category of class was insufficient because it depended on the assumption that class struggle was monolithic, constituted through an opposition that was singular and determining throughout history, whose players were predefined and invariant, and whose outcomes could be predicted. Instead, the political field was composed of multiple unstable identities, including both class and gender but not rooted in either. "[T]the decline of a form of politics for which the division of the social into two antagonist camps," they read in the historical record before and after Marx, "is *an original and immutable datum, prior to all hegemonic construction,* and the transition towards a new situation, characterized by the essential instability of political spaces, in which the very identity of forces in struggle is submitted to constant shifts, and calls for an incessant process of redefinition"[22] (emphasis in original). Antagonisms were, then, practices of articulation, where identities established a set of discursive domains as a difference from the dominant. By replacing the category of class with a linguistic structure of difference, Laclau and Mouffe distanced women as political actors from class and work as production.

Though the division-of-labor thesis did not pose women's work outside of production, neither would women's relation to production (to labor) be its defining moment. Whereas in ideology critique, a fundamental schism between production and reproduction was built on a fundamental sense that capitalism had limits—for example, that the anthropological record would teach us that patriarchal culture had a life exterior and excessive to capitalist relations—the division-of-labor thesis, like the language theories linked to deconstruction, envisioned difference as symptomatic of capitalism, that is, as an errancy, aberration, rupture, absence, limit, or crisis produced inside of it and integral to it. Though clearly the division-of-labor thesis opened up feminist analysis to a broader array of topics and perspectives, it also reinterpreted the laboring class in itself as an emptied-out and indistinct form, even conceptually unimaginable. The paradigm of ideology critique, which partitioned culture from economy to explain gender, gave way to a division-of-labor critique, which, in introducing discords and discontinuities, separated the abstract, singularizing category of class from the historical privilege granted to it by Marx.

Feminism's division-of-labor thesis foreshadows that once women and their working time could be integrated within a Marxist analysis of labor, labor itself would become an unstable or quasi-unusable category. This idea was developing at a time when manufacturing and industrial laboring were seen (however preposterously) to be disappearing, dispersing, and decentralizing in First World production. Such a formulation, however, did not take into account the continuation (and even the increase) of manufacturing and industrial production in other non–First World geographical contexts, nor the advent of other non-industrial types of labor and labor exploitation (like service), nor that working people still had a historical identity as working people (i.e., that people's working lives still defined their social place, self-conceptions, experience, and worldly relations to a great degree). Feminism's break from class analysis leaves it bereft in contesting constructions of gender that produce profits by reducing necessary labor time: the current tendency, for example, to contain inflation by keeping unemployment high, even while employing women in ever greater numbers, or mechanisms of direct Third World investment in women's labor that bypass regulatory public bodies, like microcredit financing and tax-free zones. As Martha Gimenez summarizes the "Facts on Women" of the National Council of Women's Organizations,

> the vast majority of the world's working population is female; women are the poorest of the world's poor. Seventy percent of the 1.3 billion people who live in absolute poverty are women. Women work 2/3 of the world's working hours, produce half of the world's food and yet earn only 10% of the world's income and own less than 1% of the world's property.[23]

Feminism's critique of class created a difficulty for feminism to make claims or take action on behalf of working people, even as unions and collective bargaining are attacked, benefits cut, credit dried up, jobs made less permanent, wages plateaued, and a series of other draconian maneuvers, including cutbacks in child labor protections in some states, were unleashed on working people as working people. The attack on labor has given labor an identity it did not previously or obviously have; the historical moment demands—as Marx remarked in the *Grundrisse* (and elsewhere)—that feminism rejoins work as "a *positive, creative activity*"[24] (emphasis in original) that might, under the pressure of history, remake social relations.

Notes

1. Juliet Mitchell, "Women: The Long Revolution," *New Left Review* 40 (November–December 1966): 12. Mitchell elaborates:

   > Why has the problem of women's condition become an area of silence within contemporary socialism . . . [I]t can be said with some certainty that part of the explanation for the decline in socialist debate on the subject lies not only in the real historical processes, but in the original weaknesses in the traditional discussion of the subject in the classics. For while the great studies of the last century all stressed the importance of the problem, they did not *solve* it theoretically. (12)

2. Many feminists were wary, as well, that the proletariat subject would not accommodate the specifics of gender: Leopoldina Fortunati remarks, "The woman, at the formal level, came to be excluded from any direct relation with capital" (28). Nancy Hartsock criticizes Marx's critique of capitalism because: "class [is] understood centrally . . . as the only division that counts'" and women "are profoundly absent from his account of the extraction of surplus-value" (1998: 75). There are many others.

3. Heidi Hartmann, "The Unhappy Marriage of Marxism and Feminism: Towards a More Progressive Union," in *Women and Revolution: A Discussion of the Unhappy Marriage of Marxism and Feminism*. Ed. Lydia Sargent (Montreal, QC: Black Rose Books, 1981), 20.

4. The Institute for Women's Policy Research published a report showing that the gendered wage gap is growing in all major race and ethnic groups, and that the gains of women on the labor market have been slowing since the rapid increase evident in the 1980s and early 1990s. In 2012, the overall ratio of women's to men's median full-time weekly earnings was 80.9 percent, a decline by 1 point since 2011, and the overall ratio of women's to men's median annual full-time earnings was 77 percent in 2011. What is more: "Both earnings ratios (for weekly full-time workers and for year-round full-time workers) reflect gender differences in both hourly wages and the number of hours worked each year (among full-time workers). If part-time and part-year workers were included, the ratios of women's to men's earning would be much lower" (Ariane Hegewisch, Claudia Williams, and Angela Edwards, "Insitute for Women's Policy Research Fact Sheet: The Gender Gap: 2012," http://www.iwpr.org/publications/pubs/the-gender-wage-gap-2012/, accessed: March 8, 2013). Both the US Department of Labor and the National Women's Law Center (NWLC) continue to document that women make 77 cents to a man's dollar at comparable jobs and performance levels (the percentage is even greater for women of color, down to 54 cents on the white male dollar for African American women), and average $10,784 less per year, according to Naomi Wolf in *The Guardian* ("The Paycheck Fairness Act's Realpolitik," *Guardian* (June 8, 2012), http://www.guardian.co.uk/commentisfree/2012/jun/08/paycheck-fairness-act-realpolitik, accessed: June 10, 2012).

5. Hester Eisenstein makes a related observation. Chronicling the trajectory of her own scholarly thinking when post-structuralism was gaining acceptance, she notes:

> [S]omething important had shifted in the 1970s, and . . . this change, a restricting of the global economy, had consequences for politics, culture, and, most especially, the situation of women. The period of "Fordism," the expansive industrialization of the United States and other Western countries during the Golden Age of the Long Boom from 1945 to the 1970s, had been replaced by "post-Fordism": deindustrialization, and an end to the Keynsian welfare state . . . Was it an unfortunate coincidence that women had been drawn into the economy in a productive capacity at precisely the historical moment when there was going to be such a dramatic slowdown? Or was it . . . that the slowdown caused women to become the cheap workforce of choice? . . . There seemed to be insufficient attention to the link between the massive increase in women's workforce participation, as the US economy shed manufacturing for service jobs, and the rise of feminist consciousness and activism. (Hester Eisenstein, *Feminism Seduced: How Global Elites Use Women's Labor and Ideas to Exploit the World* (Boulder, CO, and London: Paradigm Publishers, 2009), 11–12)

Eisenstein often seems to conflate post-structuralist and mainstream feminism, often oversimplifying both, and she often over-abstracts neo-liberalism to the point where it acquires overarching agency and determinism. However, the questions she raises—about the historical conjuncture of feminism and post-Fordism (or neo-liberalism)—do need further exploration.

6. Kathi Weeks, *The Problem with Work: Feminism, Marxism, Antiwork Politics, and Postwork Imaginaries* (Durham, NC, and London: Duke University Press, 2011), 9.

7. Karl Marx and Friedrich Engels, "The German Ideology, Including Theses on Feuerbach and Introduction to the Critique of Political Economy," in *The Marx–Engels Reader*, Second Edition. Ed. Robert C. Tucker (New York and London: W. W. Norton & Co., 1978), 196.

8. Annette Kuhn, "Structures of Patriarchy and Capital in the Family," in *Feminism and Materialism: Women and Modes of Production* (London, Henley, UK, and Boston: Routledge and Kegan Paul, 1978), 63.

9. Friedrich Engels, *The Origin of the Family, Private Property, and the State*. Trans. Alick West (proofed and corrected by Mark Harris, 2010), 38, www.marxists.org/archive/marx/works/download/pdf/origin_family.pdf, accessed: April 1, 2011.

10. Juliet Mitchell, *Psychoanalysis and Feminism: A Radical Reassessment of Freudian Psychoanalysis*, New Edition (New York: Basic Books, 1974), 412.

11. Gayle Rubin, "The Traffic in Women: Notes on the 'Political Economy' of Sex," in *Towards an Anthropology of Women*. Ed. Rayna R. Reiter (New York: Monthly Review Press, 1976), 157.

12. Ibid., 163.

13. Ibid., 164.

14. Louis Althusser, "Ideology and Ideological State Apparatuses (Notes towards an Investigation)," in *Lenin and Philosophy and Other Essays*. Trans. Ben Brewster (London: New Left Books, 1971), 131.

15. Hartmann, "The Unhappy Marriage," 24.

16. Iris Young, "Beyond the Unhappy Marriage: A Critique of the Dual Systems Theory," in *Women and Revolution: A Discussion of the Unhappy Marriage of Marxism and Feminism*. Ed. Lydia Sargent (Montreal, QC: Black Rose Books, 1981), 51.

17. Christine Delphy, *Close to Home: A Materialist Analysis of Women's Oppression*. Trans. Diana Leonard (London: Hutchinson, 1970), 15.

18. Ibid., 63–64.

19. Ibid., 64.

20. Ibid., 103.

21. Ernesto Laclau and Chantal Mouffe, *Hegemony and Socialist Strategy: Towards a Radical Democratic Politics*, Second Edition (London and New York: Verso, 1985), 151.

22. Ibid.

23. Martha E. Gimenez, "Connecting Marx and Feminism in the Era of Globalization: A Preliminary Investigation," *Socialism and Democracy* 18, 1 (September 2010): 98.

24. Karl Marx, *Grundrisse: Foundations of the Critique of Political Economy (Rough Draft)*. Trans. Martin Nicolaus (London and New York: Penguin Books in association with *New Left Review*, 1973), 614.

Works Cited

Althusser, Louis. "Ideology and Ideological State Apparatuses (Notes towards an Investigation)." In *Lenin and Philosophy and Other Essays*. Trans. Ben Brewster. London: New Left Books, 1971, pp. 123–173.

Delphy, Christine. *Close to Home: A Materialist Analysis of Women's Oppression*. Trans. Diana Leonard. London: Hutchinson, 1970.

DeParle, Jason. "Two Classes, Divided by 'I Do'." *The New York Times* (July 14, 2012): http://www.nytimes.com/2012/07/15/us/two-classes-in-america-divided-by-i-do.html?pagewanted=all. Accessed: July 31, 2012.

Eisenstein, Hester. *Feminism Seduced: How Global Elites Use Women's Labor and Ideas to Exploit the World.* Boulder, CO, and London: Paradigm Publishers, 2009.

Engels, Friedrich. *The Origin of the Family, Private Property, and the State.* Trans. Alick West (proofed and corrected by Mark Harris, 2010). www.marxists.org/archive/marx/works/download/pdf/origin_family.pdf. Accessed: April 1, 2011.

Fortunati, Leopoldina. *The Arcane of Reproduction: Housework, Prostitution, Labor and Capital.* Trans. Hilary Creek. Ed. Jim Fleming. New York: Autonomedia, 1995.

Gimenez, Martha E. "Connecting Marx and Feminism in the Era of Globalization: A Preliminary Investigation." *Socialism and Democracy* 18, 1 (September 2010): 85–105.

Hartmann, Heidi. "The Unhappy Marriage of Marxism and Feminism: Towards a More Progressive Union." In *Women and Revolution: A Discussion of the Unhappy Marriage of Marxism and Feminism.* Ed. Lydia Sargent. Montreal, QC: Black Rose Books, 1981, pp. 1–41.

Hartsock, Nancy. *The Feminist Standpoint Revisited and Other Essays.* Boulder, CO, and Oxford, UK: Westview Press, 1998.

Hegewisch, Ariane; Williams, Claudia; and Edwards, Angela. "Insitute for Women's Policy Research Fact Sheet: The Gender Gap: 2012." http://www.iwpr.org/publications/pubs/the-gender-wage-gap-2012/. Accessed: March 8, 2013.

Kuhn, Annette. "Structures of Patriarchy and Capital in the Family." In *Feminism and Materialism: Women and Modes of Production.* London, Henley, UK, and Boston: Routledge and Kegan Paul, 1978, pp. 42–67.

Laclau, Ernesto and Mouffe, Chantal. *Hegemony and Socialist Strategy: Towards a Radical Democratic Politics,* Second Edition. London and New York: Verso, 1985.

Marx, Karl. *Grundrisse: Foundations of the Critique of Political Economy (Rough Draft).* Trans. Martin Nicolaus. London and New York: Penguin Books in association with *New Left Review,* 1973.

Marx, Karl; and Engels, Friedrich. "The German Ideology, Including Theses on Feuerbach and Introduction to the Critique of Political Economy." In *The Marx–Engels Reader,* Second Edition. Ed. Robert C. Tucker. New York and London: W. W. Norton & Co., 1978, pp. 146–200.

Mitchell, Juliet. "Women: The Long Revolution." *New Left Review* 40 (November–December 1966): 11–37.

Mitchell, Juliet. *Psychoanalysis and Feminism: A Radical Reassessment of Freudian Psychoanalysis,* New Edition. New York: Basic Books, 1974.

Rubin, Gayle. "The Traffic in Women: Notes on the 'Political Economy' of Sex." In *Towards an Anthropology of Women.* Ed. Rayna R. Reiter. New York: Monthly Review Press, 1976, pp. 157–210.

Weeks, Kathi. *The Problem with Work: Feminism, Marxism, Antiwork Politics, and Postwork Imaginaries.* Durham, NC, and London: Duke University Press, 2011.

Wolf, Naomi. "The Paycheck Fairness Act's Realpolitik." *Guardian* (June 8, 2012): http://www.guardian.co.uk/commentisfree/2012/jun/08/paycheck-fairness-act-realpolitik. Accessed: June 10, 2012.

Young, Iris. "Beyond the Unhappy Marriage: A Critique of the Dual Systems Theory." In *Women and Revolution: A Discussion of the Unhappy Marriage of Marxism and Feminism.* Ed. Lydia Sargent. Montreal, QC: Black Rose Books, 1981, pp. 43–69.

CHAPTER 14

Criminal Class

Eric Anthamatten

Crime is a cry of distress.[1] It is the cry from the victim, but also a cry from the criminal. It is the cry of a wretched soul already imprisoned in conditions that created the need for the (cry)me. This social incarceration preexists the juridical incarceration—the formal sentencing only makes manifest the invisible walls, razor wire, and impermeable social, economic, and psychic barriers that exclude, silence, and paralyze. Crime makes visible these unseen boundaries—it is always a cry for dignity, a cry for freedom, not a cry to be apart, but a cry to be a part. The (cry)me is the sublimated scream of society's repressed desires, the irruption of a neurosis—both individual and social—that has incubated in the subterranean darkness of the unconscious. Crime is society revealing to itself the aspects of its psyche that have been silenced, oppressed, buried, those parts of the psyche that must speak, sublimate, return. (Cry)me is this treble cry: the yell of the violated, the violator, and the soul of society itself.

The social correlates of crime are well documented. Our criminals are primarily the poor, the neglected, the exploited, the alienated, the marginalized, the ignored, the forgotten. Whether or not these social factors are the "causes" of crime is a more difficult story to tell; nonetheless, the connections cannot be ignored. In his famous critique of religion, Marx uses the metaphor of escape through drugs, the "opiate of the masses," as a way of emphasizing how wretched social conditions create and perpetuate institutions and ideologies that in turn cover over the spoiled soil from which those institutions and ideologies sprouted. Instead of looking at the root socioeconomic factors that motivate the need for religion, we escape the injustices of this world and are allowed to ignore them by turning our gaze and energy to the world beyond the clouds. For Marx, religion is only the most obvious ideo-institutional symptom that is evidence of an underlying disease, and the critique of religion is the first step that begins a broader critique of other institutions that mask and perpetuate unequal, unjust, and alienating social conditions.

"It is above all the *task of philosophy*, which is in the service of history, to unmask self-estrangement in its *secular forms* once the *sacred form* has been unmasked."[2] Crime is one of those "secular" forms of self-estrangement that philosophy must unmask. Our assumptions about criminals—lazy, poor, irrational, dark—and their motivations—greed, sadism, natural depravity—cover and excuse the environmental elements that penetrate, influence, and sustain crime. We cannot exclude the role that the individual will plays in the act of crime, but we equally cannot diminish the role of various social, historic, and economic factors that shape and press upon these wills. Theories of punishment that fail to do so are not only incomplete, but culpable. These systems of "justice" that purportedly address and claim to minimize crime are the very systems that cover the conditions that generate crime, in turn, creating more crime. The "criminal" of "criminal justice system" becomes no longer an adjective describing the noun "justice," but the subject acting out the verb—the "justice" deployed by a system that is itself criminal. In this way, a tragic feedback loop begins, whereby a whole class of people emerges, not defined by their culture, their work, or their will, but by their crime. The criminal class: forever flotsam, juridical jetsam, always marginal, perpetually punished.

Crime is a symptom of society, not its cause. The "carceral boom" in the United States of the past few decades was a conscious mechanism to "treat" a symptom instead of the underlying disease from which the symptom manifests, much like unplugging the "check engine" light on the dashboard instead of opening the hood to see what might be awry. Instead of interrogating why certain marginal groups existed and why they might engage in crime, the response was simply to criminalize those groups. The criminal justice system not only responded to "crimes" as they emerged, but actively sought to create species of crime that targeted specific groups of people—especially the dark and the poor—so that the very social and economic forces—liberal, capitalist, religious—that created these marginal groups could continue unquestioned. In his *Prisons of Poverty*, Loïc Wacquant brilliantly documents this shift that begins to occur in the late 1970s from what he calls the "social state" to the "penal state."[3] In the mid-1970s, the United States was looked upon by other developed nations as a model that would eventually lead to the "decarceration" of society, one that might "end the prison as we know it." A "great leap backward" begins, however, with the Nixon administration, is perfected through the Reagan era, and continues through the Clinton era. Wacquant writes:

> Since the turnabout of the mid-1970s, the carceral system of the United States serves not only to repress crime: it also has as its mission to bolster the social, racial, and economic order via the punitive regulation of the behaviors of the populations prone to visible and offensive deviance because they are relegated to the bottom of a polarizing class and cast structure. The prison has been called upon to contain the disorders generated by the rising tide of dispossessed families, street

derelicts, unemployed and alienated youths, and the desperation and violence that have accumulated and intensified in the segregated urban core of the metropolis as the "safety net" of the U.S. semi-welfare state was torn and socialized wage labor in the low-wage service sectors has become the normal horizon of work for the deskilled fraction of the postindustrial working class.[4]

This shift in technique toward one that uses police and punishment as a way to deal with social problems reaches its perfection in New York City under the leadership of Rudolph Giuliani and chief of police William Bratton, a policy that is now being exported with gusto around the world.[5] Interestingly, the United States is now seen as both the model and the deviant when it comes to criminal "justice": as a model by neo-liberal governments beholden to free-market ideologies and a priori assumptions about the relationship of the individual to society; as deviant by intellectuals and activists who see this new system as only a smoke screen that excuses the inherent inequalities, exploitations, and alienations created and perpetuated by one of the most inefficient, unjust, ineffective, and bizarre systems of "justice."[6]

It is no accident that the carceral boom paralleled the boom in the supply-side, free-market ideologies of the Reagan era, something that continued into the Clinton era and the "end of welfare as we know it." We could "end" welfare not by genuinely addressing the failed social and economic institutions that contributed to and exacerbated these inequalities and the need for welfare, but by warehousing those aversely affected in prison—out of sight, out of mind. What "trickles down" is not the life-giving manna from Heaven, but the toxic rain of polluted clouds. It is almost as though conservative economic advisors had read their Marx very carefully, acting with the foreknowledge that their hyper-capitalist, hyper-individualist policies would inevitably produce more wretched, exploited, poor. To mask this inevitable superfluous excess, to control the potential social unrest—surveil, police, incarcerate. Michael Tonry is certain that this effort deployed by the famous euphemism of the "War on Drugs" was conscious:

> They knew that drug use was falling among the vast majority of the population. They knew that drug use was not declining among the disadvantaged members of the urban underclass. They knew that the War on Drugs would be fought mainly in the minority areas of American cities and that those arrested and imprisoned would disproportionately be young blacks and Hispanics.[7]

It would be oversimplistic and irresponsible to simply explain the carceral boom as an effect of conservative or neo-liberal policies. The criminalization of the dark and the poor follows the logic of the political-economic-religious ideologies upon which our political discourse—for both Republicans and Democrats—is founded and from which the horizon of possibilities rarely deviates. Liberal social contract theories, which reinforce capitalist economic models, tell the story of society being born as a response to the perceived threat of violent and wholly selfish individuals, the proto-criminals of the so-called "state of nature." Either society cannot get off the ground because, in the absence of some external force of fear and power, we will always lie, cheat, steal, and kill if we have the strength and cunning to get away with it (Hobbes's thesis). Or, the harmonious, egalitarian, and rational (read "God-given") state of nature is disrupted by some irrational (read "sinful") element that then must be kept in check by a minimal government and the rule of law (Locke's thesis). Though Rousseau is more attuned to the inequality and corruption created by ideologies, institutions, and "civilization" itself, even he, in his education of Émile, betrays an underlying fetishism of the individual that can somehow exist before and outside of society.[8] In all of these views, the individual somehow preexists society. The question of society then becomes a question of figuring out how to bind these individuals—externally, supposedly against nature—and how to keep them bound, as though politics is simply tying together sticks (*fasces*)[9] or constructing a castle made of many-colored, many-shaped Legos.

Because of these hyper-individualistic assumptions, it is no surprise that in all of these accounts of the "birth" of society, the question of the criminal is addressed very early. By definition, crime cannot preexist society (unless it is a "crime" against divine decree), a fact that Hobbes emphasizes. Nonetheless, liberal social contract theories always are parasitic upon some mythical proto-criminal, a radical individual whose will to power disrupts the possible formation of a stable society or some already existing pre-social harmony. Society, then, is a response, a perceived cure for these anomalous elements. Consequentially, future transgressions are always seen as transgressions by individuals—in Hobbes's case, these individuals are acting naturally; in Locke's case, they are acting irrationally. For Rousseau, the criminal is not necessarily acting irrationally, but is someone who does not understand his deep relation to the whole, who does not understand that society's freedom just *is* his freedom. In his famous and controversial statement, the deviant must be "forced to be free."[10]

The blame, then, for crime falls wholly on the criminal's individual shoulders irrespective of the social, economic, historical womb inside which he was nourished.[11] If the criminal stole because he was hungry, it is because he did not work hard enough to earn his bread. The social structures that created the conditions whereby whole classes of people do not have bread are acquitted, conditions that are very profitable to those few who literally feed off the fact that there are those who remain breadless.[12] If the criminal kills, even if it was in a moment of "passion," the responsibility falls wholly upon the murderer's shoulders. The social conditions that actively herd whole groups into ghettos, creating conditions of "passion" whereby one suffers underneath daily brow-beatings that force this passivity upon them, conditions of wretchedness whereby membership in gangs and participation in violent and illegal activity is often one of the few ways of becoming part of a community of activity and dignity at all—these facts remain ignored. The economic structures that exclude or set up de facto barriers that prevent real opportunities to "make it" in the world remain unquestioned. The educational paradigms that teach people to become mere individuals and not citizens, that emphasize the profitable over the moral, that cultivate a culture of isolation (which is not a culture) rather than community continue unperturbed.[13]

These liberal theories rest upon a limited and flawed view of the individual, a view most certainly influenced by Judeo-Christian notions of original sin, that assumes some immutable and aloof Oz behind the curtain that is not formed or affected by the world from which it grew and in which it swims. Perhaps at the birth of modernity, this thesis was necessary to liberate the individual from the tyranny of political and religious dogma. There is, however, a tyranny created of this fetishism of the individual, a tyranny whereby social influences and ideological institutions are seen to be blameless, a fact that cultivates the solipsism, cynicism, and complacency that make the ground ripe precisely for those totalitarian institutions that liberalism initially stood against.

Liberal-capitalist-religious models that hyper-emphasize the individual over society not only serve to mask the underlying social conditions of estrangement and inequality, but also exacerbate the problem of crime. The criminal is punished thrice. First, the socioeconomic prison that is poverty and the ghetto. Effectively isolated from those institutions whereby one might emerge from and minimize these pockets of poverty and neglect, for example, adequate education, access to good nutrition, physical and mental health care, the "criminal" often is incubated inside these conditions of social incarceration. Secondly, after the act of (cry)me, the actual punishment administered by the justice system is not objective but subjective, classist, racist, and multitiered—justice often peeks from beneath her blindfold to see whom it is that she weighs. There is the justice for the rich and the justice for the poor, justice for the dark and justice for the light—not only the various punishments for types of crime,[14] but access to adequate counsel, mandatory minimums, "zero-tolerance" policies, three-strikes laws. Finally, the *effects* of this multitiered system of justice only perpetuate and exacerbate the inequalities. Absentee parents (mostly fathers), backdoor sentencing, the hardening of criminals while they do their time—these are often chains and walls that are more inescapable than the actual mechanisms of restraint and isolation that are deployed by the formal mechanisms of the state. And so, punishment traverses time—past, present, future—becoming effectively eternal. Punishment is rarely about correcting a single action once and for all. The punishment preexists the crime, momentarily becomes manifest as the judge slams the gavel on the bench, then becomes invisible though no less present as it creates future crime through its various mechanisms of deployment.

We can track the history of liberal political theory as a history of defining and responding to radical individuals, individuals most often defined as criminals during their time. These radical individuals are always divided, perhaps contradictory figures. To borrow a term from Simon Critchley, the "individual" is not some perfect crystal subject, but is many-sided, fractured, more so a "dividual"—we are individual *and* social, free *and* determined, distended between where we were, where we are, and where we want to be.[15] This divided nature becomes most visible in and through these radical dividuals, our heroes, our criminals; often the line between the two is blurry, and often, as history marches onward, criminals become heroes, heroes criminals—not just world historical figures (Socrates, Luther, Hitler), but whole groups of people who have been ostracized and criminalized (minorities, immigrants, Jews, women, the poor).[16] But these "individuals" never emerge ex nihilo, for they are products of the social soup in which they are immersed. The division that constitutes an "individual" is not contradictory, but ontological, alluded to by Aristotle's notion of the *zoon politikon*, and Hegel's maxim "The I that is a We and the We that is an I," and Heidegger's notions of *Dasein* as being the structure of "Care." Though we all participate in this divided nature, it is the radical "individuals", most especially criminals, that point to these fissures, collisions, and contradictions inherent not only in our individual being but also in the existing socioeconomic order. Whether by will or accident, the criminal perhaps reveals less about his or her own individual psyche and more about the society's soul. The criminal is not an inexplicable, irrational anomaly. Rather, the criminal is precisely the rational picture of a particular society. The criminal does not point away from the social, but toward it—the cry (*logos* as speech) of the criminal reveals the logic (*logos* as logical structure) of the society in which he screams.

Crime, like any action, is carried out by an individual. But crime is rarely an action of an individual *against* society. Rather, crime is the cry by the individual demanding to be a part of society, a cry to enter the gates of the community, a cry to be recognized. Crime is the cry in the desert, "Here I am!" (*Hineni*). Not the cry of Abraham who became an individual only under God (Abraham, the greatest criminal, who had to prove himself by completely negating the ethical, the filial, the communal through the obedient murder of his son), but the cry of an individual who wants to be recognized and heard by others, who yearns deeply to be a part of the ethical, the filial, the communal. "Father! Mother! Brother! Sister! Friend! Foe! Here I am!"

Crime is not the triumph of the animalistic element of the soul over the intellectual and moral elements. It is just the opposite: crime is the moral element demanding dignity, screaming for recognition, unfortunately sometimes resorting to violent and murderous ways. It is not surprising that the word "recognition" is often heard in street slang: "You better recognize!" Even Cain, "the evil one," did not murder his brother as a result of some a priori depravity, but as a response to his rejected offerings to God. Cain was mis-recognized. God rejected Cain's offerings of his best fruit in favor of Abel's offerings of his animals. Cain's action cannot be understood simply as an act of individual jealousy. In fact, he followed most strictly that divine logic that requires sacrifice, and sacrifice is always of that thing that is most useful and dear. Cain's murder, then, was an act of love and devotion, both to God and to his brother. Abel's death was less a murder than a sacrifice, a call out to God by Cain to be recognized. "Here I am!" The murder of his brother was his individual "choice," but a choice that did not occur in a vacuum, a choice that had a history. This does not exculpate Cain; it only points to the complicated tapestry that is human action. Crime is this triple-barreled phenomenon of mis-recognition: the mis-recognition of society toward the criminal;

the mis-recognition of the criminal toward the victim; the mis-recognition of the criminal toward himself or herself.

The "crimes" of religious figures, however, are not the best examples, for the religious individual ultimately negates the social, moral, and human sphere in favor of a divine other world. By contrast, the social criminal does not try to negate the ethical world, but tries to win it back, or, in many cases, to become part of an ethical world that never was there in the first place. "Here I am!" is the demand for dignity and dialogue. It is a cry to us from us, from those that have been pushed outside the boundaries of community and call to us so that they may return. How do we respond? Do we listen? Do we open the door? Do we reinforce the locks and barricades? Do we fight back? Do we ignore?

Our response has rarely been one of understanding, compassion, or forgiveness but a response of fear, anger, and revenge. Under these individualistic, religious views—views that are becoming more prevalent and virulent in the past decade—the Other is a black box, and so, when they act "criminally," we must throw them into a black box. We cannot understand because we convince ourselves that the criminal is wholly alien, not of us, a creature from the Black Lagoon, emerging from the various isolated socioeconomic swamps with which we have no qualitative contact. We cannot have compassion (we cannot "suffer with") because we do not undergo those daily pains and injuries to dignity that they must endure. We cannot forgive because in forgiving the criminal, we implicate ourselves in the conditions that made necessary the forgiving. Perhaps, we cannot forgive because we are weak vis-à-vis the power of the criminal, and, as Nietzsche emphasizes,[17] forgiveness is an act that only the strong are capable of bestowing.

We flee the criminal. We lock him away in the caverns at the edge of society. We send him into exile. We execute him. We do all of this because we are afraid. The purported fear of the criminal seeking our annihilation only masks a deeper fear, fear of our own selves. The criminal is always of us. He looks back at us with a penetrating "J'accuse!" We flee the criminal because he always tells us something about ourselves. His existence is not on the other side of an opaque wall, but faces us, as a reflection—the criminal is society's mirror. We turn away because his gaze reveals our own blemishes and scars, and we will cover over those evidences with whatever makeup or surgery we can. We put up the walls not so we will be protected from the irrational and violent will to power of the criminal, but so we don't have to see the monstrous wounds on our own skin. The more impenetrable the walls, the more we betray the reactionary force of repression that we have deployed to keep at bay the many neuroses we nourish by that very act of repression.

Just as an individual must take heed of the manifold manifestations of neurotic impulses in our individual psyches—cries from the depths of our being—so too must we listen to the various neurotic impulses and cries of society's psyche. Both Marx and Freud use the language of "expression" and "sublimation" to describe certain institutions and ideologies that arise from underlying traumas, most especially in their rabid critiques of religion. Likewise, crime is a voice from within society, not from without. This is the distinction between a "criminal" and an "enemy." The enemy is wholly other—he threatens our mode of existence from the outside. The enemy, writes Carl Schmitt, is "in a specially intense way, existentially something different and alien, so that in the extreme case conflicts with him are possible."[18] Though the criminal creates conflicts and destabilizes society to a certain extent, he does not seek its total destruction. The criminal is always from inside, paradoxically created by the very society that seeks to punish him. The criminal is something between a friend and an enemy, but he is always more neighbor than alien. Crime is more a cancer than a virus, and its existence more often than not points to something perhaps that, though perhaps inevitable, might better be prevented than cured.[19]

The criminal always points to existing tensions and contradictions *within* society. Antigone, in her defiant burial of her brother, represents the tension between family and state, a tension that Creon attempts to bury. Socrates, Athens's greatest citizen and its most threatening criminal at once, stands at the collision between the "truth" of wisdom (philosophy) and the "appearance" of wisdom (sophistry). Luther, who initially did not want to destroy the Church but reform it, was excommunicated because he pointed to the tension between the institutional/external relationship to god and the individual/internal relationship to god. Meursault revealed the tensions between rational and accepted roles of son/lover/friend/citizen and the irreducible irrational, absurd, chaotic, and random element that is irrevocably part of what it means to be human, to be free.

What of the petty thief? What of the druglord? What of the rapist? What of the serial killer? What of the responsibility that the criminal must bear? In saying that crime is an effect of social conditions, are you not denying the criminal's individual will and freedom? Are you not denying will and freedom as such? If a "side" of this false dichotomy between individual and social must be chosen, my instinct is to first interrogate all of those conditions that surround and cultivate the individual—psychological, economic, historical—before I abstract the criminal and place all of the blame on single shoulders. Certainly, an "explanation" of the individual as *only* being the sum of various social elements does deny freedom and responsibility, thus making a theory of punishment and moral judgment as such impossible. By emphasizing the social, economic, biological, and historical elements in crime, we do not eliminate the individual. Rather, we make the individual concrete, give him substance, pulling the abstractions of "will" and "the criminal" from the clouds of ethereality down to the embodied and felt reality of ground and soil.

Though the emphasis here is on the social factors that contribute to crime, it would be equally erroneous to insist that the criminal's actions are overdetermined by natural and social forces. The discussion of "human nature" now centers around evolutionary-genetic-neurological paradigms. Obviously, the insights into human behavior offered by these paradigms must be taken seriously, for they do illuminate some elements of the complexity of the human mind and its motivations. But these natural influences on action are not adamantine laws. They are probabilistic dispositions that require certain types of environments to switch these behaviors "on" or "off"—a living organism is not a noun, but a verb, dynamically interacting with the world at every moment. The "laws" of adaptation are perhaps genuine laws, but they always occur underneath the veil, and the best we can hope for is to become aware of the types of social environment that are more likely to maximize or minimize certain behaviors, especially crime. The search for the so-called "crime gene" can dangerously slide into an essentialist narrative that excludes responsibility and more dangerously perpetuates racism and sexism in its worst form. But even those who acknowledge that certain people come into the world with certain tendencies that might make them more susceptible to criminal behavior—for example, anger, addictive behavior—these are only nascent tendencies that must become manifest or remain dormant inside of a living world.[20] Put differently, we always have that space between nature and will to understand and act, that is, to be free, responsible.

I do not seek here to eliminate the individual or the irrational and make the mistake of offering a totalizing theory that explains away all possible crime, and in so doing leaves no room for responsibility or freedom. In fact, if the utopia that ends history somehow obtains, I would perhaps encourage the irrational "criminals" that are often the protagonists of existentialist literature: the Underground Men, the Raskolnikovs, the Meursaults of the world. Perhaps there is and always must be an irreducible individual "will to power" that explains the "criminal," an element of our psyche that remains vigilant—consciously or unconsciously—over human freedom when systems of domination—religious, political, scientific— start to colonize that space of freedom, action, and responsibility. But these instances are rare. Most crime cannot be reductively explained in terms of individual psychologies, a theory of crime that is ultimately an irresponsible excuse that masks over the conditions that not only create crime, but certain types of crimes. The individual is never a button in a box—he is always in a diaphanous relationship with the world and with others, interpenetrated by various vectors of personal, familial, and social histories. The "individual" is the intersection of these threads, a complex tapestry that is constantly weaving and fraying. The "will" is simply one of these threads, the "I" the warp and woof.

There is no simple causal explanation of human action. John Dewey takes on precisely this issue in *Human Nature and Conduct*, explicitly using the image of the criminal to emphasize his point:

> Our entire tradition regarding punitive justice tends to prevent recognition of social partnership in producing crime; it falls in with a belief in metaphysical free will. By killing an evil-doer or shutting him up behind stone walls, we are enabled to forget both him and our part in creating him. Society excuses itself by laying the blame on the criminal; he retorts by putting the blame on bad early surroundings, the temptations of others, lack of opportunities, and the persecution of officers of the law. Both are right, except in the wholesale character of their recitation. But the effect of both sides is to throw the whole matter back into antecedent causation, a method which refuses to bring the matter to truly moral judgment. For morals has to do with acts still within our control, acts still to be performed. No amount of guilt on the part of the evil-doer absolves us from the responsibility for the consequences upon him and others of our way treating him, or form our

continuing responsibility for the conditions under which person develop perverse habits.[21]

The "will" does not stand over and above the body, steering it like some sober captain amidst the tempests of nature and desire. Nor can the will simply decide to disentangle itself from the many webs of historic, cultural, economic, and social strands inside which it is caught. Beware paradigms that purport to explain in dogmatic and absolutist strokes, be they religious, liberal, social, or scientific. Whoever it is that we are and whatever the "reasons" that we act cannot be explained through reductive, monolithic narratives. We are not Galileo's falling bodies dropped from the Tower of Pisa—calculable, predictable, moving in theoretical vacuum. At best, we are Copenhagen's particles, blooming, buzzing, uncertain, ambiguous. We may speak of fields of action, influences to those actions, probabilities, hypothetical "truths." The "I," especially, does not belong to Newton, but to Heisenberg.

Likewise, crime, a type of action, cannot be reduced to a simple causal story. Liberal theories of punishment emphasize the blame that must fall upon the individual. The criminal is considered an anomaly, an irrational actor that does not play by the rules, not only specific societal rules, but universal rules of reason and morality. Crime, then, is seen as a choice of the will, an exercise, however perverted and self-defeating, of freedom.[22] In fact, retributive theories of punishment, which tend to dominate the theoretical landscape, emphasize that to *not* put the whole responsibility onto the individual is to deny that individual his innate and universal dignity. But this view is at least partially, if not altogether, perverted, for dignity and responsibility are terms that are always tied to our brothers and sisters, our friends and foes, our citizens and our criminals.

Put succinctly, the purported dichotomy between individual and social is false, one that serves to cover over society's injustices at the expense of various scapegoats and bogeymen. Whole classes and races labeled "criminal" so that society and its entrenched modes of production and ideologies perpetuate—the haves remain having, the powerless remain impotent, the wretched remain damned.

Marx's great intellectual father, G. W. F. Hegel, is often considered to be one of the foundational figures in retributive punishment theory. Though there are elements of his thoughts on crime and punishment that seem to lend credence to a retributivist reading, Hegel is very interested in always thinking of the individual in and through social and historical forces. In a short text "Who Thinks Abstractly?," Hegel explicitly emphasizes the importance and necessity of the concrete. He uses the image of a criminal, a murderer:

One who knows men traces the development of the criminal's mind: he finds in his history, in his education, a bad family relationship between his father and mother, some tremendous harshness after this human being had done some minor wrong, so he became embittered against the social order—a first reaction to this that in effect expelled him and henceforth did not make it possible for him to preserve himself except through crime.—There may be people who will say when they hear such things: he wants to excuse this murderer!... This is abstract thinking: to see nothing in the murderer except the abstract fact that he is a murderer, and to annul all other human essence in him with this simple quality.[23]

By emphasizing the social, the economic, the historical, in a word, the concrete, individual responsibility does not simply fade away. Rather, we have a more mature and responsible understanding of the individual and her relation to the whole. It is certainly more complex and possibly opens another set of problems and questions, but it is a necessary complexity, one that is responsible. The false dichotomies that explain crime in reductive and simplistic ways only serve to repress the aspects of our world that crime expresses—inequality, poverty, alienation, exploitation, humiliation—thus exacerbating them so that they return in more destructive ways. Just as the criminal must be held responsible to society, so too must society be held responsible to the criminal, perhaps now more than ever.

Notes

1. "Crime" from Latin *crimen* "charge, indictment, offense," from *cernere* "to decide, to sift, to separate." Klein, however, suggests *"cri-men"*—"cry of distress."
2. Karl Marx, "A Contribution to the Critique of Hegel's Philosophy of Right: Introduction," in *Marx: Early Political Writing* (Cambridge: Cambridge University Press, 1994), 58.
3. Loïc Wacquant, *Prisons of Poverty* (Minneapolis: University of Minnesota, 2009), esp. 55–131.
4. Ibid., 149.
5. See esp. Ibid., 27–54.
6. The US Bureau of Justice and Statistics reports that nearly 2.3 million adults were incarcerated in the United States at year-end 2009, about 1 percent of the adult population. Adding the nearly 5 million on probation or parole puts nearly 7.3 million adults under correctional supervision. Globally, the United States has less than 5 percent of the world's population but 23.4 percent of the world's incarcerated population: 743 per 100,000. Compare this with Rwanda (595 per 100,000), Russia (534 per 100,000), Iran (333 per 100,000), China (122 per 100,000), Canada (117 per 100,000), and Germany (87 per 100,000), to name a few. Data from International Centre for Prison Studies, December 19, 2011.
7. Michael Tonry, *Malign Neglect: Race, Crime, and Punishment in America* (New York: Oxford University Press, 1995), 104.
8. Rousseau's *Discourse on the Origin and Basis of Inequality among Men* remains one of the most important proto-Marixst, proto-anarchist critiques of "civilization" and the assumptions about individuality and the "state of nature" that are axiomatic truths for thinkers like Hobbes and Locke, both of whom are the ancestors of present-day neo-liberal and neo-conservative thought. Rousseau, along with Aristotle and Hegel, is one of the great thinkers of the deep interconnectedness between the individual and the social, and he is very concerned about the way that society influences and shapes the individual. Nonetheless, though Rousseau seems to always to choose country over town, nature over civilization, he takes Émile out of the corrupting influence of society precisely so that he can enter back into society, or at least become an individual

who is a member of a society that is more organic and interpersonal. I take Rousseau's "general will" as an effort to think through a "social contract" that is more roots to fruits, a theory of society that is more rhizomatic and horizontal than hierarchical and vertical. This major theme of isolation and togetherness remains unresolved, not only in Rousseau's *œuvre*, but his own life as well.

9. The *fasces* was a bound bundle of wooden rods, sometimes augmented by an axe, and it was a symbol of power and jurisdiction for the magistrates in ancient Rome. It is also where the term "fascism" originates.

10. Jean-Jacques Rousseau, *The Social Contract*, trans. Maurice Cranston (New York: Penguin, 1968), 64.

11. Likewise, the praise for those "heroes" becomes wholly individual. The myth of the Horatio Alger figure who somehow does it all on his own leads precisely to the solipsistic, narcissistic, isolationist culture of greed that enables the social antecedents and consequences to remain ignored. This is precisely the kernel of truth that is illuminated by Elizabeth Warren when she said:

> There is nobody in this country who got rich on his own. Nobody. You built a factory out there—good for you! But I want to be clear. You moved your goods to market on the roads the rest of us paid for. You hired workers the rest of us paid to educate. You were safe in your factory because of police forces and fire forces that the rest of us paid for. You didn't have to worry that marauding bands would come and seize everything at your factory, and hire someone to protect against this, because of the work the rest of us did. Now look, you built a factory and it turned into something terrific, or a great idea—God bless. Keep a big hunk of it. But part of the underlying social contract is you take a hunk of that and pay forward for the next kid who comes along.

12. Trish Kahle in her blog "I Can't Believe We Still Have to Protest This Shit" makes the connection between Hugo's *Les Misérables* and the inequalities and poverty of our current day, most especially as it creates, perpetuates, and exacerbates crime. " 'A Reckoning to Be Reckoned': Les Miserables in the Age of the New Jim Crow and Occupy Wall Street," December 25, 2012, http://stillhavetoprotest.wordpress. com/tag/new-jim-crow/.

13. As of the publication of this chapter, not a single CEO or Wall St banker has been brought to trial or prosecuted for illegal activities that might have led to the recession that began in 2008.

14. The most egregious example being the infamous disparity in sentencing for possession of crack cocaine versus powder cocaine (implemented by the Anti-Drug Abuse Act of 1986), which for decades treated 100 gram of crack cocaine (cheaper, "lower class," assumed to lead to more violent actions, an assumption that obviously proved to be false) as the equivalent of 1 gram of powder cocaine (more expensive, an "upper-class" drug of choice). Possession of crack cocaine also mandated a minimum sentence of five years. The Fair Sentencing Act of 2010 lessened this disparity, but only to a ratio of 18:1. The law is also not retroactive, so if you were sentenced with crack in July 2010, the month before the legislation was enacted, then sorry, you're s.o.l.

15. Simon Critchley, *Infinitely Demanding: Ethics of Commitment, Politics of Resistance* (New York: Verso, 2007), 38–68. To be clear, Critchley is making an ethical argument for subjectivity, namely that the ethical subject arises in and through the relationship

of a subject to a demand, an infinite demand that the subject must approve despite the fact that it is infinite and impossible to achieve. At this point, I want to use the term "dividual" to make a more ontological claim, namely that the subject, the "individual," is only "unified" in and through the fact of its disunity, that its many-sided and fractured nature is in fact what makes it whole. We cannot understand the "I" without also understanding the social, economic, political, cultural, and historical elements that surround and interpenetrate the "I." Nonetheless, the ethical dimension of the "dividual" emphasized by Critchley remains important. If it is our encounter with the face of the Other that is the irritation that begins the emergence of the pearl that is an "I," it is perhaps the face of the criminal—that figure who is perceived to be most heteronomous—that is the conditions of possibility of ethics as such. If we do not face the face of the criminal—whether that "criminal" be the face of the poor, the mad, the cruel, the outlaw—then we shirk our responsibility to the infinite demand, and hence *cannot* become ethical subjects and ethical societies at all.

16. And often, some of the great "criminals" have participated in all of these categories.
17. See esp. *Genealogy of Morals*. Revenge, beyond any immediate response, is act of weakness, cowardice, and resentment.
18. Carl Schmitt, *The Concept of the Political* (Chicago: University of Chicago Press, 1996), 27.
19. With the deep interconnectedness of our world, can we speak of enemies anymore? The War against Terror is presented as a war against an enemy wholly outside, and although the radical religious ideologies are factors, so too is the poverty and alienation created by the global economic order implemented, often forcefully, by the ruling countries and their neo-liberal policies. Are Osama bin Laden, al-Qaeda, the Taliban enemies or criminals? Is he a monster from another world, or a tumor that emerged from our own body?
20. Patricia Cohen, "Genetic Basis for Crime: A New Look," *New York Times*, June 19, 2011.
21. John Dewey, *Human Nature and Conduct* (New York: Dover, 2011), 18.
22. Although the justice system does make the distinction between "crimes of passion" versus premeditated crimes.
23. G. W. F. Hegel, "Who Thinks Abstractly?," in Walter Kaufmann, *Hegel: Texts and Commentary* (New York: Anchor, 1966), 113–18.

CHAPTER 15

Consuming Class: Identity and Power through the Commodification of Bourgeois Culture, Celebrity, and Glamour

Raúl Rubio

Introduction: Class in the Current Era of Consumption

George Packer's article "Celebrating Inequality" (*The New York Times*, May 20, 2013) traces the eras of modern celebrity in order to point to its tricky relationship with class. His proposal intends to debunk the long-established positive relational link between celebrity and an individual's pursuit of the American dream, by exposing the recent branding and commodification of celebrity personae. He claims that obsession by the masses with celebrity culture stunts the aspirations of ordinary people when they adhere to and yield to the commoditized aspects of celebrity cultures. Inequality, he concludes, is what maintains the celebrity status quo. This piece acknowledges and agrees with the validity of Packer's platform but entertains the need of considering the realities associated with the other side of the coin, that of defining identity through consumption and the possible identitarian consequences (including empowerment) associated with the consuming class through the admiration, adoption, and consumption of bourgeois culture, celebrity, and glamour.

The lyrics of pop songs "Glamorous" by Fergie (*The Dutchess*, 2007) and "The Fame" by Lady Gaga (*The Fame*, 2008) exemplify the proliferation of this phenomenon. Whereas Fergie's song claims that "things don't mean a thing" and intends to unpack the allusions of glamour, Lady Gaga's song admits "I can't help myself . . . I am addicted to a life of material" while she corroborates on "Doin' it for the fame."

This chapter considers the influences of popular bourgeois and celebrity cultures, fashion, and glamour on identity and empowerment, as that representative of the conscious or unconscious efforts associated with the desires of acquiring, appropriating, faking class. What is "class," given the new realities, which entail living in imaginative or artificial worlds that span global enterprise, social media, and the meanings associated with capital?

Meanwhile, how do theories associated with Deborah Stone's concept of the *polis* that consider meanings of community, social consciousness, civic responsibility, and sustainability reconceptualize class today? What is class anyway? The idea of class is therefore subject to contemporary efforts to create class-less societies, for example, in Latin America during the last decades, where although the lines between high-class, middle-class, working-class, and the consumption-empowered lower-rungs are still clearly demarked yet individuals, many who inhabit favelas and state-supported housing are nevertheless linked to the same virtual technologies as their neighbors higher up on the ladder. Is consuming "class" an act of empowerment? How is class consumed? Is the consumption of things and access to places and knowledge significant of consuming power? My premise is that in the ongoing era of consumption, class is power, consumption is power, and therefore the existent practice is that class is gained through consumption.

The methodology and fieldwork related to defining and evaluating what things signify has a long tradition in anthropological theory, yet new analytic methods within artifact-oriented anthropology are dependent on what to make of the implications brought about by the new meanings associated with material culture. In their edited book *Thinking through Things: Theorising Artefacts Ethnographically* (Routledge, 2007), Amiria Henare, Martin Holbraad, and Sari Wastell propose that "Living in places where powder is power, where costumes allow access to other planes of existence, and where legal documents may not primarily concern reason or argument, ethnographers are obliged to question the assumptions underpinning their own surprise at such things" (1). Similarly, in what can be surmised as the artificial worlds of celebrity, fashion, and glamour, class is delineated and inequality and injustice exist nevertheless. The fashion designer Karl Lagerfeld (in his documentary *The Lagerfeld Confidential*, 2007) stated, "Fashion is ephemeral, dangerous, and unfair. To do your job you must accept injustice." Meanwhile, Condé Nast's infamous *Vogue* magazine Creative Director Anna Wintour in the documentary *The September Issue* (2009) brilliantly claimed, "The 1960s was the end of the class system." This is a key consideration given that it is historically accurate in many regards, including key accomplishments in civil rights and throughout the women's liberation movement, yet particularly in fashion, it is true given the growth of the fashion enterprise beyond the range of haute couture, particularly with the expansion of mass-produced fashion for the working class. Since the late 1960s, the production and consumption of fashion encompassed a newfound egalitarian system with the availability of fashion for all. The birth and rise of more accessible labels and fakes took a toll on the old-school classist hierarchy of fashion. The practice of consuming fashion that "looked like" name brand labels has persisted since then, through and through. The proliferation of "fakes" has increased in the last decades with Louis Vuitton and Burberry imitations globalized beyond belief, manufactured in China and sold in Chinatown, New York City, or on sidewalks around the world by impromptu and illegal (and many times immigrant) traveling salespeople.

Long-established power structures and influence also play a part in the game of the conceptualization of class and its influence on consumerist cultures. Recently, in Mexico City, an apparently simple Twitter posting had a lot more to it than the bad review offered by the disgruntled consumer. As journalist Damien Cave reported in a *New York Times* article (April 30, 2013), "Bad Reviews for a Patron at an Eatery in Mexico," the disgruntled author was Andrea Benítez, the well-connected daughter of an official at the country's main consumer protection agency, who used her influence in order to try to shut down the restaurant when she was not given the table she wanted on a Friday night at the popular Mexico City restaurant Maximo Bistrot. Ms Benítez posted the following review, "Dreadful service . . . they have no manners." The response that followed, however, was surprising, given that both Ms Benítez and her father became the targets of broad criticism, particularly via a social media campaign, which condemned their abuse of power. The public's outrage led the president's office to declare a formal investigation into allegations of abuse of power. Since then, Ms Benítez has been the subject of countless postings on Twitter (*The New York Times* article at the time of its publication listed 42,000 messages) with the hashtag #LadyProfeco in order to shed light on the long-standing and systematic abuses of power committed by upper-class Mexicans in relation to their compatriots of lower strata. This case serves as an example of the new powers of social media and "net vigilantism" as labeled by Damien Cave, *The New York Times* reporter who authored the article, but also characterizes the tightrope tensions of class relations with regard to consumer culture in this era of technological egalitarianism. Particularly it points to the continued existence of class power and influence amidst the revolutionary powers brought about by virtual and digital citizenship. However, these changing structures in relation to the powers of class, consumption practices based on the desires of assuming higher levels of class, are existent and imply identitarian mobility in relation to the commodification and significance of things.

Along similar lines are the implied meanings associated with the act of "eating" (physical consumption) and class, given the well-established tradition of metaphors associated with these types of exchanges, represented as cannibalism, communion, capital (and artistic) consumption, sex, etc. Two theoretical pieces strike a chord, first a book edited by Kristen Guest titled *Eating Their Words: Cannibalism and the Boundaries of Cultural Identity* (2001), where the historical archive on the representations of cannibalism is revisited in order to propose how this metaphor serves as a focal point for not only ideological critique but also cultural exchange, particularly in relation to the boundaries of alterity and status appropriation. Another is that presented by Devin Anthony Orgeron and Marsha Gabrielle Orgeron in their article "Eating Their Words: Consuming Culture a la Chaplin and Keaton," where they argue for the consideration of the act of eating (as observed in the films of Chaplin and Keaton) as representative of meanings of "exchange" between citizens of different social standing. The analysis this scholarship offers serves as an example of the importance of reading the nuances of consumerist "acts" in how they offer insight as to the exchanges between social classes.

This piece specifically proposes to highlight the work of two prolific Latin American authors, Guadalupe Loaeza (Mexico) and Boris Izaguirre (Venezuela), who have featured the consumption of class in their journalistic and literary work. The consideration here not only is related to the thematic topic of their writing but also is of the material success of the sales of their books based on these topics. Both Loaeza and Izaguirre have sold very well in the Spanish-language literary market and also in their respective home countries, Mexico and Spain (although Izaguirre is Venezuelan), having multiple editions published of each of their books. Therefore, the act of consuming "class" in respect to the two authors is twofold, primarily as a literary thematic topic long established in relation to the key work by these two authors, but also secondly, yet equally significant, as an important key consideration related to the amplified study of material culture in the realm of print culture, most saliently, in this case, print sales.

I Buy, Therefore I Exist: Guadalupe Loaeza and the Mexican Bourgeoisie

Guadalupe Loaeza's prolific journalism and chronicles of contemporary culture have appeared since 1982, at that time particularly in response to the Mexican economic crisis of the 1980s but later in the 1990s as a reflection upon the effects of the North American Free Trade Agreement (NAFTA) on Mexican society. Since 2008 she is a writer for Mexico City's *Reforma* newspaper, where she continues to write cultural commentary. Her work most saliently features an ironic and humorous take on the excesses of the Mexican bourgeoisie amid the crisis and serves as a vehicle to bring to light the huge gap in class differences in contemporary Mexico. Her journalistic and literary writing has been the subject of extensive scholarly work (Schaeffer-Rodríguez, 1991; Peña, 1994; VanLoan Aguilar, 1997; Shaw, 1999; Meacham, 2000; Long, 2001, among others), and her readership popularity is most impressive, as scholar Julia VanLoan Aguilar reports: "in a country where the sale of books is characteristically low and second editions uncommon, collections of Loaeza's newspaper articles and fictional caricatures are now in the 3rd, 5th, or 7th edition" (154). Perhaps this is related to the texture and weight of her subjects, the Mexican privileged elite and the upper middle class, which are presented via exaggerated and ferociously funny sketches exhibiting their social milieu, including their taste for imported things, foreign fashion, and leisure activities. Loaeza's narratives are typically firsthand and told in a self-deprecating format, which crafts satire by juxtaposing the two Mexicos—the underclass and the privileged—while in a tongue-in-cheek format then identifying and sympathizing with the latter (VanLoan Aguilar, 154).

However, as Claudia Schaeffer-Rodríguez (1991) argues, the topic of bourgeois culture in Loaeza's writing is equally a vehicle for the exploration of other important issues that are below the surface, gender and class differences, for example. On the plateau of access, two examples are necessary to consider. The first relates to the fact that in the past Mexican women had not been afforded access to publishing. Therefore, the practice of writing and publishing testimonial journalism was a key opportunity for women, as it was in the case of Loaeza at the beginning of her career. In terms of class differences, on the other hand, the availability of this type of journalism, via a mass-produced daily newspaper, allowed a more accessible means of reading, specifically for citizens of lower means. On the other hand, in terms of thematic content on class, Loaeza's writing style allowed entry into the internal thought process of the bourgeois citizen via the use of the reflective monologue. Loaeza also includes conversations with working class citizens, based on interviews with street sellers and windshield wipers, in order to offer their perspectives on the economic crisis. Race is also featured as an important topic related to class structures given customary racist attitudes held by some upper-class citizens toward the indigenous heritage of their compatriots. By exposing the inner thoughts of these citizens (mostly the bourgeoisie), her intent is to peel away the inner workings of the voiceless subject. Cherie Meacham has argued, when explaining Loaeza's writing as an offshoot of the Latin American testimonial writing of the 1970s and 1980s, that

> the use of the first-person voice of the witness who also claims to represent the experience of the broader community, the abundance of referential data, a chronological sequence, the orality of the discourse, the presence of a mediator who facilitates the expression of a voiceless subject, and the revisionary intent of the text (111)

is essential to the formulation of Loaeza's use of the "testimonial genre as a vehicle of resistance within the neoliberal agenda of Latin America" (112). I would add that the most pronounced revisionary aspect in relation to Loaeza's writing is that of the reversal of consciousness in reference to class structures, class struggles, and classist humor.

In the novel *Compro, luego existo* (1995), loosely translated as "I Buy, Therefore I Am," Loaeza exemplifies Mexican national identity through its obsession with consumerism. Within the historical context of Mexico's participation in NAFTA, Loaeza directly targets North American influence in the consumerist practices that overwhelmed the Mexican market with an increase in North American products and companies during the 1990s, when the agreement was being negotiated and went into effect. The novel is divided into six chapters and most chapter titles are geographically labeled with consumer-driven locations such as Miami, New York, and Mexico City. The cast of primary characters is from well-to-do families, some from old money and others newly rich. The narrative serves as a parody of Mexican middle and upper classes, demonstrating their consumer habits and the realities associated with these practices, including its effects on identity. Scholar Mary K. Long has categorized these habits as the love of gadgets; the addiction to shopping; and the vulnerability to advertising (122). Most importantly, Long proposes, "the novel expands the definition of 'consumer product' to other aspects of life, for example, history, love, high culture, and social status" (122). Within this proposed framework, I would argue two things are evident: first, the importance of reconsidering identity (national and beyond), and second, the clear evolution of the definitions of material and consumerist cultures in the eras of modernity and postmodernity. In other words, national identity or class identity is no longer directly related simply to national or to traditional class structures but rather to the newly defined structure of what a person owns or what a person can purchase. Class is newly defined through consumption.

It can be posited that Loaeza's readership popularity and sales success may be related to her portrayal of "class consuming class" given the excessive focus on the effects of consumerist practices in Mexico. The aforementioned metaphorical allusion of "eating" or "consuming" in the case of Loaeza's writing can be considered a representation of the appropriation or adoption (purchase) of "things" as class-related signifiers. The practice of citizens "eating themselves" (consuming signifiers pertaining to our own class) and/or "eating others" (consuming signifiers pertaining to an Other (higher) class) can be respectively considered representative of self-consumption or the consumption of difference. Loaeza's finely orchestrated narrative caricature of these characterizations and exchanges is fabricated based on the realities of the nation and keenly crafted with the use of humor, satire, and parody. Equally significant is her use of the guise of journalism or commentary in order to penetrate both high-culture consumers and the wide range of newspaper readership.

Death by Glamour: Identity, Class, and Consumer Culture in Boris Izaguirre

The book *Morir de Glamour: Crónica de la sociedad de fin de siglo* (2000) by Venezuelan author and Madrid resident Boris Izaguirre gives shape and weight to the study of the elusive notion of glamour. His narrative discourse situates "glamour" as a marker of class and taste, as an element prone to the variables of contemporary mass media, and as a vehicle dependent on globalized market culture. At first it may seem that Izaguirre is pointing to the uniqueness and individuality associated with exhibitions of glamour, specifically notions of the exotic. However, what Izaguirre so lavishly proposes in his dissertation is the opposite. Glamour has become a merchandised composite of imitation, a validation of the establishment, a predisposed regimen following prescribed formulas. Through the proposals instituted by Izaguirre in his text, it is established that glamour should not be completely held under the guise of an act of subjectivity and alterity, which has been tradition. Rather the appropriation of glamour is more along the lines of an adherence to or acceptance of collective and popular tastes, and a vehicle through which class structures are validated and social mobility is negotiated. As such, glamour has traditionally offered a sense of individuality of style, an illusion to subjectivity based on personal tastes. To a certain extent these characteristics exist, yet at the root there is an underlying adoption of that which is established as class based, merchandised and consumed with that intention.

The notion of glamour is evasive, yet its attractive nuanced meanings hold value and capital for its creators and adherents. It is widely accepted that the concept of glamour serves as a vehicle through which identity is performed and chronicled. Here, however, I propose as to whether glamour may be representative of collectivity rather than individuality. In his critically compelling history of the notion of glamour, British scholar Stephen Gundle broaches a plethora of topics, but perhaps the most resounding to my approach here is his underlying proposal as to the promise of glamour "as ultimately an illusion that can only ever be partially fulfilled" (which appears succinctly summarized on the inside flap of the monograph). Although Gundle is referring to the potentially negative effects of getting caught in the trappings of glamour, more concretely, illusions of grandeur, or the "pretend or make believe" (4) elements associated with the adherence to glamour, his focus resonates with the thesis I propose on another underlying illusion associated with glamour, that pertaining to the potentially unfulfilled aspirations to individuality. Izaguirre's chronicle best exemplifies these ideas by the use of the metaphor of death purposefully inserted into the title of the text, *Morir de glamour*. Rather than utilizing the verb "to live" (*vivir*), Izaguirre engages in the use of "to die" (*morir*) in order to point to the death of individuality when adopting (or living by) that established as glamorous.

Two philosophy scholars, Carol S. Gould and Kathleen Higgins, broach the meanings of glamour in consideration of opposing positions, both relevant to my proposal. Gould argues for the distinction between two types of glamour, "true" and "false" (238), related to various individual and cultural qualities. Her position privileges the "first person" (237) and an individual's "own symbolic field" (245) arriving at her thesis, which proposes that "glamour radiates from the complexity of an individual human character as a particular expression of imagination and personal uniqueness" (246). On the other hand, Higgins speaks of glamour as a "mirage" (105), focused on the spectator's purview, mostly a "third-person" (242) perspective, according to Gould. Both theoretical paradigms are marvelously detailed and related to philosophical postulates and theories related to the study of aesthetics. The views held by both Gould and Higgins highlight topics brought up in my reading of Izaguirre's narrative, namely the discussion as to the nature of an individual's adherence to glamour as an act (or performance) of ascribing to a cultural collective and a class hierarchy rather than an act of subjective expression. Gould's and Higgins's theories engage in two realms: first, one related to my own estimation of an individual's adherence to either collective or subjective options; and second, the important consideration of the "third-person" interpretative aspect of glamour when it is either received, invented, or understood by those (others) that are meant to grasp those "symbolic expressions" (Danto, 16–18).

I consider it important to first situate the narrative discourse of Boris Izaguirre himself, given that his referential testimony in the chronicle establishes a particular personal perspective. This perspective textures the narrative with a personal subjectivity that reformulates many of the already well-established conceptual notions he dissects. His perspective can be defined as that of a gay (or queer) Venezuelan that has adapted to a European or Spanish outlook. Equally he may be a great observer of society in general, as the subtitle of the book claims, yet his outlook may be nuanced by his own transatlantic crossing, and, of course, his educational and social upbringing. He and his narrative become an actual performative within the text, a staging of a particular moment in time that chronicles a certain frame of reference. He inserts himself into contemporary Spanish societal spaces and engages in the use of a particular voice.

Among Izaguirre's examples of objects within the framework of glamorous material cultures appear dinnerware, china, etc., all markers of individuality and social position. He claims that by observing a person's book library and video collection, as well as tableware, an established milieu of information is revealed. Arjun Appadurai's theoretical constructs of consumption as pleasure and ephemerality also support this idea of the performance of the body as a consumer subject. As such, one can deduce that Izaguirre's intent of chronicling acts of consumerism serve as testimonial of performing the collective essence of glamour.

Can glamour be symbolic of both subjectivity and collectivity? It can. The answer is dependent on the individual in question and the case at hand. Glamour can be symbolic of subjectivity and alterity when considered a vehicle by which difference is situated, disseminated, appropriated, understood, and accepted. However, Boris Izaguirre, in this text, argued for a different approach, proposing glamour as a collective and class-based culture, one that follows patterns of merchandising, or "marketing" as he calls it (76), an acceptance of mass culture, rather than true individual style (77).

Conclusion

Both Guadalupe Loaeza and Boris Izaguirre establish a framework for the reading of class through consumption-based approaches. Loaeza proposes to portray and dismantle the mystique of bourgeois culture while pointing to their class-based consumer practices, while providing insight into the huge gap of differences within the Mexican class structure. Her writing also presents the obsessive consumerist culture across the range of classes, permitting a consideration of the idea that acts of consumption are a means to establish identitarian mobility and acquire higher class. Izaguirre, on the other hand, establishes that although glamour may be empowering in an identitarian format, living the glamorous life is nevertheless an act of buying into collectivist, established, and class-oriented structures. Both authors utilize humor, satire, and parody in order to entertain and support their claims, and although their primary vehicles are print cultures, they engage in the analysis of the future amidst the changing world of virtual environments. Their writing textures the converging and conflicted realities of the worlds that inhabit class, at times imaginative and artificial, yet worlds that include ever-present poverty, the effects of global enterprise, and the changing meanings of the concepts of citizenship and nationality.

Works Cited

Appadurai, Arjun. *Modernity at Large*, Minneapolis: University of Minnesota Press, 1996.

Cave, Damien. "Bad Reviews for a Patron at an Eatery in Mexico." *The New York Times*. Tuesday, April 30, 2013.

Danto, Arthur. "Symbolic Expressions and the Self." In *Self As Image in Asian Theory and Practice*, Eds R. T. Ames and T. P. Kasulis. New York: State University of New York Press, 1998, pp. 13–26.

Gould, Carol S. "Glamour As an Aesthetic Property of Persons." *Journal of Aesthetics and Art Criticism*, Vol. 63, No. 3, 2005, pp. 237–247.

Guest, Kristen. *Eating Their Words: Cannibalism and the Boundaries of Cultural Identity*. Albany: State University of New York Press, 2001.

Gundle, Stephen. *Glamour: A History*. New York: Oxford University Press, 2008.

Henare, Amiria, Holbraad, Martin, and Wastell, Sari. *Thinking through Things: Theorising Artefacts Ethnographically*. New York: Routledge, 2007.

Higgins, Kathleen. "Beauty and Its Kitsch Competitors." In *Beauty Matters*, Ed. P. Brand. Indianapolis: University of Indiana Press, 2000, pp. 87–111.

Izaguirre, Boris. *Morir de Glamour: Crónica de la sociedad de fin de siglo*. Madrid: Editorial Espasa Calpe, 2000.

Loaeza, Guadalupe. *Compro, luego existo* (13th Edition). Mexico City: Alianza Editorial, 1994.

Long, Mary K. "Consumer Society and National Identity in the Work of Salvador Novo and Guadalupe Loaeza." *Chasqui: revista de literatura latinoamericana*, Vol. 30, No. 2, 2001, pp. 116–126.

Meacham, Cherie. "A Woman's Testimony on the Mexican Crisis: Guadalupe Loaeza's *Sin Cuenta*." *Letras Femeninas*, Vol. 26, No. 1–2, 2000, pp. 111–124.

Orgeron, Devin Anthony, and Orgeron, Marsha Gabrielle. "Eating Their Words: Consuming Class a la Chaplin and Keaton." *College Literature*, Vol. 28, No. 1, Winter 2001, pp. 84–104.

Packer, George. "Celebrating Inequality." *The New York Times*. Monday, May 20, 2013.

Peña, Luis H. "La nostalgia del milagro: Guadalupe Loaeza y la crónica como crítica cultural." *Letras Femeninas*, Número Extraordinario Conmemorativo 1974–1994, 1994, pp. 131–137.

Schaefer-Rodríguez, Claudia. "Embedded Agendas: The Literary Journalism of Cristina Pacheco and Guadalupe Loaeza." *Latin American Literary Review*, Vol. 19, No. 38, 1991, pp. 62–76.

Shaw, Deborah. "The Literary Journalism of Guadalupe Loaeza and Cristina Pacheco." *Bulletin of Latin American Research*, Vol. 18, No. 4, 1999, pp. 437–450.

Stone, Deborah. *Policy Paradox: The Art of Political Decision Making*. New York: W. W. Norton & Company, 2011.

VanLoan Aguilar, Julia. "Humor in Crisis: Guadalupe Loaeza's Caricature of the Mexican Bourgeoisie." *Journal of American Culture*, Vol. 20, No. 2, Summer 1997, pp. 153–158.

CHAPTER 16

When Prosperity Is Built on Poverty, There Can Be No Foundation for Peace, as Poverty and Peace Don't Stand Hand in Hand

Pepi Leistyna

Susan and I were walking through Siem Reap, Cambodia, two summers ago and it was oppressively hot and humid outside. The city center has a pristine, lively section of bars, restaurants, and hotels (with air conditioning, cooled-water swimming pools surrounded by fruit tress, and state-of-the-art bathrooms), which have recently been built to cater to tourists visiting the ancient temples—the remnants of a civilization in its former glory. But most of the society, as captured in a photo I took of a large neighborhood along the river that runs right through the metropolitan area, lives in abject poverty with no public utilities such as running water, sewage systems, electricity, or adequate ways to dispose of rubbish. International pressure keeps Cambodia from implementing environmental protections so that corporations can come in and exploit the cheap labor and natural resources without any reprisals as they try and tap the developing tourist and textile industry. The only places where the banks of the Siem Reap River get cleaned are in the consolidated tourist areas of the city. Susan and I have witnessed poverty like this all around the world, and my trip to India, the planet's most populated democracy, was the most traumatizing as the extreme poverty and human indifference in a country of 1.241 billion people is on a scale that is devastating beyond belief to any caring soul in search of reason, hope, and peace. Gandhi would be appalled that the old empire he sacrificed his life to displace has been replaced with new feudal lords.

While I wanted my photo of this neighborhood to capture the grim poverty and polluted waterway full of garbage and toxins—the actual image looks like a crumpled threadbare piece of paper hastily discarded on the ground—I also wanted the more vibrant colors to emphasize that, like the man in the center of the photo behind the post looking as if he's holding up his rickety home, there is life here—living and breathing people who are sweet, hardworking, family oriented, giving, and forgiving—as well as to accentuate the trees and the green grass which symbolize that life and light is trying to break through the gloom and misery. Impoverished and oppressed people of this earth don't need pity; they need social justice, and we all need to join hands and collectively realize substantive social change and the peace and prosperity that it will bring.

My original plan with this photo was to juxtapose the scene with a picture of the home of a local billionaire who lives in a small town next to ours on the South Shore of Boston. The gorgeous brick, Georgian Revival mansion is 20,000 square feet with 45 rooms and I wanted to place a photo of it on top of this one of homes in Cambodia to expose the gross inequities that exist in the world, to point out the dire global instability that this causes with the heavy weight of the bricks pushing down on the weathered stilts below, and to explain the inextricable relationship that these two apparently disparate and distant places have with each other.

The Roy family lives on this beautiful 9.4 acre estate known as "The Oaks," which was previously owned by nineteenth-century actor Lawrence Barrett, followed by Clarence Barron who made his mountain of money from owning the Dow Jones, the *Wall Street Journal*, and *Barron's* magazine, and then by the Yankee Oil & Gas Company—which sold the home to the Roys. The property, which has welcomed such esteemed guests as Frank Sinatra and Bob Hope, is tightly guarded by security and is surrounded by a massive brick and wrought iron fence with a huge front gate that is locked at all times and has ominous spikes sticking into the sky to deter uninvited outsiders from even thinking about entering the private grounds. It has perfectly kempt gardens with children laughing and roaming freely around the wonderful lush green grass, towering old-growth trees, rolling bushes, and endless flowers that flow past the pool, the tennis courts, and the three guest homes, and down to the placid harbor waters, where the family's giant yacht is sleeping next to their private dock that looks over to the local yacht club. The Roys own most of this picturesque harbor, including the Atlantica and Olde Salt House restaurants, the Cohasset Harbor Inn, and the Mill River Marina. But it's your lucky day, as this immaculate home is up for sale and is all yours if you've got a mere $55 million in your pocket to spare.

Peter Roy, cofounder, along with his brother Stephen, of Intercontinental Energy Corp., currently owns the estate. These two men and their sister, Ellen Roy Herzfelder, are the inheritors of the family fortune left by their father John Reime Roy, who made his colossal wealth with his company that built smoke stacks and power plants internationally. Ellen was part owner of this family business and she is the former State Secretary of Environmental Affairs under then Governor of Massachusetts, and GOP presidential hopeful and multimillionaire, Mitt Romney. Now there's an oxymoron: where you put a smoke stack profiteer in office as the protector of the environment . . . Romney, a shrewd businessman himself whose companies have profited handsomely by outsourcing US jobs to impoverished nations where he can exploit the poor even more, is worth an estimated $250 million. It's not exactly clear how much he is actually worth as Romney has a history of hiding his money in offshore tax-free shelters. It's ridiculous how his presidential campaign commercials painted an image of Mitt as just a regular guy.

Social class is all around us in the United States, and yet we are taught not to see or talk about it as the subject is taboo in a society that abides by a deeply engrained belief that this is the land of opportunity and individualism—all part of the myth of the American dream and meritocracy where you get what you deserve. The Roy estate is in Cohasset, an extremely wealthy New England town that borders Scituate on one side and Hull on the other. As a side note about this area that is just four towns up from Plymouth where the Pilgrims arrived on the *Mayflower* in 1620 looking for freedom: "Scituate" and "Cohasset" are Native American words, but the Natives were violently pushed out a long time ago by European settlers. If you want to see an Indian, you need to go to the Plimoth Plantation, where there are people dressed up like Pilgrims and Natives in what is a living museum, or attend one of the Thanksgiving parades in town where indigenous people show up each year to protest. Anyway, if you look at the names of these three towns' public school sports teams, the social class of each community is evident: Cohasset's high school team is known as the "Skippers." Scituate is a middle-class town that is often called the "Irish Riviera" as it was the place where the Irish from Boston came to build small vacation homes to get away from the noise of the city once they could afford to do so after a protracted, collective struggle to move from being discriminated against as "white niggers"—as the old signs said, "No dogs or Irish allowed" or "Irish need not apply"—into the middle class. But the rise in property value pushed out much of the local commercial fishing community as well as West African, Cape Verdean, working class community that farmed the land and labored on the whaling vessels and in the local cranberry bogs. Scituate is home of the "Sailors," and Hull, which is a working class town, has the "Pirates." And of course, the Roy kids don't go to public schools, but rather attend exclusive private institutions. The name of their sports team is surely something like the "Owners of cargo ships and luxury liners, with the US naval fleet at our beckon call." The Roys aren't the rich of this nation—they are the superelite: a handful of people who control much of the world's wealth. In the United States, these rare elites are not even included in the government census, as they are considered "statistically insignificant"; well, if you ask me, any small number of people that controls that much power is the most statistically significant of all!

According to Forbes, as of 2012, the list of billionaires in the world includes 1,226 individuals—an all-time high. The combined wealth of the people on this list is $4.6 trillion, which is up 2 percent from last year's tally. The average worth of a member of this esteemed club is $3.7 billion. There are now billionaires from 58 countries, including India, China, Brazil, Peru, Morocco, Georgia, and Mexico. But the United States tops the list as having the most members, with

425—12 newcomers were added from last year. And Russia and China are in a mad dash for second place: Russia has 96, and China 95.

The World Institute for Development Economics Research at United Nations University revealed that 40 percent of the world's wealth and assets is owned by 1 percent of the planet's population; 85 percent is under the control of the richest 10 percent. On the other hand, 50 percent of the people at the bottom of the global economic hierarchy own a meager 1 percent. When it comes to household assets around the world, the richest 2 percent control more than half of that as well.

By 2007, 40 percent of the value of all transnational corporations was in the controlling hands of 147 companies, and most of these operate out of the countries of the G-20—the G-20 is a group of 20 finance ministers and central bank governors of the world's largest and controlling economies. Their annual meeting this past year was held in Mexico, which should come as no surprise given that the current richest man on the planet resides there—one Carlos Slim Helu, whose net worth is 74 billion dollars: money made through his international corporation, Telmex, which is a massive global telecom business. I guess he's not so "slim" after all.

Since the birth of the nation-state, progressive and radical social activists have challenged governments and private power in an effort to ensure that the interests of the world's people and cultures are recognized and realized. However, what has dramatically changed over the years has been the power of the private sector. These days—with 51 of the planet's 100 largest economies being corporations— new global justice movements are vehemently working against the hegemony of corporate rule. Many contemporary global activists are eyeing and responding to the undemocratic governing bodies that have achieved supranational power— institutions like the G-20, the International Monetary Fund (IMF), the World Bank, and the World Trade Organization (WTO). Globalization is currently under the tight control of these governing bodies and their institutions, policies, and multilateral trade agreements that dramatically affect international affairs on every level. However, even among these power elites, there is a hierarchy in place; for example, according to Reuters, OPEC nations in 2008 had an estimated profit growth of 1,251 trillion dollars.

Meanwhile, the United Nations Commission on Human Rights has estimated that there are over 1.6 billion people on this planet who are without adequate housing, let alone the billions of people that don't have access to enough food or clean water, health care, public media, and real public education that nurtures the necessary presence of mind to be able to read the world around us and recognize our personal and collaborative political power to change it. Instead of supporting these basic human rights, global governing bodies spend trillions of dollars annually on military expenses, mostly to protect the interests of the superrich— with what are truly "soldiers of fortune." In the name of security and defending democracy, the United States alone spends over 1 trillion dollars each year to maintain its military force—more than the entire world combined. As journalist Thomas Friedman argued,

The hidden hand of the market will never work without a hidden fist. McDonald's cannot flourish without McDonnell Douglas, the designer of the F-15. And the hidden fist that keeps the world safe for Silicon Valley's technologies to flourish is called the US Army, Air Force, Navy and Marine Corps.

Of the over 7 billion people that currently live on this planet, almost half of them are under the age of 25. Half the world's 1.6 billion poor are children. Victims of the residue of a brutal history of colonial rule, sustained racism, and patriarchy, and now the imperial grasp of draconian neo-liberal mandates of deregulation and structural adjustment imposed by organizations like the WTO, the IMF, the G-20, the World Bank, and such, 11 million of these kids under the age of 5 die annually because of malnutrition; dirty water, or a lack thereof; disease; and inadequate housing. Hundreds of millions of youth around the world are not getting a formal education and millions are trapped in the sex trade and sweatshops or caught up in military conflicts where they are often forced into fighting someone else's economic and ideological wars.

The global economy, a product of the last 500 years of invention and imperialist expansion, has ushered in a new phase of social and economic relations made possible by innovative technologies, transnational institutions, and the logic of neo-liberalism. Neo-liberalism is a political and economic ideology that works to largely eliminate governments' power to influence the affairs of private business. In the name of privatization, the goal is to maximize profits—with the vague promise that wealth and prosperity will eventually make their way down to the rest of society. In order to achieve this end, standards such as a minimum wage, job security, health insurance, collective bargaining rights, and environmental protections are replaced with an unrestricted flow of production and trade, and a global division of labor. Regardless of the neo-liberal promise of peace and prosperity for all, it's more than obvious that the structural dimensions of social class within this economic logic remain profoundly in place. In fact, economic conditions for millions of people in the United States and for billions of people worldwide are worsening as a direct result of privatization, deregulation, and restructuring, as well as by the ways in which elite private powers have been successful in using the state to protect corporate interests and dismantle many of the rights and protections achieved locally and internationally by grassroots activists, organized labor, and social democracies. It is important to take a critical look at the blatant contradiction embodied in downsizing government while expanding its powers to limit democratic participation, that is, how government is being used by corporate powers to establish discriminatory and exclusionary policies and practices that work to maintain today's gross inequities.

The US private sector has been the spearhead pushing forward this neo-liberal global assault, which gained prominence in domestic politics and practice in 1979 when Nobel Prize winner Milton Friedman of the Chicago School of Economics and the Reagan administration ushered it in. Friedman is known for stating that "A society that puts equality before freedom will get neither. A society that puts freedom before equality will get a high degree of both." Indicative of his worldview and reasoning behind why the private sector should be allowed to do as it pleases, is the following quote: "That's the way the free market system distributes the fruits of economic progress among all people. That's the secret of the enormous improvements in the conditions of the working person over the past two centuries." It seems that the economist was not reading history: even Adam Smith, the father of capitalism, knew that private power left to its own devices in a so-called "free-market system" would morph into pure tyranny in no time; meanwhile, it is everyday people who have organized to fight against private and public despots that has brought about better living and labor conditions—not the unregulated market that causes the need to act up in the first place. Government in and of itself, if it is truly one "of, by, and for the people," is not bad; it's when it has been co-opted by private corporate interests who abide by the ideology of "profit over people" that the trouble really begins. The United States is the self-proclaimed apogee of democracy and opportunity and has invaded 152 countries since 1850 to impose its values and beliefs, all in the name of peace and freedom. However, since the early colonial years, the United States has largely been built on the interests of the elite business classes, which needless to say have benefited greatly from a long-standing denial of the structural realities of a class system. Their efforts may have been revolutionary against the King of England, but they were reactionary in creating an equitable society for the working class, women, indigenous populations, and enslaved Africans.

In what is now a postindustrial society—one that relies on service industries, knowledge production, and information technologies rather than industrial manufacturing to generate capital—the average wage in the United States is 29% less than it was during the days of industry. Class mobility in this country is more restricted than ever before, unless of course the direction is downward. Within these economic shifts, the middle class is imploding into the working class, which in turn is imploding into the working poor, who are literally relegated to life on the streets or in our already overpopulated prisons that have more than 2 million people locked up. Census data show that the gap between the rich and the poor in this country is the widest it's been since the government started collecting information in 1947. In fact, with the exception of Russia and Mexico, the United States has the most unequal distribution of wealth and income in the industrialized world.

As the general population of the United States is falling more and more into debt, the top 1% currently controls more than 42% of the nation's wealth and assets. The top 20% of Americans owns 85% of the country's wealth. The Congressional Budget Office revealed that between 1979 and 2007, as tax policies favored the rich (from 1997 to 2007, the top income earners enjoyed a 37% tax reduction and an income increase of 392%), 90% of Americans in the lower-economic bracket saw their income drop while the earnings at the top grew on average by 275%. Even in the recession that began in 2007, which along with the subprime mortgage scandal crushed the income and retirement savings of the average American by over 36%, the top 1% saw their wealth hold its ground. While the nation's median household income is around $50,000, the average earnings for the top 0.1% of the population is over $3 million. Only 34% of US households make more than $65,000 per year.

There are currently 27 million people in the United States who are unemployed or underemployed, and 37 million people who rely on food stamps—another social program that conservatives portray as a "handout" that should be eliminated. Funny how they call the trillions of dollars of corporate welfare given to them—which come in the form of tax breaks, subsidies, and taxpayer assistance when they fail or commit financial crimes—"stimulus packages" or "bailouts," but any money allocated to the poor, single moms, and the elderly or for retirements, unemployment compensation, health-care benefits, housing assistance, Medicare, Social Security, and food stamps is called "handouts," as if they are undeserved rather than a basic human right in any viable democracy.

If the economic model demonstrated by the United States is such a virtue, why is the nation currently 14.7 trillion dollars in debt? That's more debt than the entire "Third World" combined. This isn't the deficit—that's about trade imbalances; this is money that we've borrowed from countries like China that holds 1.7 trillion dollars of our national debt, which you, your children, and their children will have to pay back. It's ironic that the US government has been borrowing so much money from China—we take loans from this communist country so we can buy more of their cheaply produced goods. Talk about a contradictory and risky symbiosis. Meanwhile, didn't we bomb Cambodia, among many other countries, in order to fight communism? Of course, there is nothing communist about China as it's a lethal mix of state capitalism and totalitarianism—a system of elites that exploits labor on a grand scale, has no free press or Internet access, and has a harsh record of human rights abuses and crushing democratic movements. This makes for a perfect unrestrained environment for international firms to outsource production to and build factories and make profits through the roof. Susan and I witnessed the endless factories and dormitories that were built for the workers to live in just outside of Beijing. Meanwhile, China ignores its own poor people, 200 million of which are currently homeless. These downtrodden often live in villages where local corporations dump toxic waste and mountains of the world's discarded junk such as old computers, to be picked through for salvageable parts that can be resold. The cancer rates in such places are astronomical.

Funny how I can't drink Cuban rum or smoke their world-renowned cigars, or travel there, as we have had draconian economic sanctions on this tiny island-country to our south for decades since it was liberated by Castro from the clutches of US economic control in which American businessmen not only usurped the natural resources, but also turned the place into a playground for the wealthy to vacation, gamble, booze it up, do drugs, and exploit the women, while the locals lived in poverty and servitude. We even orchestrated an invasion of this impoverished nation during the Kennedy administration, but it has somehow miraculously survived all these years and has a better health-care and public education system and a far superior history of feeding the poor than we do. The worst human rights abuses in Cuba happen in the US-operated detention center at Guantanamo Bay. But China, a country controlled by a vicious despotic regime with a long track record of human rights abuses, including in occupied Tibet, is an open door for Americans. The Chinese have even been accepted as members of all the global financial governing bodies, including the World Bank, the G-20, the WTO, and the IMF; I guess that allowing a KFC (Kentucky Fried Chicken), the fastest-growing franchise in a country of over a billion people, to be just across the street from the Forbidden City and Tiananmen Square where the democratic movement was brutally crushed in 1989 makes it all fine and dandy. We've fought wars and economy-busting cold wars against communism for over six decades, and have done so at the expense of the working class in our own country who have died in such wars and found little economic support after the tax cuts needed to fund these military campaigns. And we've destroyed little democratic countries in this crusade and replaced their elected leadership with dictators, such as in Central and South America, Africa, and Southeast Asia. It's sad how after all the violence that went into the US invasion of Vietnam, where millions of people were killed supposedly because it was a communist country, that while the tiny nation is still communist in rhetoric, and, like China, while the government is hard on its own people, it is welcoming to corporations like Nike and Disney that can make shoes and kid's pajamas for 13 cents a pair. Susan and I witnessed plenty of US corporations profiting from the abuses of power of the government in Vietnam. And everyday the United States borrows more money from China to keep our failed economic system and military endeavors afloat. The United States is paying $500 million a day to cover the interest on our colossal debt. The bottom 90% of the US population has the burden of covering 73% of all national debt—and this includes the trillions owed for student loans and credit cards that have mob-like interest rates. As a result, most households have no savings, which makes many breadwinners a paycheck away from being in the streets, as one homeless man told me recently.

A total of 46.2 million people in the United States live in poverty—up 2.6 million from just last year, and the number is expected to continue to grow. Poverty in this country is the highest it's been since the census began collecting information 52 years ago. There are over 3.9 million people who are homeless in the United States (a number projected to increase 5% each year) and 39% of them are children, and over 200,000 are military veterans. There are more than 300,000 foreclosure filings a month in this country. Over 60 million Americans lack health insurance, many of them being children. This statistic is particularly interesting given that top health-care executives have an average annual income, not including stock options, of over 12 million dollars. And yet in this post-Katrina world—where federal malfeasance unwittingly exposed the raw poverty that exists in this country—support to those in great need is being cut by Washington DC elites in the name of hard economic times, the sequester being the most recent egregious example of this draconian rule; meanwhile, the stock market is the highest its ever been.

Over 80% of all political contributions in the United States now come from less than 1% of the population, and these wealthy constituencies certainly don't want their candidates to voice any real concern for everyday people. In addition to these monies, over 2 billion dollars a year are spent by K Street lobbyists. Organizations like the National Association of Manufacturers, the Business Roundtable, the National Alliance of Business, the US Chamber of Commerce, and the American Business Conference have lobbied heavily in Washington. And this consolidation of power and exposure also has the support of the private media system in the United States, which is dominated by corporations.

It is important to recognize that there is a powerful synergy among corporations, government, and media that puts a real stranglehold on the free flow of information in society and thus on democracy. Private corporate interests in the United States, which benefit from the domestic and global exploitation of labor, largely control mainstream media. Meanwhile, any public media like NPR and PBS have been enduring severe budget cuts by the feds, especially since the Reagan years, so they have been forced to rely on private funding to maintain operations. As this financial backing comes with ideological strings attached, it is no wonder that public broadcasting, as research has shown, has become less critical and more conservative in its content and tone.

Keep in mind that five massive transnational corporations largely control television in the United States: Time Warner, Disney, News Corporation, General Electric/Comcast, and Viacom. It's important for the public to understand the political economy of the mass media—that is, the ownership and regulation of this industry. While the airwaves belong to the public and are controlled by the FCC—the Federal Communications Commission—the organization has been co-opted by big-business interests and pushed into passing legislation that makes way for a handful of massive conglomerates to further monopolize the use of public airwaves and the Internet and thus to be able to more effectively circulate, legitimate, and reproduce a vision of the world that suits their ideological and economic needs. Gaining momentum during the Clinton administration's support for the Telecommunications Act of 1996, which helped usher in deregulation, and propelled forward by more recent republican efforts, this wave of power consolidation has reached such an extreme state that it now will allow a single corporate body of the likes of Rupert Murdoch's News Corp./Fox to own and operate an unprecedented combination of newspaper companies and radio and television stations within a single media market. Murdoch, the king of media moguls and one of the richest men on the planet, is not shy about his antilabor stance or other conservative views, and while Fox News describes itself as "fair and balanced," it is anything but. What's particularly frightening in this respect is that the United States, a country that prides itself as the apogee of democracy, with a constitution that protects freedom of speech and a free press, continues to move toward the Orwellian dystopia of a single organization controlling the circulation of information in society, like it is in China. It should thus come as no surprise that most of the public policy debates in this country, and ultimately their outcomes, remain in the hands of Wall Street and the Fortune 500.

The nation's wealthiest 10% own almost 90% of all stocks and mutual funds. While one in two Americans don't own stocks, the ubiquitous numbers from Wall

Street imply that the market will help those in need and the country as a whole. And of course, Republicans are working diligently to get rid of the capital gains taxes on such investments. Meanwhile, the poor and the rich are depicted as living on polar edges of society's economic spectrum that is predominantly occupied by a grand middle class—a romanticized category that works to obfuscate the realities of class conflict. According to the mythology, the rich, the middle and working classes, and the poor are not dialectically intertwined given that their class position is a product of individual efforts.

Even the current tax system in this country is structured to perpetuate the class hierarchy. The IRS revealed that workers making $60,000 pay a larger share of their income in Social Security, Medicare, and taxes than a family making $25 million. In need of government protections and tax relief, workers in the United States don't get the red carpet treatment that corporations do. 60% of US companies pay no income tax. By 2003, corporate tax revenues fell to only 7.4% of federal tax receipts. Either corporations find creative ways to keep from paying the 35% tax on profits that they are legally compelled to cover, or the government actually gives them a tax break claiming that it will help them compete and it will produce jobs. Even Exxon/Mobil (which during a time of war and during a disruption of oil production as a result of hurricanes turned its largest quarterly profits ever) was handed a generous tax break from the federal government. In fact, the government has provided billions of dollars in tax cuts to the rich, and corporations are allocated over $125 billion a year in subsidies and other forms of welfare—and this doesn't include the trillions that are funneled through the Pentagon's military industrial complex. In 2010, Obama's budget for the Department of Defense rose to $533.8 billion. If you include monies allocated to overseas contingency operations—efforts to protect US citizens, allies, and business interests from terrorists—and add in the costs for defense-related expenditures outside of the Department of Defense, then the Pentagon budget is over 1 trillion dollars. And this does not include the enormous costs for conducting military operations in the Middle East. The United States has already spent well over 1 trillion dollars on wars in Iraq and Afghanistan.

And let's not forget the billions of taxpayer dollars allocated to private US corporations to rebuild these two nations in terms of security, schools, hospitals, water supply systems, sewage treatment plants, electricity, oil production, housing, and transportation systems. So American taxpayers shell out big money to destroy a country and then they pay again to have it rebuilt. The funneling of public monies into private pockets is astounding, and war profiteering of this sort, not democracy and security, was one of the major incentives for invading and indiscriminately bombing Iraq and Afghanistan in the first place. What we have witnessed is the most contracted-out war in the history of the United States; during the height of the conflict, there were actually more private contractors in Afghanistan than there are US military personnel. Instead of granting contracts to local firms and state-owned operations, where it was estimated that it would have saved US taxpayers 90% of the costs of reconstruction in Iraq and Afghanistan and would have been much more efficient, no-bid contracts were handed out to large US corporations like Halliburton and Bechtel—so much for competition. Here the government socializes risk and investment while the public pays for research and product development, and construction costs but privatizes the profits.

The largest military contractor in Iraq—or I should say the biggest war profiteer in the form of crony capitalism—is the mega corporation, Halliburton. Halliburton is the king of the hill when it comes to oil field services in North America and it has made record profits over the past ten years. While the corporation had to pay almost $5 billion in asbestos settlement claims here at home, it was nonetheless handed a $16 billion deal to support US military operations to rebuild Iraq. Dick Cheney, one of the principal masterminds behind the war in Iraq, ran Halliburton from 1995 to 2000 and still had investments in the company while serving as Vice President of the United States—no conflict of interest or insider government favoritism there. With little State Department oversight of the use of US tax dollars and Iraqi assets intended to cover the enormous costs of reconstruction, there has been a great deal of pilfering and corruption. Congress-appointed Commission on Wartime Contracting described the Coalition Provisional Authority's loss of billions of dollars through corruption, theft, and shoddy, incomplete, over-budget, or abandoned projects as "fiscal hemorrhaging." Because of public outrage over the general situation in Iraq, the US government has been pressured to legally pursue contractors that have pocketed US tax dollars. Philip Bloom was convicted of charges of defrauding the Coalition Provisional Authority, and Bechtel, the largest engineering company in the United States—the nation's fifth-largest privately owned company—lost what was left of its 2.85 billion dollar government contract due to total mismanagement. Meanwhile, the Iraqi government has no means of recovering Iraqi assets that were stolen by US contractors: in part because civilian contractors were granted immunity from all Iraqi jurisdictions by the Coalition Provisional Authority. Halliburton has been investigated by the Securities and Exchange Commission and the Justice Department for questionable dealings in Iraq, Kuwait, and Nigeria, and its subsidiary Kellogg, Brown & Root (KBR) has been under investigation for gross mismanagement of billions of dollars of fuel, housing, and food contracts for supporting the US military on the ground in Iraq. It is well documented that KBR, on a regular basis, gave contaminated water and spoiled food to US troops. KBR is also well known for tax evasion. Of the more than 21,000 employees working for the company in Iraq, 10,500 of them were US citizens. But, regardless of their country of origin, all of these people were listed as employees of the Cayman Islands. In this way, KBR avoided paying hundreds of millions of dollars in US federal Medicare and Social Security taxes. The two companies in the Caymans that employed these workers were shells with no offices or phone numbers—a fact that the US Defense Department was well aware of since 2004. Halliburton ditched its scandal-laden subsidiary and is planning to move its CEO and corporate headquarters from Houston to Dubai in the United Arab Emirates. This not only allows it to continue to avoid paying US taxes, but the move also shields it from prosecution for corruption.

And then there's the mountain of taxpayer money that has been allocated to private security contractors like Blackwater, CACI, and Titan/L-3, all of which have been involved in the torture, abuse, and murder of Iraqi and Afghan citizens. However, these private military contractors either have not been prosecuted as they too have been granted immunity by the US government, or they have been found not guilty in US courts. You'd think that the idea of outsourcing security would be an insane proposition in this age of terrorist plots, but then again, the Bush II administration actually wanted to contract the United Arab Emirates–based company Dubai Ports World to provide port security here in the United States, even when two of the 9/11 hijackers were from the UAE. Private powers will surely push for more military exploits in the name of democracy and fighting terrorism, when these efforts are really motivated by a desire to sell weapons, control access to dwindling raw materials like oil and natural gas, garner reconstruction contracts, and crush movements of everyday people who are struggling to take control of their nations' resources and political future—in Iran, for example. Neo-liberals and neo-conservatives rely on the paradox of the stability of instability by encouraging global conflicts, pitting countries against each other, and arming them. If military intervention were really about fostering democracy then why are almost all of our so-called allies in the Middle East dictatorships, including Kuwait, which was supposedly liberated by US troops in 1991, and Saudi Arabia, where 15 of the 9/11 hijackers originated from? At the same time, using military might to secure and control access to resources contradicts the undying faith in free-market principles that neo-liberals preach.

The massive budget cuts for war and other corporate exploits and the frantic deficit spending that guts domestic funding for education, health care, and other public needs and services are part of a conscious neo-liberal effort to wipe out any money to sustain the public sector, paving the way for privatization.

In the United States, economic hardship falls particularly hard on racial minorities, women, migrant workers, and immigrants. Beyond the concocted hype about the usurping of quality employment by "outsiders," the job opportunities that are intended for this sector of the labor force consist of low-wage manual labor: cleaning crews, food service, the monotony of the assembly line, and farm work. This kind of racism is common around the world, even in Cambodia, where the extremely poor areas, like the neighborhood in my photo, are often inhabited by people who are marked as ethnic or outsiders.

It's insane that conservatives want to spend billions of dollars to build a wall between the United States and Mexico to stop illegal immigration when this money could be used to help the poor and working class on both sides of the border so there'd be no need for the mass exodus of labor. Of course, in the name of homeland security, this proposed project would line the pockets of big business with construction, service, technology, and border patrol training facility contracts. Instead of using federal agencies like the Army Corps of Engineers, the National Guard, and Border Patrol to take on these projects, guess who was solicited for these contracts under the Bush II administration—Halliburton and Bechtel—along with Lockheed Martin, Boeing, and Raytheon. Meanwhile, the push has been to train and hire private security forces, not civil servants from the US Citizenship and Immigration Services, to police the wall. So while taxpayers will fund a project to keep Mexican labor out of the United States, it's perfectly fine for the United States to exploit workers on the other side of the border with tax-free zones and free trade policies such as NAFTA—the North American Free Trade Agreement—and CAFTA—the Central American Free Trade Agreement. Meanwhile, these are not really "agreements" as the public never weighed in on the passing of such policies, and it's not free trade—if it were, then people like the elderly who have to sacrifice heat and food in order to pay for their medications would be able to get goods and services for less than they cost here in the United States. Medications are 80% cheaper in Canada and Mexico than they are here at home, but for US citizens they are illegal to purchase outside of the country. If it were an issue of public safety, then the government would put restrictions on the profit-driven health-care, pharmaceutical, and insurance companies in the United States. As research has shown, free trade initiatives just increase US corporations' ability to exploit other countries, enrich a few wealthy business elites and government authorities in those countries, while increasing poverty among the general population. Just look at the unregulated maquiladora sweatshops on the US/Mexican border. Largely owned by US businesses, they produce goods just across the boarder dirt cheap in terms of labor costs and tax relief, so they can be sold for less money back here in the States. This has weakened the Mexican economy and increased poverty in that country, which needless to say feeds into the mass migration of workers across the border.

Until just recently, Saipan, which is part of the US Commonwealth of the Northern Mariana Islands, didn't have to abide by US immigration and labor laws, and its garment industry produces clothes for such corporations as Walmart, Levi Strauss, Tommy Hilfiger USA, Gap, Old Navy, Calvin Klein, and Liz Claiborne. These clothes have a "made in the USA" tag on them and were being shipped to the States, tariff free and quota free. Saipan was a horrific model of indentured servitude in which young women, some in their early teens, were recruited from the Philippines and China to work in the garment industry. They had to agree to pay exorbitant recruiting and entrance fees, and did so with the understanding that they were going to work in the United States. Instead, they were shipped off to Saipan labor camps, where they worked for endless hours with limited days off and for half of the US minimum wage. Getting ahead financially and buying one's freedom was virtually impossible. There were reports of forced prostitution, sex acts, and abortion. Although legislation to reform the labor laws in Saipan was in the works in the US Senate—of course only after the horror story was leaked and prompted public outrage—Republican, Christian moralist Tom DeLay, the House Majority Leader from 2003 to 2005, worked behind the scenes to block this legislation from being passed. Lobbyist, now convicted criminal, Jack Abramoff illegally paid for Delay to go to the US commonwealth on a golf vacation. While there, DeLay addressed a gathering of sweatshop owners and stated with exuberance: "You are a shining light for what is happening to the

Republican Party, and you represent everything that is good about what we are trying to do in America and leading the world in the free-market system." This is a guy who was forced to step down from public office because of allegations in 2005 of breaking campaign finance laws in Texas and for money laundering. Instead of reminding the public of these criminal acts, for which he finally got some prison time, the media celebrated DeLay's participation on the popular reality TV show *Dancing with the Stars*.

With capital flight and global outsourcing, both blue-collar and white-collar jobs have been and continue to be exported by US corporations to nations that pay below a living wage and that ensure that workers have no protection under labor unions and laws that regulate corporate interests and power. By cheap labor, we're often talking between 13.5 and 36 cents an hour; we're also talking about a total disregard for child-labor laws and environmental protections. And as the Federal Reserve has noted, these jobs won't be returning even if there is a major upswing in the US economy. The working class is also blamed for not being educated enough to compete in a global economy, and yet we have one of the most educated workforces in the world regardless of the fact that our public education system is highly class based. It's also ironic that given this claim of lack of education, corporations are moving to "Third World" countries, where there is enormous illiteracy, in order to find cheap labor. In this era of globalization with enormous job loss, outsourcing, and offshoring, corporations need a scapegoat for their avarice activity, and the scapegoat is the working class who is not working hard enough, and yet, since 1975, productivity in the United States is way up (163%), who's asking for too much money, and yet wages are stagnant and profits are through the roof (758%). The last two administrations, one Republican and the other Democrat, have bragged about creating new jobs for Americans, but they have failed to inform the public that these are overwhelmingly part-time, adjunct, minimum-wage positions that provide no pension, union protection, or health-care benefits. Part-time, temp, or subcontracted jobs currently make up 30% of the workforce and this number is rapidly increasing. Meanwhile CEO pay, bonuses, and golden parachute retirements are on the rise. In 2009, just after stimulus money was allocated to corporations by the federal government, 20 billion dollars were handed out in bonuses to corporate executives, even in companies that were failing under such poor leadership. The ratio of average CEO pay in the United States to the average blue-collar pay in the same corporation is 470 to 1.

It's amazing how quickly we forget about decades of corruption here at home that have undermined our economy, such as the savings and loan scandal of the 1980s and 1990s, the Enron, Tyco, Adelphia, and WorldCom scandals in the early 2000s, and the most recent but rapidly fading crimes of the nation's major insurance and financial institutions—with the subprime mortgage and credit default swaps debacle that led to the loss of $1.75 trillion and the collapse and subsequent government bailout of those institutions; let alone the manipulation and falsification of intelligence by the Bush II administration that was used to justify the invasion of Iraq after the tragedy of 9/11. While these crimes—in which the taxpayer ends up holding the bag—are quickly erased from public memory, the stigma of organized labor is deeply planted and ever present.

As the largest employer in the country, Walmart is the perfect place to look at corporate greed and how class warfare works. As of last year, Christy Walton is worth 26.5 billion dollars and the family corporation is among the top 20 economies in the world—and its wealth and power are growing as supercenters open every 38 hours somewhere on this planet. Walmart employs 1 out of every 115 workers in the United States at an average full-time pay of around $17,000. The Walton family, which is adamantly antiunion, now makes 771,287 times more than the median US income. And yet, regardless of its colossal wealth, and its image of "looking out for America and Americans," this is a corporation that has a health-care plan that covers fewer than half its workers—46% of employees' kids rely on socialized medicine in the form of Medicaid—hence the reason that Walmart is a big supporter of Obamacare, as it loves when the government can get it off the hook of paying for its labor healthcare costs. It is an organization that has been investigated for profiting from employees' deaths, invading workers' privacy, anti-competitive activities, violating child labor laws, using undocumented immigrants to clean stores, gender and racial discrimination, and denying workers overtime pay and the right to organize. Walmart was recently found guilty in a class action suit filed by 116,000 workers who were denied the basic right to have lunch breaks; as a result, the corporation was forced to pay $172 million in fines. And that's just in the United States. Walmart is one of the richest corporations in the world that is infamous for making nothing in the United States, other than lots of money. While its ads and charity campaigns are wrapped in American flags, most of its products are made in China and in poor countries like Haiti and Vietnam, and the company refuses to inform the public where these manufacturers are located and they won't allow access to human rights inspectors.

Disney is also a miserable transnational corporation that promotes a pixie dust notion of life while profiting from the subordination and exploitation of labor. Its very founder, Walt Disney, was anticommunist, anti–organized labor, and racist toward Jews and blacks—all of which is readily apparent in his animated cartoons. He also embraced fascism and was sympathetic to Nazi Germany. He was an FBI informant, and he gladly testified in front of the House Un-American Activities Committee during the McCarthy era—giving up names of people that he suspected were communists in Hollywood.

The Disney Corporation owns islands outside of US jurisdiction to dock its cruise ships in order to put the conglomerate out of reach of US tax and environmental laws and labor rights. The company hires contractors in impoverished nations like Haiti to manufacture its promotional goods for sale here in the States and internationally and they pay their sweatshop workers as little as one dollar a day. The corporation hopes that kids around the world have sweet dreams in Mickey Mouse pajamas made by the blood, sweat, and tears of the poor— perhaps even by another child somewhere off in the dark of a "Third World" sweatshop, or in LA or New York for that matter, where such illegal manufacturing abounds. It's no wonder that virtually all of Disney's fantasy stories are about monarchies and not democracies—remember, it's the "magic kingdom." The corporation celebrates the "circle of life" in the *Lion King*, in which lions naturally rule the world and the hyenas, the bad guys, speak Black English. But Disney is supposed to be excused from its racist past with its blockbuster *The Princess and the Frog*, where the star is African American. Of course, she is a frog throughout most of the movie, the prince is not black, and, while there are racist stereotypes throughout, the issue of race is never acknowledged, let alone addressed in the film. The pendant that is worn by the princess in the movie was mass produced in some global gulag and was being sold exclusively at Walmart, but it had to be recalled by Federal Consumer Safety Regulators because of dangerously high levels of cadmium—a heavy metal carcinogen that leads to brain damage in children. We better get rid of those "big government" safety regulators as they're taking all the fun out of it . . . Disney and Walmart love the fact our government has supported a colonial ideology in Haiti through economic and foreign policy initiatives that have backed oppressive regimes, allowed US occupation of the country at one point, reinforced the oppression of workers, and helped maintain its status of being the poorest nation in the Western Hemisphere where labor is easy for corporations to exploit.

As in the past when the odds were greatly against us, in order to confront the oppressive structural economic realities that so many people face in this society, we need to work to develop class consciousness and act against the tyranny of market forces and their advocates so that in the end it's not about "free trade" but rather "fair trade." Globalization is by no means a monolithic entity, and there is a radical difference between the top-down economic versions, whose proponents are looking to ensure access to cheap labor and raw materials in order to maximize their profits, and what is being referred to as "globalization from below"—transnational networking to democratize global technologies, environmental resources, and media, information, and financial systems. As a response to the injustices produced by neo-liberal and neo-conservative versions of globalization, vast multi-interest coalitions have sprung up that include human rights, environmental, faith, indigenous, student, and consumer groups, along with trade unionists, feminists, anti-sweatshop activists, and antiwar protestors—as witnessed in the recent global "Occupy Movement." But the elite classes work diligently to suppress political and cultural dissent and the dissemination of substantive information to the public. As a response, these activist networks are using the Internet strategically to mobilize cross-border solidarity and are demonstrating how a critical and inclusive public can effectively wage a counteroffensive against abusive states and international actors and institutions. It is important to note that technology is not the problem: it is how it is installed and used, and who controls such power, and who has access to it that determine whether or not it's ethical. The Internet was funded by public monies in the United States and should be used by the general public to create dialogue, get informed, and mobilize. Confronting oppression from economic, political, technological, and cultural fronts, transnational collective action is helping people understand and fight to transform how these forces currently organize societies.

Contemporary cultural activists and social movements are adjusting to shifting power relations that are the result of globalization. What makes the global justice movement different from the nongovernmental organizations (NGOs) and international nongovernmental organizations (INGOs) that have been at the forefront of global civil society for decades is that these more traditional organizations are often less radical in their theories and strategies and focus much of their energy on working with existing governments and institutions for policy reforms. Many members of the global justice movement, on the other hand, often distrust established institutions and nation-states and generally prefer to transform, rather than merely reform, the system. The neo-liberal use of global civil society as a charity, nonprofit, voluntary "third sector" responsible for replacing the welfare state is viewed with contempt. Many advocates of the global justice movement, who are trying to democratize globalization rather than pave the way for neo-liberalism, often criticize NGOs/INGOs for merely tinkering with the machine, or for actually reinforcing the institutions of oppression that they claim to be challenging.

Recognizing that globalization is a crisis in representative democracy, global justice activists have been experimenting with novel approaches for bringing together multiple identities, issues, and alliances—doing so, in part, to balance the demands of political unity and cultural diversity. The goal has been to search out new forms of democratic and revolutionary identification, to recognize differences and commonalities within struggles for economic and social justice, and to work through dialogue and action to sustain what has become a "movement of many movements." Such solidarity, as opposed to isolated localized efforts, may present the only way of combating transnational corporations that no longer need to negotiate with local labor organizations for living wages and realistic environmental protections or with area-specific human rights groups—they just go elsewhere, leaving trade restrictions, unemployment, poverty, and political chaos in their path. Former General Electric CEO Jack Welch captured this corporate contempt for labor and human life when he spoke to a group of business elites assembled for a meeting on "World Lessons in Leadership," and stated, "Ideally, you'd have every plant you own on a barge." In other words, make sure you can access cheap labor at any time and that you can easily abandon the community that you are currently exploiting.

In November of 2006, I was invited to speak and screen my documentary on social class at the Three Screens Film Festival as part of the India Social Forum (ISF) in New Delhi. The ISF is the India chapter of the World Social Forum, where global civil society comes together annually to work for justice and peace. While there, we were driving on the outskirts of the city on the way to Agra to see the Taj Mahal, a magnificent structure that is surrounded by the worst poverty that I've ever seen: old women collecting dung in the streets to use for cooking, mangled bodies crawling up to you on their hands and feet reaching out to ask for change, children wandering about alone, and garbage everywhere. Along the way to Agra, there are endless factories that line both sides of the road that are walled in with barbwire and protected by men armed with machine guns. While watching as the downtrodden entered the gates on both sides of the highway as far as the eye could see, my car was waved over by three men in uniform with INSAS assault rifles, who emerged from a ditch next to the road. I figured from their guns that they were government forces, but was never sure. They waved their weapons in our faces and wanted to know what I was doing with the camera and they demanded money. I'm not sure what my Sikh driver said, but I was grateful that he somehow got them to crawl back into the weeds where they belong. My Sikh friend was a sweet impoverished man who could speak very little English, but we had the best conversations nonetheless. When he brought me to my hotel in Agra, I invited him in for lunch, a request that he initially refused, but I insisted. He cried at the table as he told me that he had never been in a hotel before. The Hindu staff was very cold with him and I made sure that they gave him anything he wanted and asked them, as they were hanging over the table and staring down at him in a most unfriendly and impolite manner, to leave us in peace to enjoy our meal and each other's company. Upon returning to Delhi, he brought me to his house of faith, the Gurdwara Bangla Sahib—which is the largest Sikh temple in the city. I met with the temple leadership and we spoke a great deal about globalization, US economic policies, and social injustice. They wrapped my head and kindly asked me to remove my shoes in order for us to visit the temple and pray for peace. After a long and inspiring dialogue about global inequities and ways to reconcile such problems, we took some pictures, bid farewell, and my driver dropped me off at the hotel that had been booked for me, which made me uncomfortable as it was called "The Imperial." While I didn't spend much time there, on occasion I would wander into the posh bar that was filled with international businessmen, who gathered each night to talk about their newest exploits over some expensive scotch and a cigar. I'll never forget this one man from the United States who I shared a few beers and some conversation with, as he told me with great exuberance that the poor were happy as he had seen a party of them under a plastic sheet enjoying themselves just the other night. The next day, in the extreme heat and humidity that almost made me pass out, I made my way to the forum. The area is right next to a shiny multipurpose sports arena, the Nehru Stadium, which sits beside some more of the worst poverty imaginable. I walked around these neighborhoods next to the stadium and took pictures and visited with the shy but very friendly locals who live in makeshift shacks built in dirt holes, where the few possessions they have are hanging on wobbly lines and posts. Some kids were playing in the dirt and one child in bare feet was pushing an old worn-out bike tire up the street with a stick. The juxtaposition of this child immersed in his game alongside the fancy stadium was both heartbreaking and energizing. The most inspiring part of this trip was watching these people who live in the worst possible conditions carry themselves with this amazing dignity and hope as their spirits have not been broken. I then entered the forum by going through a military gate and wandered around with my camera. The grounds of the forum were filled with military personnel with automatic rifles, and sandbag bunkers with machine guns. It was inspiring to see the plethora of movements led by people of all ages from all walks of life and from all around the world who have fearlessly mobilized against the many forms of oppression, violence, and abuse that continue to fester locally and internationally. These are sophisticated attempts to develop intra-national and international solidarity so as to build a foundation on which justice and democracy can thrive in this world—peaceful coalitions that Gandhi himself would be proud of.

I hear privileged people in the United States say all the time, when they see images of intense poverty, as in my photos of Cambodia and India, "That's why they all want to come here, to enjoy our way of life . . ." But what they either don't know about or refuse to accept is the harsh reality that while the United States has only 5% of the world's population, we consume over 25% of its natural resources, and that these vital resources that we take by corporate and/or military force from other nations—and of course exploiting the local labor to do so—are what create this apparent prosperity. The hard cold truth is that the misery of the poor of this world is in large part the very source of the prosperity that is enjoyed by those here that can afford to indulge. As Mother Teresa of Calcutta once said, "It is poverty to decide that a child must die so that you may live as you wish." Instead of being complicit in denial, the key is for us to take a stand hand in hand to stop oppression in all its forms and wherever it festers, but to never stand still in our collective struggle to realize justice, equity, and peace in the world.

(In Loving Memory of Susan Kubik—1968–2011)

CHAPTER 17

Solon the Athenian and the Origins of Class Struggle

Thomas Thorp

We are at Athens, one hundred years before the Battle of Marathon, two hundred years before the trial of Socrates, and the poet who will compose these lines:

> For to the [common] people (*dēmoi*) I gave so much power as is sufficient Neither robbing them of dignity, nor giving them too much and those who had power (*dunamin*), and were marvelously rich Even for these I contrived that they suffered no harm. I stood with a mighty shield in front of both classes.[1]

has just been declared "archon" with the authority and special powers necessary to remake the Athenian constitution.[2] Attica, the region whose center is Athens, is in crisis. The rich are getting richer while increasingly many are being impoverished and as a result are being enslaved. Solon's extraordinary appointment is a clear indication that the competing parties, including specifically the powerful and wealthy, have recognized that they are powerless to achieve any resolution to the crisis through traditional means, in part at least because the economic landscape is shifting. Population pressures have assured that all arable lands are now being farmed and still the Athenians are being forced to import grain. The lack of available lands has now forced Athenians to consider taking up a trade, a step likely to produce if not actual political disenfranchisement then something close to dishonor according to traditional standards, where political power passed through the aristocratic associations and clubs, the phratries. Finally this political economy, formerly based almost solely in agricultural production—with some of the best lands being held in common—has just begun to see the possibility of wealth through trade, and this "globalization" effect has put pressures on a traditional village-based system that had located authority in the hands of a leading family or *genos* through their control of cult practices and of public lands.

In short, while Solon's laws are usually described as reforms, it is important to note that the granting of extraordinary powers itself proves that he was being asked to deal with changes to economic conditions and political forces that were both already well under way, and were beyond the capacity of the old order (*politeia*) to manage or control. To comprehend Solon's changes to the Athenian constitution requires, first, challenging our own view of what is meant by the word "constitution" (*politeia*), and second, realizing that Solon's work pivots around the reinvention of what we now call class.

* * *

Class conflict is the term traditionally employed to describe the conditions that caused the Athenians to appoint Solon as archon with special powers.[3] And yet the problem that immediately and persistently arises when the notion of class struggle is invoked in this context is that since the time of Aristotle[4] it has proven to be nearly impossible actually to identify those "classes" whose conflict was tearing apart the Athenian polis in the first decades of the sixth century.

> [T]here was civil strife (*stasiasai*) for a long time between the nobility (*gnōrimous*) and the common people (*plēthos*). For the whole political setup (*politeia*) was oligarchic, and, in particular, the poor (*plusiois*) together with their wives and children were serfs ('*edouleuon*) of the rich.[5]

Here we have the account from Aristotle's *Constitution of the Athenians* of the conditions that lead to Solon first becoming, it says, a leader (*prostatēs*) of the people (*tou dēmou*). Who are the people, the *demoi*? Note the complexity of the overlapping categories and terms just in this passage. There are "the people" (who must at least overlap with "the many"), yet "the many" are first defined in opposition to "the nobility." The nobility in turn seem to be the rich, and then the rich are of course defined in opposition to the poor, but that does not seem to preclude the possibility of a noble who is poor. Solon himself was an example, as he was known to have been descendant of an old established family, but was by wealth only middle class.[6]

And bear in mind that to this point we are examining the words employed by the author of the *Constitution of the Athenians*. When Solon's own poetry describes his actions, the terms for these groups do not simply proliferate but they clearly begin to overlap, with, for example, the critical term "*demoi*" referring at one point to the poor and at another to the citizens.[7] In short, this nominal complexity is not an indication of the weakness of the analysis but in fact reflects the vocabulary employed by Solon himself in the poetry he wrote as he reflected upon his own actions. Perhaps what appears to be a confused and overlapping demography reflects rather the imposition of an anachronistic notion of class.

Questions regarding who exactly comprised the various classes in the dramatic political struggle that Solon resolved have been discussed since the fourth century BC and we are not going to resolve them here.[8] Instead I'd like to take a slightly different tack by shifting the discussion of class struggle initially at least away from the question of class to the matter of the struggle or conflict. The account in the *Constitution of the Athenians* says that citizens transformed into "serfs" were working the land of the rich, paying them a rent, and it says that many citizens were going into debt. Then it says that if and when they were unable to pay, then the rich would sell them into slavery: for, until the time of Solon, "loans were contracted on the person."[9] My suggestion is that were we to take up the class struggle question and radicalize it, then we might find ourselves in a position to rethink not only Solon's reforms but also a much better known version of the class struggle thesis, the version advanced by Marx and Engels. What I expect to be able to show is that our traditional understanding of class morphs inevitably into a discussion of class interests. By contrast, an examination of some of Solon's better-documented reforms should support the view that they were democratic precisely because they pushed the Athenians, all of them, the rich and the poor, the well-born and the commoners, to divorce themselves from their class interests and to constitute themselves instead as the *demoi*, as a citizen body, and thus to rule themselves democratically.

We too live in a time when "the whole political setup was oligarchical." What it means to view oneself as "a people" can perhaps, then, be reconnected to a rethinking of the Marxian tradition of class and class struggle and to an understanding of our own revolutionary position.

*   *   *

The history of all hitherto existing society is the history of class struggles (*Klassenkampfen*).[10]

For Marx, which is to say of course for Marxism, the term class is meant to seamlessly join two notions. In fact the very notion of class requires that these two notions be effectively identified as expressions of a singular truth.

1) The first is the notion that *class is a representation of the system of production*. But this first notion has to be read carefully for it harbors a double; a specter is haunting the Marxist account of class struggle.

On the one hand there is a need to identify class divisions with the roles played by capital and labor in the system of production. On this first reading the antagonism between capital (the bourgeoisie) and labor (the proletariat) in the system of production *is* the class struggle.

On the other hand, however, there is an accompanying and necessary second reading of the notion that *class is a re-presentation of the system of production*. On this second reading class cannot be simply identified with economic relations but is their re-presentation, in consciousness. That this representation "in consciousness" should be reduced to a form of identity—in other words the idea that class consciousness could be false consciousness unless the representation were identical to the conflict or struggle within the system of production that it represents—is both necessary and, of course, impossible. Both necessary and impossible since the re-presentation (in consciousness) of the conflict inherent in the economic sphere both cannot be (because it is a re-presentation) and must be (in order to be true) identified with what it would represent.[11] We will be following this moment of repressed re-presentation.

2) The second notion that has to be identified with the (already doubled) notion that class is a representation of the system of production is the notion that classes, thus determined, are inherently in conflict. The singular truth that subtends the seamless identification of these two notions is called, by Marx–Engels, simply history.[12] History *is* the history of class conflict, that is to say of the inevitable clash between the class of those who own the means of production and the class of those who must sell their labor to the class of property owners.

Now Weber was only the earliest and most effective of a long line of commentators who criticized historical materialism by pointing to other factors constituting one's class. Religious affinity, traditional forms of prestige, individual honors, along with race and gender would have to be included alongside the matter of one's position in the labor market or production process. And a Marxist theory of class can accept or reject such additions more or less indifferently just as long as these elective affinities[13] are viewed as mere adumbrations of a law-governed history of class conflict. Weber's critique of the Marxist theory of class consciousness would suggest, however, not that the range of factors defining class be expanded beyond simply one's place in the means of production, but would challenge the very foundation of the Marxist theory itself: namely the fundamental truth that history *is* the history of class conflict.

At issue, in short, is the nature of the bond between the two notions that defined the Marx–Engels thesis. If history is the history of class conflict, it is because class consciousness is properly understood as a product. A class simply is the designation of a class interest, and class interests are expressions of the relations of production at a given time. Once again we arrive at the conclusion that the conflicts inherent in capitalist production, between the interests of those who purchase and the interests of those who sell labor, are the class conflicts that constitute history. Marxism is bound to the notion of class interest.

It has been noted often enough that this theory of inevitable class conflict between the bourgeoisie (capital) and the proletariat (labor) is itself a bourgeois theory. That is, it bears all the characteristic features of a modernist, scientistic empiricism: the belief that understanding a phenomenon such as class conflict involves tracing the phenomenon back to a set of laws. Now the Marxist interest in such a theoretical move has little to do with any fetishization of modern science (though this was a weakness that afflicted Engels certainly) but is in fact the expression of a properly political imperative.

To the extent that the class conflict can be shown to be a matter of tensions inherent in a law-governed economic system, to that same extent can the analysis assert the inevitability of a revolutionary response. In other words Marxism is bound to view history as a clash of class interests (class struggle) not for theoretical but for political reasons.[14] The political imperative that drives the apparently "scientific" analysis is the need to describe a revolt against the capitalist system as a dialectical feature of that very system. This is what political philosophers call the problem of immanent critique,[15] by which they mean that either a critical transformation takes place as a result of some contradiction inherent in the system or the revolutionary transformation comes about due to some outside force, where the outside force is the insight of the critic of that system. If the critical moment that triggers reform comes from the outside, then it is declared voluntarist, meaning it lacks any force other than the rhetorical power of the critic to convince others to take action. If, on the other hand, the critical moment really is inherent in the system—so, for example, the system of production produces its own revolutionary cadre with a built-in revolutionary consciousness—then the critic is out of a job and we are forced simply to sit back and await history's own decisions.

Why then, one might well ask, bother with the notion of class consciousness at all? If the consciousness of a given class is determined by its role in the system of production and if the dialectical contradictions characterizing the system of production define the consciousness of the class (e.g., the dialectical relation between the exploitation of labor and labor's conscious awareness of and resistance against that exploitation), then why not simply cut out the recourse to consciousness altogether and adopt a positivistic account of history as a series of causes and effects?

In part because it is a full-blown assertion of historical materialism, *The German Ideology* can be read against the grain to suggest that class consciousness is not simply an, as it were, automatic dialectic inherent in the systematic relation of base to superstructure, but requires reference as well to a ruling class and its power to determine the scope of available ideas. This notion that relations of production can be "mystified" to a degree that a ruling ideology might overwhelm the effects of one's actual role in the system of production is in fact an acknowledgment that something occurs in the transition from material conditions to class consciousness. The question is whether or not Marxism is able to account for it. The determinism of the *German Ideology* and of the "mature" Marx–Engels suggests that it cannot and the reasons are primarily, again, political. But here, and as a result, the determinism of the theory of class consciousness runs squarely up against the apparent recalcitrance of history to play by the dictated rules. The proletariat did not rise up, or if they did they were wearing brown shirts. In short, the identification of that "something" connecting the consciousness of a class to the truth of its conditions, and then to a revolutionary response, became the Holy Grail of all Marxian theory even before the midpoint of the twentieth century.

All of this is well known of course. In fact in the 1980s, the last decade where Marx was still being regularly taught in most American universities, the tension described here was represented by the division between the "critical Marxists" (Horkheimer) and the so-called "scientific Marxists." But it is also worth noting, here in the twenty-first century as global-historical conditions prompt a return to Marx in both academic and activist circles, that the debate framed in those terms was never resolved but gave way instead to a novel form of critical social science (Habermas). So this might be the moment for a return to this problem, but framed differently. And that novel return would begin as we have begun here, noticing that while a long tradition has tended to treat these Marxisms as two, the recognition that consciousness of the truth does not in fact constitute the truth of consciousness is already present in the most empirical and materialist version of the theory of class consciousness.

In short, the political or "critical" Marx shares with the scientific Marx a common need to repress the difference between the economic base and its re-presentation. This repression of an unacceptable difference, like all effective repression, screens itself behind an acceptable assertion of difference. In this case, clearly, the acceptable difference is the one between the base and the superstructure (between the conflict inherent in the system of capitalist produc-tion and its public, political, or ideological expression). But both the political and the scientific versions of the story rest firmly upon the conviction that the act of representation involves the repetition in a secondary realm of the original.

The unacceptable and repressed difference is the struggle within the notion of class representation itself. But why concern ourselves with this sort of semiotic analysis? Isn't this just a theoretical observation, detached from the political strug-gle? What would be remarkable is if what is still sought by Marxism—the spark that would ignite the class struggle, raising it from a fact to an acknowledged truth and thus making it a cause of action—were to be found not in the first difference (the inherent tensions between the means of production and their revolutionary expression) but in the second (internal to the movement of representation itself). And even more remarkable but perhaps not surprising would be if that second moment of difference, in which the moment of re-presentation is purged of class interest, turned out the be the key moment in Solon's reconstitution of Attica.

To make good on that suggestion we will need a reading of Solon's reformation of the constitution that shifts our focus, first, from the *politeia* understood as a noun to its verbal sense ("constitution of"), and that shift will require, second, a regard for the *politeuma*, the citizenry or the polity. It will turn out that Solon reformed the *politeia* only in order to make possible the reformation of the *poli-teuma* for he understood the term "constitution" to refer primarily to the reform of the citizens, not in their laws.

* * *

Aristotle calls Solon a *nomothete*, a lawgiver, and he is credited with having instituted many laws governing everything from restrictions on agricultural exports (only olive oil could be exported), to the standardization of weights in the market, to the establishment of a penalty for anyone who, during a time of political crisis, refused to take sides. Despite their value to the thesis I'm advancing regarding class, a full discussion of these many laws and reforms would be too lengthy and involved, and so the argument would be well served instead if we focus only on the best documented of Solon's so-called political or constitutional reforms, his reinvention of political classification, that is, of a system of wealth-based ranking defining qualification for political office. Aristotle describes this particular element of the new constitution:

> And he arranged the constitution in the following way: he divided the people by assessment into four classes (*eis tettara telē*), as they had been divided before, five-hundred measure man (*pentakosiomedimnōn*), horseman (*hippea*), teamster (*zeugitēn*), and laborer (*thēta*) and he distributed the political offices . . . assigning each office to the several classes in proportion to the amount of their assessment; while those rated in the Laborer class he admitted to the membership in the assembly and law-courts alone. Any man has to be rated as a Five-hundred-measure man the produce from whose estate was five hundred dry and liquid measures jointly, and at the cavalry rate those who made three hundred . . . And men had to be rated in the Teamster class who made two-hundred measures, wet and dry together; while the rest were rated in the Laborer class, being admitted to no office.[16]

Now the term that gets translated here as "class" (he divided the people, by assessment, into four classes) is *telē*, which shares a root with the familiar word *telos*, end or completion, and which shares this unusual meaning (class) with the verb *telein*, meaning to be rated, as attested by the same Athenian practice we are discussing. This old term, which Solon picks up and reorients, probably means class in the sense that, like a telos, it sums you up. Your class, *telē*, is the sum of who you are. This is what Aristotle means when he says of this novel constitutional change introduced by Solon "as they had been divided before": that is, the terms of classification had been used before Solon, with only the political inclusion of the Thetes, the Laborer class, being novel to Solon's laws. In other words, the people of Attica had long been divided into four tribes (*teleō*), and now Solon was repeating that same division, only with a difference. And it is that difference within the same that we need to unpack if we are to recognize the power of Solon's conception of "class." The standard interpretation places the emphasis on the granting of limited political franchise to the previously disenfranchised Thetes. And this reading would be more or less in line with the Marxist thesis that discerns in history the struggle of class interests.

These four classes clearly are a straightforward ranking according to agricultural wealth (dry or wet means any combination of grain, wine, or oil) but we should resist too quickly seeing them as the apportionment of political power on the basis of class. In fact, Solon's reform has the opposite effect to reinforcing class interest, and only partly due to the radical inclusion of the poor. Solon undercut the power of the wealthy by most of his other political reforms. He cancelled debts, freed citizens from debt slavery, and even brought back to Attica citizens who had been sold. He outlawed debt slavery, Aristotle says, making "the people (*dēmon*) free both at the time and for the future by prohibiting loans secured on the person,"[17] and, most critically democratic in Aristotle's view, he granted to each citizen the power to bring a suit in court on behalf of any other injured party.[18]

If it can be argued that Solon has radically altered the prior system of political classification, it is because what is properly democratic in these reforms is not the expansion of the existing system through the addition of an additional "class" but, rather, the banishment of class from the political sphere. The argument would be that the principle common to all of Solon's reforms, whether viewed as economic or political reforms, can be seen here in the fact that the Solonian classification system effectively altered the meaning of qualification for office.[19] Indeed, that was probably the entire purpose behind the classification, not the creation of classes (these already existed of course) nor the effort to offer some offsetting benefits to the aristocracy, splitting the difference as it were between the rich and the poor, but the transfer of the question of qualification for political office from the Areopagus to a public and neutral determination.

Prior to Solon it had been the right of Areopagus, the traditional aristocratic council, made up of prior archons, to pronounce finally upon the qualification of any candidate for office.[20] Note that in this case, and unlike with the matter of initiating lawsuits and appealing rulings of the archons, Solon's new law did not amount to taking the power from the Areopagus and handing it over to the people, but consisted rather in taking it out of the hands of any party, the many or the few, the wealthy or the poor, the well-born or the commoners, and installing it, rather, precisely nowhere. Instead of a determination by one party or another, Solon's classification system establishes a neutral standard. It does not appear to be neutral to us, since it is pegged to wealth, but it is pegged to land-based wealth precisely to banish class interest from the political sphere. The reform has to be understood in the specific context of the change it instituted, and that change, again, was to establish a public and, relative to the specific prior history of Athens, a neutral measure for public office. Anyone who attains a given measure of production is qualified to serve. This determination does not merely break the control of the aristocracy over the determination of political qualification; it alters fundamentally what the term "qualification" means. Indeed, this neutralization of the meaning of qualification for political office is in fact the very invention of the idea of political office, since prior to Solon a qualification always entailed a reference to *genos*, to clan or phratry. The idea of qualification through accomplishment rather than heredity or class affiliation did not spring from Solon's head but was probably viewed by him as a return to an earlier healthier tradition, a view that finds some support in a politological reading of Homeric epic poetry.[21] The idea about the creation of a no-where place, "*es meson*," in the middle of the polis, and the suggestion that it is the key to comprehending the relation of class to democracy will perhaps seem a little less far fetched if the same general logic can be shown to be at work in Solon's other reforms.

And the connection is quite simple to establish because the same fundamental gesture that explains the political reforms is at work simultaneously in the so-called economic and land reforms. If the heart of the "political" reforms is the creation of a neutral ground to which the established political powers-that-be, the aristocracy, not only had access but had privileged access by virtue of their wealth, but to which any other individual too might have access, depending solely on his neutral qualification as measured by his net worth, then what we have is an instance of the re-presentation of class as traditionally understood, a re-presentation of class that just happens to cause the withdrawal of the erstwhile principle of class. The established phratries or corporations had exercised their political control primarily through two mechanisms, their control of the duties of religious cult and their control of corporate or common lands. In other words, the same aristocratic families whose membership in the phratries gave them political authority in the villages of Attica that comprised the Athenian polis were also the priests, and they passed on their control of both common lands and cult to their sons and family friends.[22] In short, the same logic of aristocratic authority that was undercut by Solon's neutralization of political qualification was overthrown in Solon's most famous reform, the so-called "throwing off of debts" (the *seisachtheia*) that was celebrated in Attic villages for centuries after, and involved the throwing off of both public and private debt.[23] In the same way Solon relieves the burden of unjust debt by revoking the power of the landed aristocracy to demand security for loan "on the person."[24] Notice that Solon does not outlaw slavery but only the power of the traditional aristocracy to declare a citizen a slave, that is, to permit private economic interests to impose upon and alter a citizen's political being. The constitution, *politeia*, is, it seems less a collection of laws, than it is the *politeuma*, the citizen body.

Solon's objective, in a word, was to identify the class basis of civil strife but then to show that the solution to civil strife was not the erasure of class divisions but rather their banishment from the political sphere. Thus do we resolve the apparent confusion of overlapping "classes"; thus do we resolve the vexing question of the imposition of class-based qualifications for political office; and thus do we discover a way out of the Marxian dilemma of material-historical determinism and the formation of consciousness. It is not necessary to shut down the moment of re-presentation through the idealized straitjacket that is historical materialism. Private property and capital can be consistent with human dignity and economic liberty just so long as corporate interests—and every other economic interest group—are banished from the site of political self-representation.[25]

* * *

Solon knows that while the polis comprises classes, it is the very purpose of the *politeuma* (the citizens constituted as citizens) and thus of the constitution (*politeia*) to create a sphere in which those same individuals, all of them members of various overlapping classes, can nevertheless act "as if" they were citizens. Here we encounter the political significance of the repressed difference internal to representation itself. The people become a *politeuma* (citizenry) only through an act of self-representation and what this means is that the moment of the "as if" is the properly political and revolutionary moment sought by Marxism. The difference within the moment of representation divorces political representation from the epistemic or scientific sense of the word whereby the representation is true if it repeats the base facts without difference. The difference within the moment of representation is the moment of the "as if," which moment casts the citizen into an active engagement with the economic reality but which moment of engagement takes him beyond his economic interests. This imaginary stance—what Castoriadis calls the social imaginary—places the citizen outside of the temporal order that governs his economic (from *oikos*, household) life and places him within this artificial sphere. Two things happen here: the citizen is formed, not by the causal forces that determine her as an economic being, defining her as a mere effect of her class position; rather, the citizen is formed "as such." Free by virtue of being artificially unconditioned and thus free to consider what is best not for her class and her economic interest but for the polis, it is this act of imaginary self-representation (not the erasure of class differences) that *is* democracy.

Solon did not "split the difference" between the interests of the rich and the poor, and to frame the matter thus is to miss the point in its entirety. What Solon did was to prohibit both the rich and the poor from allowing their interests to define the political-civic sphere, and in doing so he invented the notion of a democratic constitution. Not a set of laws, though those were his tools, but a space of artificial freedom in which alone political action is possible. What Solon clearly understood was that the revolutionary reforms required to return justice to the polis would have their effect not in the administration of the laws but in the capacity of the polity for self-representation. And this means, finally, the revolution would have to occur in "each one."[26] Democracy is the self-representation of the self-interested beings we are "as if" we were political beings. The goal cannot be to become beings without class interests but to act as if we might be. And the reason that this apophantic self-representation is so critical to the definition of democracy is that democracy is not one form of constitution among others, but is the condition itself of that act of impossible but necessary self-representation.

Notes

1. Solon's words are preserved, when they are, only because they were cited by ancient scholars, whose works were then cited and preserved. The definitive compilation is M. L. West's *Iambi et Elegi Graeci* (Oxford: Oxford University Press, revised edition, 1992), and West's numbers are now standard. This passage is *Solon 5. 5–6*. West, of course, does not translate the passages. An excellent study of those surviving poems and fragments, a study attuned to the political question of class and conflict and its resolution, is John Lewis, *Solon the Thinker: Political Thought in Ancient Athens* (London: Duckworth, 2006). I've relied on Lewis's study both for his political

insights and especially for his sensitive translations. I have also regularly consulted, and will occasionally be citing, Solon's poetry from the Loeb edition: *Greek Elegiac Poetry*, edited and translated by Douglas E. Gerber (Cambridge: Harvard University Press, 1999). In nearly every case I have altered the translations I cite and, occasionally, especially in the case of citations from Aristotle, the translations are my own.

2. Scholars differ as to whether Solon's laws and reforms should be associated with his appointment as Archon in 594 BC or with a second special appointment perhaps 20 years later. For the purpose of this discussion, it does not matter.

3. It is safe to say that what we know about Solon comes from two basic sources: Aristotle's *The Constitution of the Athenians*, and the chapter on Solon in Plutarch's *Parallel Lives*. In addition, however, the field of comparative or interdisciplinary archeology has provided over the past several decades considerable information and occasional insight regarding the political significance of land-use and agrarian practices as well as burial practices and cult. In my view, still the most insightful deployment of the former is Philip Book Manville, *The Origins of Citizenship in Ancient Athens* (Princeton, NJ: Princeton University Press, 1997).

4. Whether authored by Aristotle or at his direction, the account of Solon's archonship in the *Constitution of Athens* is our best source, if only because it was written about 200 years after the events by Athenians who still saw themselves as living in a political system, and had at hand some documentation that could claim a historical continuity with Solon.

5. Aristotle, *Constitution of Athens and Related Texts*, translated by Kurt von Fritz and Ernst Kapp (New York: Hafner Press, 1974): 69.

6. Ibid., 23

7. On *demoi* as "masses," see Solon's poetry cited in *Greek Elegiac Poetry*, edited and translated by Douglas Gerber (Cambridge, MA: Harvard University Press, 1961): 120; on *demoi* as citizens, see Gerber, *Greek Elegiac Poetry*, 112.

8. Two recent and expansive studies of Solon in English are Elizabeth Irwin, *Solon and Early Greek Poetry: The Politics of Exhortation* (Cambridge: Cambridge University Press, 2005), and the study by John Lewis (*Solon the Thinker*).

9. Aristotle, *Constitution of the Athenians*, 21.

10. Karl Marx and Friedrich Engels, *Manifesto of the Communist Party*, the English edition of 1888, edited by Friedrich Engels, in Robert C. Tucker, ed., *The Marx Engels Reader* (New York: Norton, 1978): 473.

11. An epistemologist would protest that validity does not require that the representation of X be "identical" with X. Rather they simply have to match up. Of course this viciously begs the question. In order to constitute a valid match the representation must be different from what it would represent. In the political sphere, where representation is not merely a theoretical game, that difference cannot be a matter of indifference but in fact constitutes the political space itself.

12. "The history of all hitherto existing society is the history of class struggles . . . Freeman and slave, patrician and plebeian, lord and serf, guild-master and journeyman, in a word, oppressor and oppressed, stood in constant opposition to one another, carried on an uninterrupted, now hidden, now open fight, a fight that each time ended, either in a revolutionary reconstruction of society at large, or in the common ruin of the contending classes . . . The modern bourgeois society that has sprouted from the ruins of feudal society has not done away with class antagonisms. It has but established new classes, new conditions of oppression, new forms of struggle in place

of the old ones. Our epoch, the epoch of the bourgeoisie, possesses, however, this distinctive feature: it has simplified class antagonisms. Society as a whole is more and more splitting up into two great hostile camps, into two great classes directly facing each other: Bourgeoisie and Proletariat." Marx and Engels, *The Communist Manifesto*, in Tucker, *The Marx Engels Reader*, 473–74.

13. The term "elective affinities" in the context of a critique of economic determinism is properly attributed to Weber in *The Protestant Ethic and the Spirit of Capitalism* (1905) but Weber purposefully borrowed the term from a novel by Goethe, *Die Wahlverwandtschaften*, in which Goethe proposes to describe the laws governing love and romance *as if* they were a series of chemical reactions.

14. Study carefully the differences between *The Economic and Philosophic Manuscripts of 1844* and *The German Ideology* of 1846 and you will see the nuanced critiques of Hegel and Feuerbach giving way to a full-throated campaign rhetoric.

15. Dick Howard, *The Politics of Critique* (Minneapolis: University of Minnesota Press, 1988).

16. Aristotle, *Constitution of the Athenians*, 27.

17. Ibid., 23.

18. What Solon granted the many, it seems, was the right to initiate such cases and perhaps to appeal the decisions of archons or even decisions of the Areopagus, and perhaps the invention of a new form of assembly whereby the assembled citizens could act as a law court in those same cases. See Martin Ostwald, *From Popular Sovereignty to the Sovereignty of Law: Law, Society, and Politics in Fifth-Century Athens* (Berkeley: University of California Press, 1986): 12–13.

19. "By making the qualification for the arkonship landed wealth instead of birth and wealth, Solon was not only breaking the Eupatrid monopoly of the arkonship but was also broadening the most powerful institution in Athens, the Areopagas. For arkhons passed into the Areopagos after their year of office." G. R. Stanton, *Athenian Politics c.800–500 BC: A Sourcebook* (London: Routledge, 1990): 71, n. 8.

20. ". . . for in ancient times the Council of the Areopagus used to issue a summons and select the person suitable for each of the offices, and commission him to hold office for a year." Aristotle, *Constitution of the Athenians*, 29.

21. See the discussion in chapter three of Brian Seitz and Thomas Thorp, *The Iroquois and the Athenians: A Political Ontology* (Lanham, MD: Lexington Books, 2013).

22. See Manville's discussion of the public lands issue: Manville, *The Origins of Citizenship*, 115.

23. On public land and debt, see Aristotle's summary of Solon's actions: "he laid down laws, and enacted cancellation of debts both private (*idiōn*) but public (*dēmosiōn*)" Aristotle, *Constitution of the Athenians*, 23.

24. *Cf.* Manville's contention that debt slavery affected not sharecroppers on private or public land, but only small landholders who would have to borrow year to year in order to survive: Manville, *The Origins of Citizenship*, 116.

25. Castoriadis, commenting on the integrity of the Athenian polis, relates the "fantastic clause" referenced by Aristotle in the *Politics* to the effect that inhabitants of a region bordering a neighboring polis should be barred from voting on a resolution of war against that neighboring polis, since it is simply wrong to ask them to vote for the probable destruction of their own farms and houses, or, worse, to tempt them to fail to set aside their interests as the political-civic realm demands. Then Castoriadis writes:

To glimpse the gulf separating the Greek political imaginary from the modern political imaginary, let us try to imagine for an instant what would happen today if someone had the preposterous (and quite evidently *politically just*) idea of proposing that, in votes of the French National Assembly concerning the growing of wine, the deputies from the wine-growing districts should be forbidden from voting.

26. "The raging civil strife comes 'to the home of each one', oikad' hekastōi (4.26. Hekastos is one of Solon's favorite words; he uses it six times, always to stress that 'each one of us' is responsible and pays the price for a wider crime": Lewis, *Solon the Thinker*, 44.

CHAPTER 18

Memories of Class and Youth in the Age of Disposability

Henry A. Giroux

In spite of being discredited by the economic recession of 2008, market fundamentalism or unfettered free-market capitalism has once again become a dominant force for producing a corrupt financial service industry, runaway environmental devastation, egregious amounts of human suffering, and the rise of what has been called the emergence of "finance as a criminalized, rogue industry."[1] The Gilded Age is back with huge profits for the ultrarich, banks, and other large financial service institutions while at the same time increasing impoverishment and misery for the middle and working classes. The American dream, celebrating economic and social mobility, has been transformed into not just an influential myth but also a poisonous piece of propaganda.

The class-based power of the new financial services, banks, and investment industries works its way through the American landscape like an electric current destroying all those public spaces that speak to the common good and embrace the ideals of economic justice. America now "has the highest level of inequality of any of the advanced countries."[2] One measure of the upward shift in wealth is evident in Joseph E. Stiglitz's claim that "in the 'recovery' of 2009–2010, the top 1% of US income earners captured 93% of the income growth."[3] The vast inequities and economic injustice at the heart of the mammoth gap in income and wealth become even more evident in a number of revealing statistics. For example, "the average pay for people working in U.S. investment banks is over $375,000 while senior officers at Goldman Sachs averaged $61 million each in compensation for 2007."[4] In addition, the United States beats out every other developing nation in producing extreme income and wealth inequalities for 2012. It gets worse. The top 1% now owns "about a third of the American people's total net worth, over 40 percent of America's total financial wealth . . . and half of the nation's total income growth."[5] At the same time, political illiteracy and religious fundamentalism have cornered the market on populist rage, providing support for an escalating crisis that Alex Honneth has termed the "failed sociality" characteristic of neo-liberal states.[6]

It is important to note that the violence of unnecessary hardship and suffering produced by neo-liberal ideology and values is not restricted to the economic realm. The crisis of class is not restricted to an economic crisis. Workers are not merely exploited; they are also under assault through forms of neo-liberal intellectual violence that diminish their sense of agency and depoliticize the spaces in which they may produce the language and social relations necessary to resist the ravages of economic Darwinism. It is important to note that neo-liberal violence wages war against the modernist legacy of "questioning the givens, in philosophy as well as in politics and art."[7] Ignorance is no longer a liability in neo-liberal societies but a political asset endlessly mediated through a capitalist imaginary that thrives on the interrelated registers of consumption, privatization, and depoliticization. Manufactured ignorance is the new reigning mode of dystopian violence and class warfare, spurred on by a market-driven system that celebrates a passion for consumer goods over a passionate desire for community affairs, the well-being of the other, and the principles of a democratic society. As the late Cornelius Castoriadis brilliantly argues, under neo-liberalism, the thoughtless celebration of economic progress becomes the primary legitimating principle to transform "human beings into machines for producing and consuming."[8]

Under neo-liberalism with its class-specific pedagogical practices, acts of translation become utterly privatized and removed from public considerations. Public issues now collapse into private problems. One consequence is not only the undoing of the social bond, but also the endless reproduction of the narrow register of individual responsibility as a substitute for any analyses of wider social problems, making it easier to blame the poor, homeless, uninsured, jobless, and other disadvantaged groups for their problems while reinforcing the merging of a market society with the punishing state. Accordingly, zones of social abandonment now proliferate, and the varied populations made disposable under casino capitalism occupy a globalized space of ruthless politics in which the categories of "citizen's rights," "social protections," and "democratic representation," once integral to national politics, are no longer recognized. Disposable populations are less visible, relegated to the frontier zones of relative invisibility and removed from public view. Punishment creep and the "machinery of social death" now work their way from the prison to the halls and classrooms of public education.[9]

Everywhere we look, the power of the megacorporations and financial elite aggressively promotes failed modes of governance and massive human hardship and suffering. This is particularly clear in the attempts by the bankers, hedge fund operators, and their corporate cohorts to dismantle regulations meant to restrict their corrupting political and economic power while enacting policies that privilege the rich and the powerful. In this instance, casino capitalism produces an autoimmune crisis in which a social order attacks the very elements of a democratic society that allow it to reproduce itself, while at the same time killing off any sense of history, memory, and social and ethical responsibility. As social protections are dismantled, public servants denigrated, and public goods such as schools, bridges, health-care services, and public transportation deteriorate, the current apostles of neo-liberal orthodoxy embrace the cruel and punishing values of economic Darwinism, with its survival of the fittest ethic and its winner-take-all belief system.

One consequence is that many working class and poor minority youth today live in an era of foreclosed hope, an era in which it is difficult either to imagine a life beyond capitalism, or to get beyond the fear that any attempt to do so can only result in a more dreadful nightmare. But for such youth, there is more at work here than dystopian nightmares concerning the future—there is also an overwhelming catalogue of evidence that reveals that many neo-liberal societies are at war with their children, and that the use of such violence against young people is a disturbing index of a society in the midst of a deep moral and political crisis.[10] Beyond exposing the moral depravity of a nation that fails to protect its youth, especially those marginalized by race and class, the violence waged against many young people speaks to nothing less than a perverse death wish, especially in light of the fact that, as Alain Badiou argues, we live in an era in which there is zero tolerance for poor minority youth and youthful protesters and "infinite tolerance for the crimes of bankers and government embezzlers which affect the lives of millions."[11]

Poor minority and low-income youth, especially, are often warehoused in schools that resemble boot camps, dispersed to dank and dangerous workplaces far from the enclaves of the tourist industries, incarcerated in prisons that privilege punishment over rehabilitation, and consigned to the increasing army of the permanently unemployed. Rendered redundant as a result of the collapse of the social state, a pervasive racism, a growing disparity in income and wealth, and a take-no-prisoners neo-liberalism, an increasing number of individuals and groups are being demonized, criminalized, or simply abandoned either by virtue of their status as immigrants or because they are young, poor, unemployed, disabled, homeless, or confined to low-paying jobs. The new face of class exclusion can be found in what Joao Biehl has called "zones of terminal exclusion," which now accelerate the disposability of the unwanted.[12]

The human face of this process and the invisible others who inhabit its geography is captured in a story told by Chip Ward, a former librarian, who writes poignantly about a homeless woman named Ophelia, who retreats to the library because like many of the homeless she has nowhere else to go to use the bathroom, secure temporary relief from bad weather, or simply be able to rest. Excluded from the American dream and treated as both expendable and a threat, Ophelia, in spite of her obvious mental illness, defines her existence in terms that offer a chilling metaphor that extends far beyond her plight. Ward describes Ophelia's presence and actions in the following way:

Ophelia sits by the fireplace and mumbles softly, smiling and gesturing at no one in particular. She gazes out the large window through the two pairs of glasses she wears, one windshield-sized pair over a smaller set perched precariously on her small nose. Perhaps four lenses help her see the invisible other she is addressing. When her "nobody there" conversation disturbs the reader seated beside her, Ophelia turns, chuckles at the woman's discomfort, and explains, *"Don't mind me, I'm dead. It's okay. I've been dead for some time now."* She pauses, then adds reassuringly, *"It's not so bad. You get used to it."* Not at all reassured, the woman gathers her belongings and moves quickly away. Ophelia shrugs. Verbal communication is tricky. She prefers telepathy, but that's hard to do since the rest of us, she informs me, "don't know the rules." (emphasis added)[13]

Ophelia represents just one of the 200,000 chronically homeless, or growing members of the underclass—the new disposables—who now use public libraries and any other accessible public space to find shelter. Many are often sick, are disoriented, suffer from substance abuse, or are mentally disabled and on the edge of sanity due to the stress, insecurity, and danger that they face every day. And while Ophelia's comments may be dismissed as the ramblings of a mentally disturbed woman, they speak to something much deeper about the current state of American society and its desertion of entire populations that are now considered the human waste of a neo-liberal social order. People who were once viewed as facing dire problems in need of state intervention and social protection are now seen as a problem threatening society. This becomes clear when the war on poverty is transformed into a war against the poor; when the plight of the homeless is defined less as a political and economic issue in need of social reform than as a matter of law and order; or when government budgets for prison construction eclipse funds for higher education. Indeed, the transformation of the social state into the corporate-controlled punishing state is made startlingly clear when young people, to paraphrase W. E. B. Du Bois, become problem people rather than people who face problems.

Already disenfranchised by virtue of their age, poor minority and low-income youth are under assault today in ways that are entirely new because they now face a world that is far more dangerous than at any other time in recent history. Not only do they live in a space of social homelessness in which precarity and uncertainty lock them out of a secure future, but they also find themselves inhabiting a society that seeks to silence them as it makes them invisible. Victims of a neo-liberal regime that smashes their hopes and attempts in order to exclude them from the fruits of democracy, young people are now told not to expect too much. Written out of any claim to the economic and social resources of the larger society, they are increasingly told to accept the status of "stateless, faceless, and functionless" nomads, a plight for which they alone have to accept responsibility.[14] Like Ophelia, increasing numbers of youth suffer mental anguish and overt distress even, perhaps especially, among the college-bound, debt-ridden, and unemployed, whose numbers are growing exponentially.

If youth were once viewed as the site where society deposited its dreams, that is no longer true. Too many are now viewed mostly as a public disorder and inhabit a place where society increasingly exhibits its nightmares. Many young people now live in a post-9/11 social order that views them as a prime target of its governing through crime complex. This is made obvious by the many "get tough" policies that now render poor minority and low-income youth as criminals, while depriving them of basic health care, education, and social services. Punishment and fear have replaced compassion and social responsibility as the most important modalities mediating the relationship of youth to the larger social order. When war and the criminalization of social problems become a mode of governance, youth are reduced to a target rather than a social investment. As anthropologist Alain Bertho points out, "Youth is no longer considered the world's future, but as a threat to its present."[15] The only political discourse available for young people is a disciplinary one. Poor minority and low-income youth now represent the absent present in any discourse about the contemporary moment, the future, and democracy itself and increasingly inhabit a state that mimics what Michel Foucault calls "an absolutely racist state, an absolutely murderous state and an absolutely suicidal state."[16] Before I take up this theme in more detail, I want to say something about my own working class youth as a way of illustrating that how young people are represented in both historical and contemporary terms tells us a lot about "the social and political constitution of society" and what I call the contemporary war on youth.[17]

Memories of Youth

Beneath the abstract codifying of youth through the discourses of law, medicine, psychology, employment, education, and marketing statistics, there is the lived experience of being young. For me, youth invokes a repository of memories fueled by my own journey as a working class youth through an adult world that largely seemed to be in the way, a world held together by a web of disciplinary practices and restrictions that appeared at the time more oppressive than liberating. Dreams for young people living in my Smith Hill neighborhood in Providence, Rhode Island, were contained within a limited number of sites, all of which occupied an outlaw status in the adult world: the inner-city basketball court located in a housing project, which promised danger and fierce competition; the streets on which adults and youth collided as the police and parole officers harassed us endlessly. These were class-based sites, defined by the jobs our parents had, the level of poverty that marked our lives, and the cultural capital that was imprinted on the way we talked, dressed, and manifested our individual and collective presence in the world.

Lacking the security of a middle-class childhood, my friends and I seemed suspended in a society in which the constraints of class neither accorded us a voice nor guaranteed economic independence. Identity didn't come easy in my neighborhood. It was painfully clear to all of us that our identities were constructed out of daily battles waged around masculinity, the ability to mediate a terrain fraught with violence, and the need to find an anchor through which to negotiate a culture in which life was fast and short-lived. I grew up amid the motion and force of mostly white and black working-class male bodies—bodies asserting their physical strength as one of the few resources we had control over. Job or no job, one forever felt the primacy of the body: the body flying through the rarefied air of the neighborhood gym in a kind of sleek and stylized performance; the body furtive and cool existing on the margins of society filled with the possibility of instant pleasure and relief, or tense and anticipating danger and risk; the body bent by the weight of grueling labor.

I saw a lot in that neighborhood, and I couldn't seem to learn enough to make sense of it or escape its pull. My youth was lived through class formations that I felt were viewed by others as an outlaw culture. Schools, hospitals, community centers, and surely middle-class social spaces interpreted us as alien, other, and deviant because we were from the wrong class and had the wrong kind of cultural capital. As working class youth, we were defined through our deficits. Class marked us as poor, inferior, linguistically inadequate, and often dangerous. Our bodies were more valued than our minds, and the only way to survive was to deny one's voice, experience, and location as a working class youth.

We lacked the political vocabulary and insight that would have enabled us to see the contradiction between the brutal racism, violence, and sexism that marked our lives and our constant attempts to push against the grain by investing in the pleasures of the body, the warmth of solidarity, and the appropriation of neighborhood spaces as outlaw publics. As kids, we were border-crossers and had to learn to negotiate the power, violence, and harshness of the dominant culture through our own lived histories, restricted languages, and narrow cultural experiences. Recognizing our fugitive status in all of the dominant institutions in which we found ourselves, we were suspicious and sometimes vengeful of what we didn't have or how we were left out of the representations that seemed to define American youth in the 1950s and early 1960s. We listened to Etta James and hated both the music of Pat Boone and the cultural capital that for us was synonymous with golf, tennis, and prep schools. We lost ourselves in the grittiness of working class neighborhood gyms, abandoned cars, and street corners that offered a haven for escape but also invited police surveillance and brutality. Being part of an outlaw culture meant that we lived almost exclusively on the margins of a life that was not of our choosing. We lived in the present tense, and the present never stopped pulsating. Like most marginalized youth cultures, we were time bound. The memory work, for me, would have to come later. But when it came, it offered me a newfound appreciation of what I learned in those neighborhoods about solidarity, trust, friendship, sacrifice, and most of all individual and collective struggle.

I eventually left my neighborhood, but it was nothing short of a historical accident that allowed me to leave. I never took the requisite tests to apply to a four-year college. When high school graduation came around, I was offered a basketball scholarship to a junior college in Worcester, Massachusetts. After violating too many rules and drinking more than I should have, I left school and went back to my old neighborhood hangouts. But my friends' lives had already changed. Their youth had left them and they now had families and lousy jobs and spent a lot of time in the neighborhood bar, waiting for a quick hit at the racetrack or the promise of a good disability scheme. After working for two years at odd jobs, I managed to play in a widely publicized basketball tournament and did well enough to attract the attention of a few coaches who tried to recruit me. Following their advice, I took the SATs and scored high enough to qualify for entrance into a small college in Maine that offered me a basketball scholarship. While in school, I took on a couple of jobs to help finance my education, and eventually graduated with a teaching degree in secondary education. In the grand scheme of things, I was lucky because I experienced my youth at a time when postwar America was imbued with optimism. Moreover, the utopian thrust of the early 1960s offered up a set of ideals that provided a critique of poverty, inequality, and racism. Hence, youth in my neighborhood were feared but at the same time we were defined through what Jean and John Comaroff have termed a kind of doubling in which we were perceived ambiguously as both a threat and a promise.[18] While this was not true of poor minority youth at that time, some of us still occupied that middle ground between being seen as a nightmare and a "source of yet-to-be-imagined futures."[19] Privileged by gender and race and part of a generation in the 1960s that was as political as it was utopian, I was able to make my way out of an existence that otherwise by contemporary standards would have been bound and sealed by class and material deprivations.

The social contract, however feeble, came crashing to the ground in the late 1970s as Margaret Thatcher and soon afterward Ronald Reagan in the United States, both hard-line advocates of market fundamentalism, announced respectively that there was no such thing as society and that government was the problem, not the solution. Democracy and the political process were soon hijacked by corporations, and hope was appropriated as an advertisement for the whitewashed world of Disney. At the same time, larger social movements fragmented into isolated pockets of resistance mostly organized around a form of identity politics. Given the deepening gap between the rich and the poor, a growing culture of cruelty, and the dismantling of the social state, I don't believe youth today will have the same opportunities I had, although undoubtedly they will have struggles similar to mine and much more. The promise of youth has given way to an age of market-induced angst, a view of many young people as a threat to short-term investments, rampant self-interest, and fast profits.

Today's young people inhabit an age of unprecedented symbolic, material, and institutional violence—an age of grotesque irresponsibility, unrestrained greed, and unchecked individualism—all of which is rooted in an antidemocratic mode of economic globalization. Poor minority and low-income youth are now removed from any talk about democracy. Their absence is symptomatic of a society that has turned against itself, punishes children it defines through their alleged deficits, and does so at the risk of crippling the entire body politic. Many working class youth are now disappeared from the neo-liberal landscape of quick profits, short term investments, and gated communities.

Under such circumstances, all bets are off regarding the future of democracy. Besides a growing inability to translate private troubles into social issues, what is also being lost in the current historical conjuncture is the very idea of the public good, the notion of connecting learning to social change, and developing modes of civic courage infused by the principles of social justice. Under the regime of a ruthless economic Darwinism, we are witnessing the crumbling of social bonds and the triumph of individual desires over social rights, nowhere more exemplified than in the gated communities, gated intellectuals, and gated values that have become symptomatic of a society that has lost all claims to democracy or for that matter any sense of utopian thrust.

The eminent sociologist Zygmunt Bauman is right in claiming that "Visions have nowadays fallen into disrepute and we tend to be proud of what we should be ashamed of."[20] Politics has become an extension of war, just as state-sponsored violence increasingly finds legitimation in popular culture and a broader culture of cruelty that promotes an expanding landscape of fear and undermines any sense of communal responsibility for the well-being of others. Too many young people today learn quickly that their fate is solely a matter of individual responsibility, legitimated through market-driven laws that have more to do with self-promotion, a hyper-competitiveness, and surviving in a society that increasingly reduces social relations to social combat. Young people today are expected to inhabit a set of relations in which the only obligation is to live for oneself and to reduce the obligations of citizenship to the demands of a consumer culture. There is more at work here than a flight from social responsibility. Also lost is the importance of those social bonds, modes of collective reasoning, and public spheres and cultural apparatuses crucial to the formation of a sustainable democratic society. "Reality TV's" mantra of "war of all against all" brings home the lesson that punishment is the norm and reward the exception. Unfortunately, it no longer mimics reality: it is the new reality.

The War against Youth

In what follows, I want to address the intensifying assault on young people through the related concepts of "soft war" and "hard war," which I developed in my two recent books, *Disposable Youth* and *Youth in a Suspect Society*. *The idea of soft war* considers the changing conditions of all youth within the relentless expansion of a global market society. Partnered with a massive advertising machinery, the soft war targets children and youth of various class positions, devaluing them by treating them as yet another "market" to be commodified and exploited, and conscripting them into the system through relentless attempts to create a new generation of consuming subjects. This low-intensity war is waged by a variety of corporate institutions through the educational force of a culture that commercializes every aspect of kids' lives, using the Internet and various social networks along with the new media technologies such as cell phones to immerse young people in the world of mass consumption in ways that are more direct and expansive than anything we have seen in the past.

The influence of the new screen and electronic culture on young people's habits is disturbing. For instance, a study by the Kaiser Family Foundation found that young people of ages 8–18 now spend more than seven and a half hours a day with smartphones, computers, televisions, and other electronic devices, compared with less than six and a half hours five years ago.[21] When you add the additional time youth spend texting, talking on their cell phones, and doing multiple tasks at once, such as "watching TV while updating *Facebook*—the number rises to 11 hours of total media content each day."[22] There is a greater risk here than what seems to be emerging as a new form of depoliticization conveniently renamed as attention deficit disorder, one in which youth avoid the time necessary for thoughtful analysis and engaged modes of reading the word and the world. There is also the issue of how this media is conscripting an entire generation into a world of consumerism in which commodities and brand loyalty become both the most important markers of identity and primary frameworks for mediating one's relationship to the world. Many young people can only recognize themselves in terms preferred by the market. This only makes it more difficult for them to find public spheres where they can locate metaphors of hope.

The stark reality here is that the corporate media are being used to reshape kids' identities into that of consumers rather than critically engaged citizens. The means and objects of consumption now define life and politics, just as reality TV provides the legitimating mix of a culture of cruelty and a survival-of-the-fittest ethic as the driving motifs of neo-liberal culture. One consequence is the selective elimination and reordering of the possible modes of political, social, and ethical vocabularies made available to youth. Corporations have hit gold with the new media and can inundate young people directly with their market-driven values, desires, and identities, all of which fly under the radar, escaping the watchful eyes and interventions of concerned parents and other adults. Of course, some youth are doing their best to stay ahead of the commodification and privatization of such technologies and are using the new media to assert a range of oppositional practices and forms of protest that constitute a new realm of political activity.

The hard war is more serious and dangerous for certain young people and refers to the harshest elements of a growing crime-control complex that increasingly governs poor minority and low-income youth through a logic of punishment, surveillance, and control.[23] The youth targeted by its punitive measures are often young people whose work is not needed, youth who are considered failed consumers and who can only afford to live on the margins of a commercial culture of excess that eagerly excludes anybody without money, resources, and leisure time to spare. Or they are youth considered both troublesome and often disposable by virtue of their ethnicity, race, and class. The imprint of the youth crime-control complex can be traced in the increasingly popular practice of organizing schools through disciplinary practices that subject students to constant surveillance through high-tech security devices while imposing on them harsh and often thoughtless zero-tolerance policies that closely resemble the culture of the criminal justice system. In this instance, poor and minority youth become the object of a new mode of governance based on the crudest forms of disciplinary control.

As is evident in the killing of 17-year-old Trayvon Martin, working class minority youth are not just excluded from "the American dream" but are relegated to a type of social death, defined as waste products of a society that no longer considers them of any value. Under such circumstances, matters of survival and disposability become central to how we think about and imagine not just politics but the everyday existence of poor white, immigrant, and minority youth. Too many young people are not completing high school but are instead bearing the brunt of a system that leaves them uneducated and jobless, and ultimately offers them one of the few options available for people who no longer have available roles to play as producers or consumers—either poverty or prison.

How else to explain the fate of generations of many young people who find themselves in a society in which 500,000 youth are incarcerated and 2.5 million are arrested annually, and that by the age of 23, "almost a third of Americans have been arrested for a crime."[24] What kind of society allows 1.6 million children to be homeless at any given time in a year? Or allows massive inequalities in wealth and income to produce a politically and morally dysfunctional society in which "45 percent of U.S. residents live in households that struggle to make ends meet, [which] breaks down to 39 percent of all adults and 55 percent of all children"?[25] stocks_and_economy/#.T3SxhDEgd8E. Current statistics paint a bleak picture for young people in the United States: 1.5 million are unemployed, which marks a 17-year high; 12.5 million are without food; and, in what amounts to a national disgrace, one out of every five American children lives in poverty. Nearly half of all US children and 90 percent of black youngsters will be on food stamps at some point during childhood.[26]

The Youth Crime-Control Complex

Against the idealistic rhetoric of a government that claims it venerates young people lies the reality of a society that increasingly views working class and poor minority youth through the optic of law and order, a society that appears all too willing to treat youth as criminals and when necessary make them "disappear" into the farthest reaches of the carceral state. Under such circumstances, the administration of schools and social services has given way to modes of confinement whose purpose is to ensure "custody and control."[27] Hence, it is not surprising that "school officials and the criminal justice system are criminalizing children and teenagers all over the country, arresting them and throwing them in jail for behavior that in years past would never have led to the intervention of law enforcement."[28]

For instance, as the logic of the market and crime control frame a number of school policies, students are now subjected to zero-tolerance rules that are used primarily to humiliate, punish, repress, and exclude them.[29] What are we to make of a society that allows the police to come into a school and arrest, handcuff, and haul off a 12-year-old student for doodling on her desk? Or, for that matter, a school system that allows a 5-year-old kindergarten pupil to be handcuffed and sent to a hospital psychiatric ward for being unruly in a classroom? Where is the public outrage when two police officers called to a day care center in central Indiana to handle an unruly 10-year-old decide to taser the child and slap him in the mouth? How does one account for a school administration allowing a police officer in Arkansas to use a stun gun to control an allegedly out of control 10-year-old girl? One public response came from Steve Tuttle, a spokesman for Taser International Inc., who insisted that a "Stun gun can be safely used on children."[30] Sadly, this is but a small sampling of the ways in which children are being punished instead of educated in American schools, especially inner-city schools.

Racial and class-specific state violence waged against young people is also evident in the fact that the United States engages in "the widespread use of solitary confinement on youth under the age of 18 in prisons and jails across the country [regardless of] the deep and permanent harm it causes to kids caught up in the adult criminal justice system."[31] Not only are poor work-ing class and minority youth disproportionately put in adult jails, sentenced to life imprisonment while still children, but also locked up in cells for up to 23 hours at time, cut off from other inmates, their families, and the most basic rehabilitative services. Many of these young people are prone to mental ill-ness, self-inflicted harm, and, in too many cases, suicide. These are the wages that young people pay because they occupy a lower rung on the socioeconomic ladder.

All of these examples point to the power of class discrimination in America, the growing disregard American society has for poor young people, and the number of institutions willing to employ a crime-and-punishment mentality that consti-tutes not only a crisis of politics, but the emergence of a new politics of educating and governing through crime.[32] Of course, we have seen this ruthless crime optic in previous historical periods, but the social costs of such criminalization were viewed as a social issue rather than as an individualized problem, that is, in which crime and reform were viewed as part of a broader constellation of socioeconomic forces. For one historical example of this broader understanding of crime, I want to turn to Claude Brown, the late African American novelist, who understood something about this war on youth. Though his novel, *Manchild in the Promised Land*, takes place in Harlem in the 1960s, there is something to be learned from his work. Take for example the following passage from his book, written in 1965:

> If Reno was in a bad mood—if he didn't have any money and he wasn't high—he'd say, "Man, Sonny, they ain't got no kids in Harlem. I ain't never seen any. I've seen some real small people actin' like kids, but they don't have any kids in Harlem, because nobody has time for a childhood. Man, do you ever remember bein' a kid? Not me. Shit, kids are happy, kids laugh, kids are secure. They ain't scared a nothin'.

You ever been a kid, Sonny? Damn, you lucky. I ain't never been a kid, man. I don't ever remember bein' happy and not scared. I don't know what happened, man, but I think I missed out on that childhood thing, because I don't ever recall bein' a kid."[33]

In *Manchild in the Promised Land*, Claude Brown wrote about the doomed lives of his friends, families, and neighborhood acquaintances. The book is mostly remembered as a brilliant, but devastating portrait of Harlem under siege—a community ravaged and broken by drugs, poverty, unemployment, crime, and police brutality. But what Brown really made visible was that the raw violence and dead-end existence that plagued so many young people in Harlem stole not only their future but their childhood as well. In the midst of the social collapse and psychological trauma wrought by the systemic fusion of racism and class exploitation, children in Harlem were held hostage to forces that robbed them of the innocence that comes with childhood and forced them to take on the risks and burdens of daily survival that older generations were unable to shield them from. At the heart of Brown's narrative, written in the midst of the civil rights struggle in the 1960s, is a "manchild," a metaphor that indicts a society that is waging a war on those children who are black and poor and have been forced to grow up too quickly. The hybridized concept of "manchild" marked a liminal space if not liminal drift in which innocence was lost and childhood stolen. Harlem was a well-contained, internal colony and its street life provided the conditions and the very necessity for insurrection. But the many forms of rebellion young people expressed—from the public and progressive to the interiorized and self-destructive—came with a price, which Brown reveals near the end of the book: "It seemed as though most of the cats that we'd come up with just hadn't made it. Almost everybody was dead or in jail."[34]

Childhood stolen was not a plea for self-help—that short-sighted and mendacious appeal that would define the reactionary reform efforts of the 1980s and 1990s, from Reagan's hatred of government to Clinton's attack on welfare reform. It was a clarion call for condemning a social order that denied children a viable and life-enhancing future. While Brown approached everyday life in Harlem more as a poet than as a political revolutionary, politics was embedded in every sentence of the book—not a politics marked by demagoguery, hatred, and orthodoxy, but one that made visible the damage done by a social system characterized by massive inequalities and a rigid racial divide. *Manchild* created the image of a society without children in order to raise questions about the future of a country that had turned its back on its most vulnerable population. Like the great critical theorist C. Wright Mills, Claude Brown's lasting contribution was to reconfigure the boundaries between public issues and private sufferings. For Brown, racism was about power and oppression and could not be separated from broader social, economic, and political considerations. Rather than denying systemic causes of injustice (as did the discourses of individual pathology and self-help), Brown insisted that social forces had to be factored into any understanding of both group suffering and individual despair. Brown explored the suffering of the young in Harlem, but he did so by utterly refusing to privatize it, or to dramatize and spectacularize private life over public dysfunction, or to separate individual hopes, desires, and agency from the realm of politics and public life.

Nearly 50 years later, Brown's metaphor of the "manchild" is more relevant today than when he wrote the book, and "the Promised Land" more mythic than ever as his revelation about the sorry plight of low-income and poor minority children takes on a more expansive meaning in light of the current economic meltdown and the dashed hopes of an entire generation now viewed as a generation without hope for a decent future. Youth today are forced to inhabit a rough world where childhood is nonexistent, crushed under the heavy material and existential burdens they are forced to bear.

What is horrifying about the plight of youth today is not just the severity of deprivations and violence they experience daily, but also how they have been forced to view the world and redefine the nature of their own childhood within the borders of hopelessness, cruelty, and despair. There is little sense of a hopeful future lying just beyond highly policed spaces of commodification and containment. An entire generation of youth will not have access to decent jobs, the material comforts, or the security available to previous generations. These children are a new generation of youth who have to think, act, and talk like adults; worry about their families, which may be headed by a single parent or two out of work and searching for a job; wonder how they are going to get the money to buy food and how long it will take to see a doctor in case of illness. These children are no longer confined to so-called ghettos. As the burgeoning landscapes of poverty and despair increasingly find expression in our cities, suburbs, and rural areas, these children make their presence felt—they are too many to ignore or hide away in the usually sequestered and invisible spaces of disposability. They constitute a new and more unsettling scene of suffering, one that reveals not only the vast and destabilizing inequalities in our economic landscape but also portends a future that has no purchase on the hope that characterizes a vibrant democracy.

Defending Youth and Democracy in the Twenty-First Century

Finally, I want to suggest that while it has become more difficult to imagine a democratic future, we have entered a period in which young people all over the world are protesting against neo-liberalism and its class-based pedagogies and politics of disposability. Refusing to remain voiceless and powerless in determining their future, these young people are organizing collectively in order to create the conditions for societies that refuse to use politics as an act of war and markets as the measure of democracy. They are taking seriously the words of the great abolitionist Frederick Douglass, who bravely argued that freedom is an empty abstraction if people fail to act, and "if there is no struggle, there is no progress."

Both the Occupy and Quebec movements suggest that the young people are once again a source of creativity, possibility, and political struggle. Moreover, the movement points to a crucial political project in which new questions are being raised by many young people about emerging antidemocratic forces in both the United States and Canada that threaten the collective survival of vast numbers of people, not exclusively through overt police violence or worse, but also through an aggressive assault on social provisions, higher education, health care, pensions, and other social programs on which millions of young and older Canadians and Americans depend. What is partly evident in both movements is both a cry of collective indignation over class-based economic and social injustices that pose a threat to humankind, and a critical expression of how young people and others can use new technologies, develop democratic social formations, and enact forms of critical pedagogy and civil disobedience necessary for addressing the diverse antidemocratic forces that have been poisoning North American politics since the 1970s.

The current protests in the United States, Canada, Greece, and Spain make clear that this is not—indeed, *cannot be*—only a short-term project for reform, but a political movement that needs to intensify, accompanied by the reclaiming of public spaces, the progressive use of digital technologies, the development of public spheres, the production of new modes of education, and the safeguarding of places where democratic expression, new identities, and collective hope can be nurtured and mobilized. A formative culture must be put in place pedagogically and institutionally in a variety of spheres extending from churches and public and higher education to all those cultural apparatuses engaged in the production and circulation of knowledge, desire, identities, and values. Clearly, such efforts need to address the language of democratic revolution rather than the seductive incremental adjustments of liberal reform. This suggests not only calling for a living wage, jobs programs, especially for the young, the democratization of power, economic equality, and a massive shift in funds away from the machinery of war and big banks, but also a social movement that not only engages in critique but makes hope a real possibility by organizing to seize power. There is no room for failure here because failure would cast us back into the clutches of authoritarianism—that, while different from previous historical periods, shares nonetheless the imperative to proliferate violent social formations and a death-dealing blow to the promise of a democracy to come.

I realize this sounds a bit utopian, but we have few choices if we are going to fight for a future that does a great deal more than endlessly repeat the present. Given the urgency of the problems faced by those marginalized by class, race, age, and sexual orientation, I think it is all the more crucial to take seriously the challenge of Derrida's provocation that "We must do and think the impossible. If only the possible happened, nothing more would happen. If I only did what I can do, I wouldn't do anything."[35] We may live in dark times as Hannah Arendt reminds us, but history is open and the space of the possible is larger than the one on display.

Notes

1. Charles H. Ferguson, *Predator Nation* (New York: Crown Press, 2012), 21.
2. Joseph E. Stiglitz, "The Price of Inequality," *Project Syndicate*, June 5, 2012, http://www.project-syndicate.org/commentary/the-price-of-inequality.
3. Ibid.
4. Ferguson, *Predator Nation*, 8.
5. Ibid.
6. Alex Honneth, *Pathologies of Reason* (New York: Columbia University Press, 2009), 188.
7. Cornelius Castoriadis, *A Society Adrift: Interviews & Debates 1974–1997*, trans. Helen Arnold (New York: Fordham University Press, 2010), 7.
8. Ibid., 8.
9. Joao Biehl, *Vita: Life in a Zone of Social Abandonment* (Berkeley: University of California Press, 2005), 14.
10. J. F. Conway, "Quebec: Making War on Our Children," *Socialist Project*, E-Bulletin No. 651, June 10, 2012, http://www.socialistproject.ca/bullet/651.php.
11. Alain Badiou, *The Rebirth of History*, trans. Gregory Elliott (London: Verso, 2012), 18–19.
12. Biehl, *Vita*.
13. Chip Ward, "America Gone Wrong: A Slashed Safety Net Turns Libraries into Homeless Shelters," *TomDispatch.com*, April 2, 2007, www.alternet.org/story/50023.
14. Zygmunt Bauman, *Wasted Lives* (London: Polity Press, 2004), 76–77.
15. Jean-Marie Durand, "For Youth: A Disciplinary Discourse Only," trans. Leslie Thatcher, *TruthOut*, November 15, 2009, http://www.truthout.org/11190911.
16. Michel Foucault, *Society Must Be Defended: Lectures at the College de France, 1975–1976* (New York: Picador, 2003), 260.
17. Jean and John Comaroff, "Reflections of Youth, from the Past to the Postcolony," in *Frontiers of Capital: Ethnographic Reflections on the New Economy*, eds Melissa S. Fisher and Greg Downey (Durham, NC: Duke University Press, 2006), 267.
18. Ibid., 280.
19. Ibid.
20. Zygmunt Bauman, "Introduction and in Search of Public Space," *In Search of Politics* (Stanford, CA: Stanford University Press, 1999), 8.
21. Tamar Lewin, "If Your Kids Are Awake, They're Probably Online," *New York Times*, January 20, 2010, A1.
22. C. Christine, "Kaiser Study: Kids 8 to 18 Spend More Than Seven Hours a Day with Media," Spotlight on Digital Media and Learning: MacArthur Foundation, January 21, 2010, http://spotlight.macfound.org/blog/entry/kaiser_study_kids_age_8_to_18_spend_more_than_seven_hours_a_day_with_media/.
23. See, for example, Angela Y. Davis, *The Meaning of Freedom* (San Francisco, CA: City Lights Books, 2012); Michelle Alexander, "Michelle Alexander, The Age of Obama As a Racial Nightmare," *Tom Dispatch*, March 25, 2012, http://www.tomdispatch.com/post/175520/best_of_tomdispatch%3A_michelle_alexander,_the_age_of_obama_as_a_racial_nightmare/; Anne-Marie Cusac, *Cruel and Unusual: The Culture of Punishment in America* (New Haven, CT: Yale University Press, 2009); Michelle Brown, *The Culture of Punishment: Prison, Society and Spectacle* (New York: New York University Press, 2009).
24. Erica Goode, "Many in U.S. Are Arrested by Age 23, Study Finds," *New York Times*, December 19, 2011, A15.

25. Reuters, "45% Struggle in US to Make Ends Meet," *MSNBC: Business Stocks and Economy*, November 22, 2011, http://www.msnbc.msn.com/id/45407937/ns/business

26. Lindsey Tanner, "Half of US Kids Will Get Food Stamps, Study Says," *Chicago Tribune*, November 2, 2009, http://www.chicagotribune.com/news/chi-ap-us-med-children-food,0,6055934.story.

27. Bauman, *Wasted Lives*, 82.

28. Bob Herbert, "School to Prison Pipeline," *New York Times*, June 9, 2007, A29.

29. For an extensive treatment of zero-tolerance laws and the militarization of schools, see Christopher Robbins, *Expelling Hope: The Assault on Youth and the Militarization of Schooling* (Albany: SUNY Press, 2008); and Kenneth Saltman and David Gabbard, eds, *Education as Enforcement: The Militarization and Corporatization of Schools* (New York: Routledge, 2003).

30. Carly Everson, "Ind. Officer Uses Stun Gun on Unruly 10-Year Old," *AP News*, April 3, 2010, http://hosted.ap.org/dynamic/stories/U/US_POLICE_SHOCK_CHILD?SITE=FLPLA&SECTION=HOME&TEMPLATE=DEFAULT.

31. Jean Casella and James Ridgeway, "Kids in Solitary Confinement: America's Official Child Abuse," *Alternet*, October 11, 2012, http://www.alternet.org/civil-liberties/kids-solitary-confinement-americas-official-child-abuse. This is documented extensively in *Growing Up Locked Down*, a report released in 2012 by the American Civil Liberties Union.

32. Jonathan Simon, *Governing through Crime: How the War on Crime Transformed American Democracy and Created a Culture of Fear* (New York: Oxford University Press, 2007), 5.

33. Claude Brown, *Manchild in the Promised Land* (New York: Signet Books, 1965).

34. Ibid., 419.

35. Jacques Derrida, "No One Is Innocent: A Discussion with Jacques about Philosophy in the Face of Terror," *The Information Technology, War and Peace Project*, 2.

Notes on Contributors

Eric Anthamatten is currently a PhD candidate at the New School for Social Research in New York City. His works focus on philosophy, education, and social justice, more specifically on issues surrounding education in marginal, nontraditional, and nonacademic settings: the prison, adult education, the homeless. He is writing a dissertation titled "Pedagogy of the Condemned," which explores the intersections of education, criminality, punishment, and the "therapeutic" possibilities of philosophy. Using a deep reading of Aristotle's notion of habit and virtue education, as well as the theories in various critical philosophies of education (Dewey, Buber, Freire, Rancière), he seeks to develop the concept of "habilitation" (as opposed to *re*-habilitation) as a way of approaching pedagogy, most especially pedagogy in the context of marginalized or condemned communities.

Stanley Aronowitz has taught at the Graduate Center of the City University of New York since 1983, where he is Distinguished Professor of Sociology and Urban Education. He received his BA at the New School in 1968 and his PhD from the Union Graduate School in 1975. He studies labor, social movements, science and technology, education, social theory, and cultural studies and is director of the Center for the Study of Culture, Technology and Work at the Graduate Center. He is author or editor of 25 books including *Against Schooling: For an Education That Matters* (2008), *Left Turn: Forging a New Political Future* (2006), *Just Around Corner* (2005), *How Class Works* (2003), *The Last Good Job in America* (2001), *The Knowledge Factory* (2000), *The Jobless Future* (1994, with William DiFazio), and *False Promises: The Shaping of American Working Class Consciousness* (1973, 1992).

M. Lane Bruner (PhD, University of Washington) is Professor of Rhetoric and Politics in the Department of Communication at Georgia State University in Atlanta, Georgia. He is the coeditor of *Market Democracy in Post-Communist Russia* and the author of *Strategies of Remembrance: The Rhetorical Dimensions of National Identity Construction*, *Democracy's Debt: The Historical Tensions between Political and Economic Liberty*, *Repressive Regimes, Aesthetic States, and Arts of Resistance*, and dozens of essays and book chapters on the relationship between communication and political power.

Kevin Bruyneel is Associate Professor of Politics at Babson College. He wrote *The Third Space of Sovereignty: The Postcolonial Politics of US–Indigenous Relations* (University of

Minnesota Press, 2007), and has published articles in such journals as *Studies in American Political Development*, *New Political Science*, *Canadian Journal of Political Science*, and *Settler Colonial Studies*.

Jon Dietrick is Associate Professor of English at Babson College in Wellesley, Massachusetts. He is the author of *Bad Pennies and Dead Presidents: Money in Modern American Drama* (Cambridge Scholars Publishing). His work has also appeared in journals such as *American Drama*, *Twentieth-Century Literature*, and the *Journal of International Women's Studies*.

Emily M. Drew is Associate Professor of Sociology and American Ethnic Studies at Willamette University in Oregon. She teaches courses about racism, immigration, mass media, and social change. Her primary areas of research involve understanding how racism operates inside institutions and strategies for interrupting it. She has been actively engaged in anti-racism organizing and activism for over 20 years, and serves as a facilitator of "Understanding Institutional Racism" workshops for Crossroads Anti-Racism Organizing and Training.

Henry A. Giroux currently holds the Global TV Network Chair Professorship at McMaster University in the English and Cultural Studies Department and a Distinguished Visiting Professorship at Ryerson University. His most recent books include *On Critical Pedagogy* (Continuum, 2011), *Twilight of the Social: Resurgent Publics in the Age of Disposability* (Paradigm, 2012), *Disposable Youth: Racialized Memories and the Culture of Cruelty* (Routledge, 2012), *Youth in Revolt: Reclaiming a Democratic Future* (Paradigm, 2013), and *The Educational Deficit and the War on Youth* (Monthly Review Press, 2013); "America's Disimagination Machine" (City Lights) and "Higher Education after Neoliberalism" (Haymarket) will be published in 2014. Giroux is also a member of Truthout's Board of Directors. His web site is www.henryagiroux.com.

Robin Truth Goodman is Professor of English at Florida State University. Her publications include "Gender Work: Feminism after Neoliberalism" (Palgrave, forthcoming); *Feminist Theory in Pursuit of the Public: Women and the "Re-Privatization" of Labor* (Palgrave, 2010); *Policing Narratives and the State of Terror* (SUNY Press, 2009); *World, Class, Women: Global Literature, Education, and Feminism* (Routledge, 2004); *Strange Love: Or, How We Learn to Stop Worrying and Love the Market* (Rowman and Littlefield, 2002; with Kenneth J. Saltman); and *Infertilities: Exploring Fictions of Barren Bodies* (University of Minnesota Press, 2001).

bell hooks is an American author, feminist, and social activist. She took her *nom de plume* from her maternal great-grandmother, Bell Blair Hooks. Her writing has focused on the interconnectivity of race, capitalism, and gender and what she describes as their ability to produce and perpetuate systems of oppression and class domination. She has published over 30 books and numerous scholarly and mainstream articles, appeared in several documentary films, and participated in various public lectures. Primarily through a postmodern perspective, hooks has addressed race, class, and gender in education, art, history, sexuality, mass media, and feminism.

Dick Howard is Distinguished Professor Emeritus at Stony Brook University. He is the author of 14 books, the most recent ones being *The Primacy of the Political. A History* *of Political Thought from the Greeks to the American and French Revolutions* (2010), *The Specter of Democracy* (2002), and *Political Judgments* (1997). He has also written several books in French, most recently, *La démocratie à l'épreuve* (2006) and *Aux origines de la pensée politique américaine* (2004, 2008). He is a member of several editorial committees, most actively those of *Constellations* and *Esprit*. He is a frequent commentator on everyday politics for Francophone radios, including a 15-month stint of weekly commentaries on the US elections of 2012 for Radio Canada. Since retirement he has written on the arts and culture in a regular "Chronique transatlantique," first for *Esprit* and presently for the monthly *Philosophie Magazine*. Details and links can be found at www.dickhoward.com.

Ted Kafala completed a PhD in Media and Technology Studies, with cognate area in arts education and curriculum and instruction. He teaches digital and experimental media, interactive media, visual communication, and media aesthetics as Associate Professor at the College of Mount Saint Vincent in NYC. He was formerly Associate Professor at the University of Cincinnati. Ted has published critical articles on contemporary new media thinkers, as well as papers on aesthetics, computing, cultural studies, and qualitative research. He has published in the *Journal of Curriculum Theory* and in various cinema journals.

Kristin Lawler is Assistant Professor of Sociology at the College of Mount Saint Vincent in New York City and has worked as a union organizer and an environmental advocate. Her first book, *The American Surfer: Radical Culture and Capitalism*, was published by Routledge in 2011 and examined the subversive politics of the pop culture image of surfing during the twentieth century. Her essay "Fear of a Slacker Revolution: Occupy Wall Street and the Cultural Politics of the Class Struggle" was published by the Social Science Research Council in its "Possible Futures" Digital Forum on Occupy Wall Street. Another essay, "The Politics of Austerity and the Ikarian Dream," was published in the March 2013 issue of *Z Magazine*. Dr. Lawler is currently at work on a new book, "Less Is More: American Labor and Shorter Hours," with Michael Roberts. She lives in Brooklyn with her husband and two children.

Pepi Leistyna is Professor of Applied Linguistics Graduate Studies at the University of Massachusetts, Boston, where he coordinates the research program; teaches courses in cultural studies, critical pedagogy, media literacy, and language acquisition; and is the director of the Center for World Languages and Cultures. He is a research fellow for the National Education Policy Center at the University of Colorado Boulder. Pepi speaks internationally on issues of cultural politics, democracy, and social justice. His books include *Breaking Free: The Transformative Power of Critical Pedagogy*, *Presence of Mind: Education and the Politics of Deception*, *Defining and Designing Multiculturalism*, *Corpus Analysis: Language Structure and Language Use*, and *Cultural Studies: From Theory to Action*. He was the recipient of the Studs Terkel Award for Media and Journalism in 2007 for his documentary film *Class Dismissed: How TV Frames the Working Class*.

Lisa Nel lives in Cape Town, South Africa, and is currently researching and writing about dimensions of cultural perspectives. She has been involved with higher education, communications, and self-help organizations in Botswana and South Africa. She holds a degree in English Literature from Middlebury College. She was a Peace Corps Volunteer in a rural village in Botswana in the early 1980s and has been involved with multicultural teaching of English language and literature since then.

Ann Neumann, a hospice volunteer, has written for *Guernica* magazine, *The Nation*, *New York Law Review*, and other publications and appears regularly on Voice of America. She edits *The Revealer*, a publication of the Center for Religion and Media at New York University, and teaches journalism at Drew University.

Ravi K. Perry is Assistant Professor of political science, Yasmiyn Irizarry is Assistant Professor of sociology, and Timothy J. Fair is a PhD student in the Department of Political Science and Public Administration—each at Mississippi State University.

Raúl Rubio is Associate Professor of Foreign Languages and Literature at John Jay College of the City University of New York (CUNY). A Hispanist and cultural studies scholar, his research is grounded in the emerging interdisciplinary field of material culture, which examines a wide range of artifacts, from cultural commodities to the museum archive. Professor Rubio received a doctorate in Latin American Literature and Cultural Studies from Tulane University in New Orleans and earned a master's degree in Spanish from Middlebury College of Vermont. He completed his undergraduate degree at Barry University in Miami Shores, Florida. He is a Cuba Project Fellow of the Bildner Center for Western Hemisphere Studies at the Graduate Center of the City University of New York. He serves on the Board of Directors of the National Association for Ethnic Studies (2010–2014) and served on the 2012 jury committee of the prestigious Lora Romero Prize of the American Studies Association.

Ron Scapp is founding director of the Graduate Program in Urban and Mulitcultural Education at the College of Mount Saint Vincent, the Bronx, where he is also Professor of Humanities and Teach Education. He is the author and editor of a number of books, including *Teaching Values: Critical Perspectives on Education, Politics, and Culture* (Routledge). He is currently serving as president of the National Association for Ethnic Studies. He is a founding member of Group Thought, a philosophy collective based in Red Hook, Brooklyn, and continues to collaborate with Brian Seitz.

Brian Seitz is Professor of Philosophy at Babson College. He is the author of numerous articles in social and political philosophy, continental philosophy, and environmental philosophy. He is coauthor, with Thomas Thorp, of *The Iroquois and the Athenians: A Political Ontology* (Lexington Books). He is also author of *The Trace of Political Representation* (SUNY Press), and coeditor, with Ron Scapp, of *Living with Class: Philosophical Reflections on Identity and Material Culture* (Palgrave Macmillan), *Fashion Statements: On Style, Appearance, and Reality* (Palgrave Macmillan) *Etiquette: Reflections on Contemporary Comportment* (SUNY Press), and *Eating Culture* (SUNY Press). He is currently writing *Double or Nothing: A Troubled Subject*. He is a founding member of Group Thought, a philosophy collective based in Red Hook, Brooklyn, and continues to collaborate with Ron Scapp.

Thomas Thorp is Professor of Philosophy at Saint Xavier University in Chicago, a student of Archaic Greek politics, and a researcher and activist in the Yellowstone area. He is the founding director of Greater Yellowstone College. He is coauthor, with Brian Seitz, of *The Iroquois and the Athenians: A Political Ontology* (Lexington, 2013). His recently published essays include a study of hyperbolic wolf-loathing, "Eating Wolves" (in *Environmental Ethics, Old World and New*, Drenthen and Keulartz, eds, Fordham University Press), and " 'til human voices wake us': the Aporia-fish in the *Meno*" (in *Plato's Animals*, Naas and Bell, eds, Indiana University Press).

Index

Printed and bound in Great Britain by
CPI Group (UK) Ltd, Croydon, CR0 4YY